Time, Space and Phantasy

GW00644990

Time, Space and Phantasy examines the connections between time, space, phantasy and sexuality in clinical practice. It explores the subtleties of the encounter between patient and analyst, addressing how aspects of the patient's unconscious past are actualized in the present, producing new meanings that can be retranslated to the past.

Perelberg's analysis of Freud's Multi-dimensional model of temporality suggests that he always viewed the constitution of the individual as non-linear. In Freud's formulations, the individual is de-centred and ruled by different temporalities, most of which escape their consciousness. Perelberg identifies the similarities between this and Einstein's theory of relativity which states that rather than being absolute, time depends on the relative position and speed of the observing individual suggesting that rather than being a reality, time is an abstraction, connecting objects and events.

Throughout this text, Perelberg draws together connections between time, mental space, and phantasy showing how time is constantly reshaped in the light of new events and experiences. This book will be of interest to psychoanalysts, psychotherapists, psychologists, and social workers.

Rosine Jozef Perelberg, PhD is a Training Analyst and Supervisor, and Member of the British Psycho-Analytical Society. She is Visiting Professor in the Psychoanalysis Unit, Division of Psychology and Language Sciences at University College, London. She undertook her PhD in Social Anthropology at the London School of Economics. Amongst her publications, *Psychoanalytic Understanding of Violence and Suicide, Time and Memory* and *Freud: A Modern Reader*.

This is an exceptional volume that establishes lines of communication between colleagues from countries that are marked by different traditions. Through this, Rosine Perelberg makes her own original and creative contribution to psychoanalysis.

From the Preface by **Andre Green**, *Past President of the Société Psychanalytique de Paris; International Psychoanalytic Association Outstanding Scientific Achievement Award*

Time, Space and Phantasy is a *tour de force* of psychoanalytic and anthropological scholarship and clinical acumen. The reader is taken through the history of the development of psychoanalytic thinking about time, space and phantasy from Freud to the present day, the representation of these concepts in tribal cultures, and a consideration of the interplay between different notions of time in Gabriel García Márquez's *One Hundred Years of Solitude*. Perelberg explains and elaborates many of the psychoanalytic concepts that are crucial to our understanding of what it means to be human. The discussions of these theoretical concepts are beautifully linked to case presentations (10 cases in all) and an infant observation in such a way that the concepts help make sense of the clinical phenomena while the clinical work illuminates the nature and value of the concepts. To take just one example from among many of Perelberg's original contributions, the concept of a *dynamic après coup* is particularly useful in clinical work because, as she observes, après coup, a retrospective meaning in the moment to moment progress of a session, also has a prospective function. By identifying the bi-directionality of après coup, she helps us to see how the here and now experience of the transference not only illuminates the nature of the trauma of an event in the past, but can also reflect back and shed new light on the present. I highly recommend *Time, Space and Phantasy* to all those who want to deepen their understanding of the theory and practice of psychoanalysis.

Donald Campbell, *Past President of the British Psycho-analytical Society*

This is a deeply intelligent and original book yet written in a clear and simple style which avoids jargon. Reading *Time, Space and Phantasy* gives you the feeling that you are discovering ideas that were never brought together in quite this way . . . This exceptional book has many remarkable clinical illustrations and closes with a beautiful chapter, written with Bella Jozef . . . followed by thoughts on creativity in psychoanalytical research.

Marilia Aisenstein, *Past President of the Société Psychanalytique de Paris,*

The breadth of Rosine Perelberg's anthropological and cultural background makes her one of the most interesting voices in analytic writing today. Both in theoretical discussions and with vivid extended case histories, she reveals the many ways that time as a subjective experience and temporality as a concept pervade psychoanalytic thinking. The comparison of psychoanalytic and scientific views of time, and a remarkable discussion of time in Latin American fiction, makes for a complex and rewarding mixture.

Michael Parsons, *Training Analyst, Fellow of the British Institute of Psycho-Analysis*

THE NEW LIBRARY OF PSYCHOANALYSIS
General Editor   Dana Birksted-Breen

The New Library of Psychoanalysis was launched in 1987 in association with the Institute of Psychoanalysis, London. It took over from the International Psychoanalytical Library which published many of the early translations of the works of Freud and the writings of most of the leading British and Continental psychoanalysts.

The purpose of the New Library of Psychoanalysis is to facilitate a greater and more widespread appreciation of psychoanalysis and to provide a forum for increasing mutual understanding between psychoanalysts and those working in other disciplines such as the social sciences, medicine, philosophy, history, linguistics, literature and the arts. It aims to represent different trends both in British psychoanalysis and in psychoanalysis generally. The New Library of Psychoanalysis is well placed to make available to the English-speaking world psychoanalytic writings from other European countries and to increase the interchange of ideas between British and American psychoanalysts.

The Institute, together with the British Psychoanalytical Society, runs a low-fee psychoanalytic clinic, organizes lectures and scientific events concerned with psychoanalysis and publishes the *International Journal of Psychoanalysis*. It also runs the only UK training course in psychoanalysis which leads to membership of the International Psychoanalytical Association – the body which preserves internationally agreed standards of training, of professional entry, and of professional ethics and practice for psychoanalysis as initiated and developed by Sigmund Freud. Distinguished members of the Institute have included Michael Balint, Wilfred Bion, Ronald Fairbairn, Anna Freud, Ernest Jones, Melanie Klein, John Rickman and Donald Winnicott.

Previous General Editors include David Tuckett, Elizabeth Spillius and Susan Budd. Previous and current Members of the Advisory Board include Christopher Bollas, Ronald Britton, Catalina Bronstein, Donald Campbell, Sara Flanders, Stephen Grosz, John Keene, Eglé Laufer, Juliet Mitchell, Michael Parsons, Rosine Jozef Perelberg, David Taylor and Mary Target, and Richard Rusbridger, who is now Assistant Editor.

ALSO IN THIS SERIES

TITLES IN THE NEW LIBRARY OF PSYCHOANALYSIS TEACHING SERIES

THE NEW LIBRARY OF PSYCHOANALYSIS

General Editor: Dana Birksted-Breen

Time, Space and Phantasy

Rosine Jozef Perelberg

Routledge
Taylor & Francis Group

LONDON AND NEW YORK

First published 2008
by Routledge
27 Church Road, Hove, East Sussex BN3 2FA

Simultaneously published in the USA and Canada
by Routledge
270 Madison Avenue, New York, NY 10016

Routledge is an imprint of the Taylor & Francis Group, an Informa business

Typeset in Bembo by RefineCatch Limited, Bungay, Suffolk
Printed and bound in Great Britain by
TJ International Ltd, Padstow, Cornwall
Paperback cover design by Sandra Heath

This publication has been produced with paper manufactured to
strict environmental standards and with pulp derived from
sustainable forests.

British Library Cataloguing in Publication Data
A catalogue record for this book is available from the British Library

Library of Congress Cataloging-in-Publication Data
Perelberg, Rosine Jozef.
Time, space, and phantasy / Rosine Jozef Perelberg.
p. ; cm.
Includes bibliographical references and index.
ISBN 978-0-415-46321-8 (hardback) – ISBN 978-0-415-46322-5 (pbk.)
1. Psychoanalysis. 2. Time perception. 3. Space perception. 4. Fantasy.
I. Title.
[DNLM: 1. Psychoanalysis. 2. Imagination. 3. Memory.
4. Sexuality–psychology. 5. Space Perception. 6. Time Perception.
WM 460 P437t 2008]
RC506.P38 2008
616.89′17—dc22

2007043071

ISBN: 978-0-415-46321-8 (hbk)
ISBN: 978-0-415-46322-5 (pbk)

'The only reason for time is so that everything doesn't happen at once'

Albert Einstein

To Sergio, naturally.

Contents

About the authors

Rosine Jozef Perelberg, PhD, is a Training Analyst, Fellow of the British Institute of Psychoanalysis. She is Visiting Professor in the Psychoanalysis Unit, Division of Psychology and Language Sciences at University College, London. Between 2003 and 2007 she was Chair of the Curriculum Committee and served on the Admissions and Education Committees of the Institute of Psychoanalysis. She is currently a member of the Training Staff Committee. She undertook her PhD in Social Anthropology at the London School of Economics. Between 1989 and 1999 she was an Associate Editor of the New Library of Psychoanalysis and sat on the Editorial Board of the International Journal of Psychoanalysis.

She is on the advisory board of numerous international journals. Since 1997 she has convened, with Monique Cournut and Chantal Lechartier-Atlan from the Société Psychanalytique de Paris, the British–French Colloquium on Sexuality. As well as numerous publications in the *International Journal of Psycho-Analysis, Nouvelle Revue de Psychanalyse, Psychiatrie de l'Enfant, Revue Francaise de Psychosomatique, Actualités Psychosomatiques, Jornal Brasileiro de Psicanálise Trieb* and *Kinderanalyse*, she has also edited the following books: *Female Experience: Three Generations of British Women Psychoanalysts on Work with Women* (1997, co-edited with Joan Raphael-Leff), *Psychoanalytic Understanding of Violence and Suicide* (1998), *Dreaming and Thinking* (2000), *Freud: A Modern Reader* (2005) and *Time and Memory* (2007).

In 2007 she was named one of the Ten Women of the Year by the National Council of Women in Brazil.

Bella Jozef is Emeritus Professor of Hispano-American Literature at the Federal University of Rio de Janeiro. She has won numerous prestigious international prizes, including the Academic Palms (France), the Order of the Sun (Peru), the Order of May (Argentina), the Book Prize (Organization of American States) and the Medalha Pedro Ernesto da Câmara dos Vereadores awarded by the Brazilian Academy of Writers. Between 2005 and 2007 she was Vice President of PEN Club do Brasil. She has also been Vice President of the Instituto Internacional de Literatura Iberoamericana (Mexico).

She has been visiting Professor at the following universities: Hebrew University of Jerusalem (1972–1973), Universidad Complutense de Madrid (1977) and the Romulo Gallegos Centre for Study (Caracas, Venezuela, 1986). She is also Honorary Professor of the Universidad Nacional Mayor de San Marcos, Peru (the oldest in Latin America). For several years, she has been a judge for several international awards, most notably the International Juan Rulfo Prize for Latin-American Literature (Mexico) and the International Romulo Gallegos Prize (Venezuela). She has written hundreds of papers and twelve books, amongst which are *História da Literatura Hispano Americana, Antología General da Literatura Brasileira, A Máscara e o Enigma, O Espaço Reconquistado* and *Borges*. She has translated the work of Jorge Luis Borges, Mario Vargas Llosa, Jorge Ibargüengoitia, José Luis Romero and Antonio Skármeta into Portuguese. She lives and teaches in Rio de Janeiro, Brazil.

Preface

Rosine Perelberg is a celebrated psychoanalyst from the British Society, well-known internationally, and frequently invited to lecture and to participate in international meetings. Her career has some interesting characteristics. Before training at the British Psychoanalytical Society she read social anthropology at the Federal University of Rio de Janeiro, Brazil and is a member of several scientific groups in Latin America. When she came to England she undertook a PhD in social anthropology at the London School of Economics.

Following the tradition of her native country, she has been in close contact with the work of French psychoanalysts. Her deep knowledge of the French tradition is quite remarkable, as her bibliography shows. She is currently a Senior Lecturer in psychoanalytic theory at University College, London. She has already published on British women psychoanalysts and her contribution to the understanding of violence and suicide is internationally respected. She has edited *Freud: A Modern Reader* (2005), an impressive volume that establishes a dialogue between psychoanalytic cultures.

In this collection of papers, Rosine Perelberg displays first and foremost a very deep knowledge of Freud's ideas, something relatively uncommon in current British psychoanalytic literature. Notions that are sometimes neglected, such as 'désir' and 'jouissance', are explored; other topics such as absence, predominant in French psychoanalysis, are also clarified. In addition to considering concepts of Freud's metapsychology, the author also takes into account the important influence of Winnicott as well as others such as Bion. Beyond the psychoanalytic field, Rosine Perelberg's comments on the work of

Claude Lévi-Strauss are also thought provoking. Throughout the book the clinical material is a testimony to her sensitivity, the openness of her listening and her courage in treating very difficult individuals.

The reader should pay special attention to Chapter 2: 'Après coup'. The author prefers to use the French term rather than the traditional English version: 'deferred action', and presents incisive clarification of the subject. As all those who are interested in this concept will know, the notion is already present in Freud's *Draft* and then in the case of the Wolf Man. This implies a conception of discontinuity of our mental life. In a letter to Fliess, Freud mentions things 'heard but understood *subsequently*', just as unconscious phantasies sometimes take place retrospectively.

This aspect of time organization can also be applied to dreams that are predictive of the future course of analysis. This original view proposed by Rosine Perelberg does not understand dreams as related only to situations in the past; they are sometimes forerunners of the future and relate to clinical material which is announced by them and will be apparent only *a posteriori*.

In Chapter 5, the author considers the relationship between identification and identity. Identification is a mode of thinking about objects in the unconscious; it is also closely linked to the primal scene and shows alternating oscillations between masculine and feminine positions. Identity is another kind of process that seeks unity; it is meant to receive projective identifications and contain them. Identity is a defence that protects from the fear of intrusion and maintains a distance toward the analyst, as Bouvet showed in his concept of object relationships in France in the late fifties. It can also be related to Sandler's concept of safety. In other words, it is opposed to the dynamic fluidity between masculine and feminine, which is a characteristic of identification. Identification is built through the relationship with the mother's body and can lead to delusional constructions. As Rosine Perelberg suggests, identity is a factor of stability that in the end is an illusion when it is put in perspective with bisexual identification.

Rosine Perelberg quotes Rosenfeld's ideas on 'thin or thick skins' that have enlightened our understanding of borderline conditions. Although I believe that the main value of this volume lies in its treatment of time, it also contains interesting thoughts on space, particularly the opposition between, to quote Rosine Perelberg, 'patients who create an empty space in the analyst's mind' and 'patients who fill the consulting room not only with their emotions and actions, but also with their words, dreams and associations'. She further suggests that both of these types of patients 'share an experience of something un–representable in their internal world, which is expressed in terms of either an absence or an excess of affect. . . . Many patients may alternate between these two types of experience. We are all familiar with patients who fill a session in order to empty it, or those who fill a session with their sense of emptiness. . . . One of the most significant changes in the analytic process in recent decades has been the way in which we all focus less on analysing detailed content and more on the way in which the internal world is actualised in the transference and countertransference.'

In Chapter 7, Rosine Perelberg gives a detailed account of the Controversial Discussions, using as her source the book published by King and Steiner. Hers is a most precise and clear account of the different ways of thinking closely related to 'après coup': later phantasies acquire aspects of earlier ones so that what one has access to is a retrospective modification of earlier phantasies. The distinction proposed by Perelberg between descriptive and dynamic après coup is compelling, as well as her idea of a 'structure with dominance'. The contributions of Jones, Rivière, Heimann and also Friedlander, Brierley, Sharpe, Hoffer and Glover are all sensitively distinguished in a text that breaks with traditional views about the Controversial Discussions.

The next chapter brings more precision to the meaning of what is happening at the moment it is happening as well as later on. Referring to Lacan, Rosine Perelberg argues that the symbolic offers a triangular perspective 'which refers to the structure of the alliance between mother, father and child', which always brings the third into the analytic situation. This topic is also expanded in the chapters entitled 'What Can You Possibly Learn From Babies?' (which won the Cesare Sacerdoti prize at the IPA Congress in Buenos Aires in 1991) and 'The Infant And The Infantile'. These two chapters further the debate on child observation and research and their place in the training of psychoanalysts in the British tradition.

I have only introduced some of the issues that are dealt with by this very rich book; I am sure the reader will enjoy reading the detailed development of all the themes Rosine Perelberg has chosen to treat. This is an exceptional volume that establishes lines of communication between colleagues from countries that are marked by different traditions. Through this, Rosine Perelberg makes her own original and creative contribution to psychoanalysis.

André Green

Acknowledgements

This book is the outcome of a journey on which I have been privileged to be accompanied by many inspiring friends and colleagues.

I would pinpoint the National Museum of Social Anthropology at the Federal University in Rio de Janeiro as the starting point. The museum buzzed with intellectual activity in the 1970s and this is where I firmly internalized the rigour of academic reading and writing. Being such an exotic discipline, anthropology had been virtually ignored until then under the prevailing political repression in Brazil; in the 1970s, apparently trivial aspects of daily life were elevated to the status of objects of study. Roberto Da Mata and Gilberto Velho were particularly inspiring teachers and introduced me to the rigour of qualitative research, as well as the importance of the creative construction of one's subject of study. Their influence has remained with me over the years and especially during the last decade as a supervisor of students' dissertations in the psychoanalysis unit at University College London.

My PhD research at the London School of Economics was a natural next step. Arriving at LSE was an anthropological experience in itself. The faculty seemed to have taken on an uncanny resemblance to the 'natives' they had been studying: James Woodburn to the hunter gatherer group he had worked with, and David McKnight, who was my first tutor, to the Australian aborigines. Maurice Bloch, who was studying the Marina of Madagascar, was one of the inspiring forces in the department. He was fiercely against psychoanalysis, so I felt I had truly landed among a foreign tribe. Jean la Fontaine and Ioan Lewis, my two doctoral supervisors, were in many ways as curious about me as I was about them. Our partnership was very successful and enjoyable and a PhD in Social Anthropology was the outcome. My personal rite of passage was the presentation of my research project, when I had to argue that the natives in England could be studied from an anthropological perspective, being as exotic as traditional societies in the eyes of the observer. Elizabeth Bott-Spillius had undertaken early anthropological research at LSE with English families, and she was one of the first people I met when I arrived in London.

The next stage on my journey comprised five years of training in family therapy at the Institute of Family Therapy and then the Tavistock Clinic, followed by a decade of work in the NHS, at the Maudsley Hospital and the Marlborough Family Service. These were fantastic years of learning about clinical practice with dear friends and colleagues: Alan Cooklin, Gill Gorel-Barnes, John Byng Hall, Christopher Dare, Eia Asen, and Ann Miller. Working with families and their networks enabled me to have a clear vision of systems, something that now comes easily to me, and is so useful in the understanding of organizations.

Training at the Institute of Psychoanalysis was a long-awaited goal. The British tradition manages to combine rigour in clinical practice with detailed listening to the patient's material through the analyst's free-floating attention. My supervisors Joseph Sandler and Pearl King and my consultants Harold Stewart and Anne-Marie Sandler each taught me through the sensitivity of their listening. My teachers and colleagues have been too numerous to mention individually. However, I am especially grateful to Don Campbell, Gregorio Kohon, and Sira Dermen for an environment in which we can all constantly refine our thinking. Other groups of colleagues that over the years have had an impact on my thinking include the Spanish Club and the Young Adults Research Group.

My participation in the Scientific Committee in the British Society and Admissions and Education committees of the Institute of Psychoanalysis gave me an experience of the positive impact that diversity and debate can bring to the furthering of psychoanalysis. My years as Chair of the Curriculum Committee enabled me to contribute to the continuous thinking on the curriculum of the training of the British Society.

André Green was the first to invite me to present a paper to the Société Psychanalityque de Paris. Over the years his work has been inspirational. He has been pivotal in the many invitations to present my work in France. It was at these events that several of the papers in this book were first presented.

Monique Cournut, Chantal Lechartier-Atlan and Danielle Kaswin have been my co-convenors of the British French Colloquium on sexuality that has alternated between London and Paris since 1997. Together with the Anglo-French Colloquium organized annually by Anne-Marie Sandler and Haydee Faimberg since 1992, these have been opportunities to explore in depth French psychoanalytic thinking and practice. Jean Luc Donnet's invitation to open the Colloques de Deauville in 2005 challenged me to write a chapter that had been waiting to be written for a long time. Marilia Aisenstein has also been a source of inspiration with her pioneering work and our ongoing conversation on questions of psychoanalytic practice and ethics.

My thanks go to Dana Birksted Breen for her support of this project and her incisive comments, and to my anonymous readers for their comments on the manuscript.

With Marion Burgner I experienced what it all meant in practice.

My patients consistently guide me through their thoughts and feelings into new journeys and explorations.

My students at Federal University of Rio de Janeiro, University College London and the Institute of Psychoanalysis continuously stimulate my thinking with their questions and their enthusiasm.

To Hélène Martin and Saven Morris, librarians of the British Society, for their availability and skills in finding much needed books and articles.

Thanks to Rabbi Thomas Salomon for a fascinating conversation about the notion of time in ancient Judaism.

Judith Perle is my friend and editor, with whom I learnt much about the English language over the past 30 years, since our first encounter at LSE.

Georges and Bella introduced me to the dimensions of space and time where phantasy takes place.

Sergio and Daniel have been with me in this journey, throughout which desire, knowledge and growth have been facilitated.

Thanks are also due to the following publishers:

- **The International Journal of Psycho-analysis** for permission to reprint the following papers:

    Perelberg, R. J. (1999) The Interplay Between Identifications and Identity in the Analysis of a Violent Young Man: Issues of Technique. 80: 31.

    Perelberg, R. J. (2003) Full and Empty Spaces in the Analytic Process. 84: 579–592.

    Perelberg, R. J. (2006) Controversial Discussions and *Apres-Coup*. 87: 1199–1220.

    Perelberg, R. J. (2007) Time and Space in Analytic Listening. 88: 1473–1499.

- **Karnac** for permission to reproduce the following:

    The chapter entitled 'The oracles in dreams: the past and the future in the present', originally published in Perelberg, R J (Ed) (2003) *Dreaming and Thinking*.

    The discussion in Sandler, J. Sandler, A-M and Davies, R (Eds) *Clinical and Observational Psychoanalytic Research: Roots of a Controversy: Andre Green and Daniel Stern* London: Karnac pp 91–99, that constitutes part of Chapter 11.

- **Routledge** for permission to quote from King, P and Steiner, R. (Eds.) (1991) *The Freud-Klein Controversies 1941–1945*, London, Routledge in association with the Institute of Psycho-Analysis.

- Gabriel García Márquez for permission to quote from *Cien Años de Soledad*. © Gabriel García Márquez, 1967.

Introduction

Time and space are central dimensions in psychoanalysis, indissolubly linked to each other. The enigma of one's origins, the origins of desire, sexuality and loss, introduces the individual to the dimensions of space, time and phantasy. They constitute the fundamental questions that human beings have asked about themselves since the beginnings of time, the answers to which ultimately provide a view of the individual that is not constituted solely in terms of a linear line of development. The individual in psychoanalytic formulations is de-centred and ruled by different temporalities, most of which escape conscious awareness.

If one attempts to summarize some of the crucial ideas that psychoanalysis has contributed to the understanding of the individual, one would include ideas on the different rhythms and temporalities co-existing within the individual, the importance of the presence and absence of the other for one's sense of time and space, the role of dreams and of repetitions, the role of mourning at the loss of the object, the crucial importance of sexuality (especially infantile sexuality) and the role of phantasy in psychic life and the retrospective importance of psychic events like the temporal perspective of the narrator in Proust's masterpiece *In Search of Lost Time* (1913–1927).

In observing the game played by his 18-month-old grandson, Freud noticed that he threw the cotton reel and said *fort* (disappeared), and then pulled it back and said *da* (found). This is understood by Freud as an attempt to master the comings and goings of the mother. It is in the space created by the absence of the object that a sense of time is instituted and the activity of phantasy takes place. Recent discussions of this game have stressed how the child is indeed throwing

1

the cotton reel inside the cot and thus, perhaps, also exploring the nature of his own disappearance from the mind of the mother. Who is she with when she is gone? The beginnings of the awareness of time, linked to the comings and goings of the mother, are also linked to the awareness of the existence of the father. In the space that is thus constructed the Oedipal situation also finds its origins. Time, space, phantasy and sexuality are completely intertwined.

The discovery of transference, and later of the compulsion to repeat, with the realization that the past is relived in the presence of the analyst was revolutionary, and perhaps paralleled the discovery of the unconscious itself. In the subtlety of the encounter between patient and analyst, aspects of the unconscious past of our patients are actualized in the present that itself produces new meanings that, in turn, retranslate the past. Gestures, affects and ideas within the process of free association give rise to a movement whereby meaning is progressively constructed.

Chapter 1 explores Freud's work and identifies a multi-dimensional model of temporality. The developmental and the structural models of the mind, the timelessness of the unconscious and repetition compulsion are some of the temporal dimensions discussed; the whole of psychic reality, in its positive and negative aspects, is structured in terms of time and space. The unconscious is only identifiable through its derivatives, as it is by definition invisible and unknowable. Freud tells us that it is only accessible in the gaps between the observable; the absence of time is its hallmark.

Chapter 2 outlines the complexity of Freudian notions of time, and suggests the structural determinacy of the concept of après coup.[1] Freud at times has been seen as a biologist of the mind, emphasizing a

---

[1] Throughout the book I have chosen to use the concept in French, instead of the German *nachträglich* (adjective) or *Nachträglichkeit* (noun) because 'après coup' evokes an intellectual field of debate in France, where the concept was not only first recovered by Lacan, but has been more centrally discussed than in any other country. Haydee Faimberg suggested that the fact that these are common words in the German language perhaps may be one explanation of why the concept has not acquired the same importance in the German psychoanalytic culture as it has in France. The very process of translation has demanded reflection (see Faimberg, 2005: 1). Laplanche also suggested: 'It is therefore in France, and in close relation to the problems of translation, that the importance of Nachträglichkeit has made itself felt' (1999: 26). The suggestion is that one is already dealing with an *interpretation* of a concept, which implies a particular understanding of it (Laplanche, 1999: 263).

biological and genetic model of development and the various phases of development (oral, anal, phallic, genital). Others have seen him as teleological, with his notion of primary unconscious phantasies. The richness of Freud's formulations is centred in the complexity of all these perspectives on time, which perhaps might be considered as more revolutionary than those of any of his followers. An analysis of Freud's views suggests that he did not regard time as an absolute entity but as something that is constantly interpreted in terms of the individual's existence. In this way, Freud constructed a real anthropology of time.

Psychoanalysis has brought about a revolution in the modern understanding of time and space in the constitution of the individual. Einstein's theory of relativity, written in 1905, discovered that time is not absolute, maintaining fixed values (as Newton had previously proposed), but depends on the relative position and speed of the observing individual. Some 10 years later, in 1915 (the same year that Freud wrote his metapsychological papers), Einstein was to further propose the general theory of relativity, indicating that the time interval between two events is measured differently according to the observer's perspective. Time ceased to be a 'reality' that existed in itself, and became an abstraction that connected objects and events (Hawking, 1988: 24). Different observers will attribute different times and positions to the same event (ibid.: 25). Freud developed a similar formulation when he indicated that the individual is not at the centre of himself, but is ruled by temporalities that escape his awareness. More specifically, the notion of après coup, which is discussed in several chapters in this book, illuminates the constant reshaping of time in the light of new events and experiences.

In Chapter 3, I suggest that in the early stages of the analysis of many patients, their dreams are predictive of the future course of the analysis. These dreams contain a condensed account of the transference relationship and encapsulate a narrative that unfolds as the analysis progresses. Although the analyst may be aware of the crucial relevance of such dreams at the time they occur, it is only retrospectively, at a later stage in the analysis, that these dreams are more fully comprehended. The paradox contained in the title of the chapter is that if *dreams predict the future, one is only aware of their 'prediction' more fully retrospectively (in terms of après coup)*. There is a specific experience that is conveyed in the account of these dreams that is felt by the analyst in the counter-transference but only slowly understood as the analysis unfolds. The analytic task is to change the course anticipated by these dreams, and introduce a difference in the 'prediction' these dreams make.

Some authors have suggested that the body of the dream is in itself inextricably linked to the body of the mother, and the wish to return to it. Is this not what the character Aurealiano Buendia explains, at the end of Gabriel García Márquez's seminal novel *One Hundred Years of Solitude* (1970): 'We are fighting this war ... so that a man can sleep with his mother'. The process of writing the novel implies the re-creation of a lost world that is perhaps at the basis of any process of creation. However, psychoanalysis has also discovered that one can only create what one has renounced.

Chapters 4, 5 and 6 present detailed analyses of four patients. In different ways they illustrate how I articulate the connections between time, mental space and phantasy in my clinical practice. A method that characterizes psychoanalytic work by members of the British Society can be identified – namely, paying attention to what takes place in the minutiae of the interaction between patient and analyst in the vicissitudes of the transference and counter-transference. The dimensions of space and time find meaning in the here and now of the transference situation, which by definition cannot be reduced to the present of the analysis. Transference is in itself guided by the compulsion to repeat, which indicates that the past is implicitly present in the present.

In Chapter 4, I present the analysis of Maria, who attempted to live in an endless present. Throughout my therapeutic work with her, I was consistently struck by the two-dimensionality that followed Maria into the consulting room, through which the past was eradicated and a sense of time and history was also lost. My patient's world had to be repetitive so that the experience of differences – between past and present, male and female, inside and outside, love and hate, her and me – was avoided. The past was privileged as opposed to the present and future. This past, however, was presented in a reified, stilted way, through repetitive and predictable accounts that contained no enlargement or new information. It had no depth and was simply presented as the opposite of now; events and sequences of events had no place.

In Chapter 5, I propose a distinction between 'identification' and 'identity'. Identification is a process that takes place in the unconscious and is the stuff of phantasies. Throughout his work Freud postulated the fluidity of identificatory processes. Identity, in contrast, is an attempt that each individual makes to organize these conflicting identifications in order to achieve an illusion of unity, which allows an individual to state 'I am this (and not that)'. A fundamental characteristic present in some violent patients is an attempt by an individual, potentially overwhelmed by the extreme fluidity between masculine and feminine identificatory processes, to establish a persona, an identity. Furthermore, in the analysis of Karl, a violent young man, the physical act of violence was an attempt to create a mental space in relation to confusing internal primary objects.

In the analysis of the borderline patient, identifying and keeping in mind the shifts between the identificatory processes and formulating them in terms of interpretations represent a technical challenge for the analyst. As the analyst is progressively better able to identify the patient's internal movement between different states and identificatory processes, and is able to integrate these into interpretations to the patient, the patient is himself more able to tolerate the internal fluidity between identificatory processes. The account of this successful analysis indicates that the individual is thus placed in a chain of reciprocity in relation to their internal and external objects. Karl's fundamental concern in his analysis was to regulate his distance from his analyst. I now understand this as representing his conflict about entering a chain of reciprocity that is, ultimately, the force of the life instinct itself. It was Karl's inability to take part in this system of exchange that condemned him to death itself, to his coffin. In his analysis we were able to reach representations of this enclosure, which, by definition, indicates his progressive entrance into the symbolic sphere, with its associated dimensions of time and space.

In Chapter 6, I explore the idea that the analyst's counter-transference may be a crucial pathway that enables the analyst to understand their patients' mental states in the analytic treatment. I discuss two categories of patients who differ in terms of the impact they have on the counter-transference. On the one hand, there are patients who create an empty space in the analyst's mind. The response they provoke is a kind of depressive feeling that remains after they leave. The patient may bring dreams and associations, but they do not reverberate for the analyst. The experience is of dryness, a dearth of memory that may – at times – leave the analyst with a sense of exclusion from the patient's internal world. At the other extreme there are patients who fill the analyst's mind. They do that not only with their words, dreams and associations but also with their emotions and their actions. The analyst feels over-included in the patient's world. The pathway through which the analyst can understand both of these types of patients is via the counter-transference. Both types of patients find it difficult to deal with absence, and lack a 'capacity to be alone in the presence of the analyst'. The emphasis is on actions, rather than representations.

In Chapter 7, the concept of après coup is revisited and expanded. Some of the ideas contained in this chapter were originally presented in October 2005 to the opening of the Colloquium of Deauville, organized by Jean Luc Donnet on the theme of 'Après Coup Revisited'. In Chapter 2 of this book, I have already suggested that the concept of après coup was not mentioned even once during the Controversial Discussions in London between 1942 and 1944. Yet, when over 20 years ago I first read the text of these discussions, I thought that the concept would have shed further light onto the controversies in terms of issues of temporality. Moreover, in contrast to predominant views in the British Society, who maintain that the controversies were mainly between Anna Freud and Klein, I found that some of the analysts in the 'middle' had made some of the most profound criticisms of Kleinian views on temporality expressed at the time. This chapter is an exploration of these ideas.

In Chapter 8, I provide clinical illustrations of my understanding of the concept of après coup. Particularly relevant to the example I discuss is the primacy of sexuality, the erotic passivation in the transference that evokes the childhood traumatic sexual scene. In the Freudian model, sexuality and sexual phantasies are at the centre of the re-elaboration of meaning. All these experiences, however, acquire fuller meaning in the present. It is by interpreting the transference that an experience of the past makes sense in the present, which in turn gives new meaning to the past. This chapter is also illustrative of the pace of an analysis, of how the patient's free association finds shape and meaning in the analyst's listening. It is in this process that something new and surprising takes place that had not been expected by either patient or analyst, and yet had been present from the beginning of the analysis.

In Chapter 9, written together with Bella Jozef, we explore the work of the great contemporary Latin American novelist Gabriel Garcia Márquez, and examine the way in which he has utilized the interplay between different notions of time to construct his narrative.

6

We study *Cien Anos de Soledad (One Hundred Years of Solitude)* and suggest that through its use of time the novel deals with major and universal problems, such as a search for one's origins, incest, endogamy, separation, procreation and death. More specifically we suggest that there is a relationship between time and the formation of a couple that has allowed Márquez to write a novel that has become a myth of origins. These ideas are inspired by psychoanalytic and anthropological thinking, and a profound knowledge of Hispanic American literature. The novel encapsulates a myth that constitutes a longing for a return to a primary relationship. Freud has suggested that a passionate sexual union constitutes a re-finding of the primary object. The end of the novel presents the passion of an incestuous relationship, which brings with it the beginnings of time and also its end. The process of writing itself implies the re-creation of a lost world, as one can only create what one has renounced.

The myths created by this and other Latin American novels have been termed 'magical realism': the characters are ambiguous, past and present become blurred and life and death complement and are in a dialogue with each other. There is no escape from 'reality' to an imaginary world where daily life is forgotten. In the process, the cartography of a continent, with its particular history and struggles, is delineated.

Lesser has discussed the capacity of fiction to telescope time:

In a sense the feat which fiction performs with time is comparable to that which cartographers perform with space by the device of scale. Just as a map helps us to visualize things our unaided eyes could never perceive – for example, the contours of a continent – so a story helps us to overcome the limitations of our eyes, minds and memories and see in a single instant the connections among events sprawling over decades of time. . . . Fiction compresses time and still manages to convey the 'feel' of time itself, its relentlessness, its indifference to man and his purposes . . .

(1962: 169)

Chapter 10, written in 1986 and chronologically the earliest chapter in this book, is derived from a paper written for the Baby Observation Seminars, in my first year of training in the British Society. The issue of the Baby Observation Seminars captures some of the controversies in psychoanalytic thinking in terms of temporality.

7

What is at stake is not only the model of temporality adopted by the specific teacher, but also the differentiation between the infant and the infantile (an issue that will be discussed in Chapter 11). Some may think that one can learn about the development of the internal world of the baby, and they emphasize a great deal of conceptual speculation in their seminars. Others underline the developmental model, whereas still others tend to speculate about the potential structuring of the mind of the infant. In the chapter, I present observations of a baby in the context of his relationship with his mother in the first year of development. The theoretical point I propose is that although I observe a phenomenon of regression in an 8-month-old baby, it is only retrospectively, and at a much later stage, that one will be able to see how crucial this was for the internal world of the baby (in terms of après coup). Because we are observing a baby for a period of only one year, we cannot know what the influence of future experiences will be. Our experience with patients indicates that even if they bear the mark of past unprocessed materials, their experiences will have been rearranged and reorganized in terms of après coup.

The final chapter links the issue of temporality with research, and combines two papers presented at two different debates at the University of London. The first involved a debate between André Green and Daniel Stern, at which I was one of the discussants (the others being Irma Brenman Pick and Anne Alvarez). The second was a paper presented in 1999, again on the debate between research and psychoanalysis, with the participation of Peter Fonagy and André Green. Green warns us that there is a profound difference between the infant, who can be observed in the course of development, and the infantile, which is a construction of the analyst in the context of the analysis of adults.

Stern suggests throughout his work that he has been able to navigate some of the uncharted territory of infancy. Green, for his part, warns us not to confuse the infantile (in all of us) with the infant. Green's thesis is that psychoanalysis is incompatible with observation. Observation cannot tell us anything about intrapsychic processes, which are the true characterization of the subjective experience. Stern asks if a baby's experience can be structured at the very moment in which it is being produced, the moment of 'coup', he suggests. He proposes the notion of 'musical contours', which, like musical phrases, are structured as they are being experienced. In listening to music, the form of a phrase is captured while it is being heard. It is not, Stern suggests, structured après coup, even though its perceived structure can be modified in the light of later musical phrases.

I suggested on that occasion, and in this chapter, that in his monumental series of volumes on the analysis of myths in South America, Claude Lévi-Strauss suggested that 'one cannot translate music into *anything other than itself*'. Music cannot be reduced or transformed into anything that might be expressed verbally. Lévi-Strauss further suggested that it is the audience that invests music with one or various virtual meanings. It is the listener who is compelled to make up for the absent sense, and who attributes meaning to it in terms of their own previous experiences. Meaning is thus ultimately produced by interaction between the listener and the music.

This analogy allows us to think that there is a meaning that is produced by the interaction between mother and baby that does not relate to 'what is going on in the baby's mind', which is by definition unknowable and unreachable and, to use Lévi-Strauss's analogy of music, is irreducible to verbal understanding. This perspective is radically different from that which stresses the mother as the interpreter of her baby's behaviour. The mother's reinterpreting of her baby's feelings and thoughts is not solely an act of translation; it also actually produces meaning. This view highlights the essential importance of the mother's state of mind in the constitution of the child's sense of his own mind.

Through two brief clinical examples I indicate how several concepts are necessary and serve as intermediaries in our attempt to understand observations. Representations cannot be inferred by observation, but can only be surmised through other representations. From the examples presented, I suggest that if some shapes and rhythms of a primitive mode of relating to the external object can be alluded to and grasped in analysis, meaning can only be derived après coup, after the emergence of symbolic representations and genital sexuality has retranslated earlier experiences.

★   ★   ★

This book represents an intellectual and emotional journey over a period of many years. Its preparation has allowed me to express the coherence of this path, where some of the same theoretical and clinical preoccupations centred on time, spacc and phantasy have guided my route from its very beginning, and appear in different forms, informing my questions and preoccupations about other themes.

Meanings are also transformed from one chapter to the next, acquiring new depths and dimensions as we move from clinical practice to theory, and back again.

The chapters are not presented in chronological order. Chapter 2 on après coup, for instance, was written after several of the subsequent chapters. It outlines, nevertheless, a theoretical construct that has been paradigmatic to my thinking and has illuminated my clinical praxis. It thus seemed natural to me that it should open the book. In the next three chapters I indicate how these theoretical ideas have guided my thinking in my clinical practice. The intensive, long-term analyses of 10 patients are presented. These chapters could also serve as illustrations of my thinking about the compulsion to repeat in the analyses of borderline patients, as well as about a theory of technique that emphasizes the analyst's listening, infantile sexuality, the patient's response to the presence and absence of the analyst, and the thirdness of the analytic setting.

Chapter 6 was presented to the Colloque de Deauville, and is my review of the 1942 Controversial Discussions in the British Society in the light of the concept of après coup. In many ways, however, it is the oldest in my mind, although it had to wait for many years to be written. The bi-directionality of the concept of après coup, discussed in Chapters 6 and 1, is exemplified in the very arrangements of the chapters in this volume. Like the mode of functioning in any analysis itself, one can have access to what took place, to the reasons that led us to interpret in the way we chose to do at a specific time, only après coup, as there is always an unconscious dimension to the interpretation that we do not have access to at the time itself.

PART ONE

Theory and Clinical Practice

1

Time and space in psychoanalysis and anthropology

Two temporal axes permeate Freud's work: the genetic, which articulates development with the biological dimension of the individual's life, and the structural, present in Freud's various models of the mind. They are associated with different spatial configurations: unconscious, preconscious and conscious in the topographical model of the mind (from 1900 until 1923), and the id, ego and superego in the structural model (from 1923 onwards).

Freud's letter to Fliess of 6 December 1896 announces the mapping of the mind that he intended to develop in Chapter VII of *The Interpretation of Dreams*:

> As you know, I am working on the assumption that our psychic mechanism has come into being by a process of stratification: the material present in the form of memory traces being subjected from time to time to a rearrangement in accordance with fresh circumstances – to a retranscription. Thus what is essentially new about my theory is the thesis that memory is present not once but several times over, that it is laid down in various kinds of indications . . . I do not know how many of these registrations there are – at least three, probably more.
>
> (Masson, 1985: 207)

Whilst starting with an archaeological metaphor that underlined a linear conception of time, in this passage Freud indicates a progressive complexification of his model that will understand temporality along several axes (a central theme developed in Chapters 2 and 7 of this book). *The Interpretation of Dreams* establishes a link between space and time, as Freud refers to a topographical model, using a spatial metaphor in an attempt to map the mind. Freud suggests (1900b: 536) that 'the scene of action of dreams is different from that of waking life'. This statement includes the notion of two moments in time, between which there is a period of 'latency' and elaboration. This spatial disjunction parallels a temporal one, elaborated in the process of après coup.

Freud refers to the mind in terms of a 'physical locality', although he is careful not to link it to any anatomical location. Thoughts are 'never localised in organic elements of the nervous system but, as one might say, between them' (1900b: 611). Each space is ruled by a certain type of temporality, and here Freud further develops his distinction between primary and secondary processes, calling the rules that govern the unconscious 'primary process'. Unconscious thoughts must undergo a process of transformation or distortion before they are accessible to consciousness. Primary process concerns the rules or grammar of that transformation. These rules disguise unacceptable or traumatic unconscious ideas, which can only be understood via a process of interpretation.

Primary process is ruled by displacement, condensation and conditions of representability. Displacement allows an apparently insignificant idea or object to be invested with great intensity that originally belonged elsewhere. Condensation is the means by which, according to Freud, thoughts that are mutually contradictory make no attempt to do away with each other, but persist side by side. They often combine to form condensations just as though there were no contradictions between them, or arrive at compromises that our conscious thoughts would never tolerate. Condensation is another way of disguising unacceptable thoughts pushing through into consciousness. Conditions of representability indicate why dreams represent words in figurative form, in images. Another rule of primary process is the *absence of chronological time*. Timelessness characterizes the unconscious mode of functioning. Different times co-exist, and this is what allows one to dream that one is a child, a baby or an older person all at the same time.

The association between dreams and earlier experiences, between the present and the past, is at the core of Freud's thinking about dreams: 'A dream might be described *as a substitute for an infantile scene modified by being transferred onto a recent experience*. The infantile scene is unable to bring about its own revival and has to be content with returning as a dream' (1900b: 546).

14

Dreaming, Freud adds later, 'is a piece of infantile life that has been superseded' (1900b: 567). It is this characteristic that creates the sense of timelessness in dreams. The childhood wish, however, 'is only represented in the dream's manifest content by an allusion, and has to be arrived at by an interpretation of the dream' (1900a: 199).

Other modes of functioning typical of the unconscious are an absence of negation (in the unconscious 'No' does not exist, and contradictory ideas persist side by side), and representability, whereby abstract ideas are replaced in dreams by pictorial expressions.

Freud contrasted the rules of primary process with secondary processes that exercise a regulatory function over the primary process, through the establishment of the ego (or the person's self).

Freud also introduced the progression and regression that occur in the movement between the different psychic 'localities'. Progression moves from the unconscious to the preconscious–conscious; regression moves from the preconscious–conscious towards the unconscious, as happens in dreams.

Once the baby has an experience of satisfaction, such as the primary experience of feeding at the breast, a trace is laid down in the memory, which Freud designated the memory trace. When the baby is next hungry he will wish to repeat that same experience at the breast that satisfied his hunger. The object – the breast – is now sought, and provides the prototype for all further experiences, including that of love. The finding of the object is always a re-finding:

> An essential component of this experience of satisfaction is a particular perception (that of nourishment, in our example), the mnemic image of which remains associated thenceforward with the memory trace of the excitation produced by the need. As a result of the link that has thus been established, next time this need arises a psychical impulse will at once emerge, which will seek to recathect the mnemic image of the perception and to re-evoke the perception itself, that is to say, to re-establish the situation of the original satisfaction. An impulse of this kind is what we call a wish; the reappearance of the perception is the fulfilment of the wish . . . Thus the aim of this first psychical activity was to produce a 'perceptual identity' – a repetition of the perception which was linked with the satisfaction of the need.
>
> (Freud, 1900b: 565–566)

15

and:

> No one who has seen the baby sinking back satiated from the breast and falling asleep with flushed cheeks and a blissful smile can escape the reflection that this picture persists as a prototype of the expression of sexual satisfaction in later life.
>
> (Freud, 1905: 182)

And later:

> This satisfaction must have been previously experienced in order to have left behind a need for its repetition.
>
> (Freud, 1905: 184)

This primitive experience takes place in the intimacy of the contact with the body of the mother. The 'right' amount of eroticism is crucial, so that it is not too much, overexciting the child, or too little, without an erotic investment by the baby or its relationship with his/her own body. Inevitably, however, the mother oscillates between 'excess of gratification and excess of frustration' (Green, 1986b). This erotic dimension lies at the basis of what Laplanche (1997) has referred to as the seduction of the child by the adult, through the enigmatic message addressed, unilaterally, by the adult to the child, and which is to be found at the very heart of the 'primal fantasies' (see Chapter 2).

In *The Two Principles of Mental Functioning*, Freud (1911c) extended the distinction he had pointed out 15 years earlier between the 'primary system' and 'secondary system' of mental functioning and introduces the term 'reality testing'.

In the primary system, such as operates in the young infant, in dreams and to a large extent in waking phantasies, the pleasure principle dominates the scene. The baby's needs can, in the first instance, be satisfied in terms of hallucinatory wish fulfilment. It is its failure to procure adequate satisfaction, with subsequent frustration, that compels the further step of taking reality into account. One can see here the precursors of Winnicott's ideas on disillusionment. Now it is no longer only what is pleasurable that counts; reality also has an important role. Freud (1911c) indicates that it is in the process of waiting that *attention* is developed, so as to be prepared for the new impressions. Motor discharge, instead of being inchoate as earlier, is organized in the direction of behaviour. This is carried out through a process of thought. The link is thus established between time (waiting), space and the beginnings of thought.

It is with the appearance of the reality principle that one species of thought activity was split off and kept free from reality testing: phantasy life, the continuation of play in children. There is a link between the wish, the intervention of the reality of waiting and phantasy life.

'In the absence of a real object, the infant reproduces the experience of the original satisfaction in a hallucinated form' (Laplanche, in Steiner, 2003: 13). Laplanche suggested that:

> This is 'a myth of origin': by this figurative expression Freud claims to have recovered the very first up urgings of desire. It is an analytic 'construction', or fantasy, which tries to cover the moment of separation between before and after, whilst still containing both a mythical moment of disjunction between the pacification of need (*Befriedgung*) and the fulfilment of desire (*Wunscherfullung*), between the two stages represented by real experience and its hallucinatory revival. It is here that the notion of space, separation from the object, is instituted, and also the beginnings of phantasy life.
>
> (Steiner, 2003: 13)

Winnicott's work on the function and development of play was inspiring for the understanding of mental space, phantasy and dreaming and their function in mental life and development. Winnicott pointed out the mother's facilitating function in enabling the child to have an illusion of omnipotence. Development takes place in the slow process of disillusionment that needs to be well modulated in the relationship with the mother. Winnicott (1971: 13) viewed potential space as 'The intermediate area . . . that is allowed to the infant between . . . primary creativity and objective perception based on reality testing'. It is 'unchallenged in respect of its belonging to inner or external reality, [it] constitutes the greater part of the infant's experience, and throughout life is retained in the intense experiencing that belongs to the arts, religion and imaginative living' (1971: 16). 'It is intermediate between the dream and the reality that is called cultural life' (1971: 150). 'In so far as the infant has not achieved transitional phenomena I think the acceptance of symbols is deficient, and the cultural life is poverty stricken' (Winnicott *et al.*, 1989: 57).

The infant should not wait too long, or too little. If he waits too much the negative of the object, its absence, will be over-emphasized in relation to its presence. What is also evoked is the multitude of registrations in this first experience of the mother: sounds, smells, textures and rhythms that constitute the baby's environment. Anne Dennis refers to this as an 'archaic temporality' based on rythmic experiences, inseparable from auto eroticism. It lacks the characteristics of Pcs/Cs thought (linearity, structuring in terms of part, present and future, order, and abstract representation) (1995). Botella and Botella (2005), exploring the links between trauma, the negative and the difficulties in the emergence of the experience of intelligibility, have suggested the potential role of transformation that psycho-analysts can perform in a session through the work of *figurability*. This arises from a state of formal regression in the analyst, which allows access to a state of 'memory without recollection', when something emerges that has not been able to be represented (2005: XV). In their view, the absence of representable content does not mean an absence of an event (2005: 164).

Kristeva describes the tasting of Proust's madeleine in the following way: 'Soaked in tea, the morsel of cake touches the palate. This point of contact (the most infantile and archaic that a living being can have with an object or a person, since food, along with air, is that exquisite need that keeps us alive and curious about other people) . . .' (1996: 17). Proust's *search for lost time* is a never-ending search for the 'lost, invisible temple of the *sensory time of our subjective memories*' (1996: 171). Sensory time, so much of which is pre-verbal and archaic, is perhaps some of what will be found and given words in an analysis in terms of après coup.

In the metapsychological papers, Freud introduces the concept of primary phantasies (*Urphantasien*) that are there from the beginning, but can only be 'reactivated' so to speak in the life of each individual in terms of après coup (see Freud, 1915a–e, 1916–17, 1918; Laplanche and Pontalis, 1973; Perron, 2001; Steiner, 2003; Perelberg, 2006). Laplanche and Pontalis (1973) view these primary phantasies, which are transmitted philogenetically, as structuring experience. Green suggests the notion of *the disposition to re-acquisition* (2002a). Primal phantasies are re-actualized through individual experience. These ideas will be further explored in Chapter 2.

Freud's paper *Mourning and Melancholia* (1915d) introduces a major shift in his work away from a theory that predominantly accounted for the vicissitudes of the drives and their representations toward a theory concerned with the internal world and identifications. It is the absence of the object that opens the space for the beginnings of thinking and, one can suggest, of time. Freud had already discussed the role of incorporation whereby the individual would identify in the oral mode with the lost object; the constitution of the internal world was made through identifications. In *Beyond the Pleasure Principle* (1920a), Freud interprets his grandson's game with a cotton reel as the child's attempt to master his mother's absence. In *The Loss of Reality in Neurosis and Psychosis* (1924b), Freud states: 'But it is evident that a precondition for the setting up of reality is that the objects have been lost which once brought real satisfaction' (1924b: 183). In *Negation* (1925b), Freud puts forward the formulation that thinking begins 'when the omnipotent control over the subjective object is shattered'. The absence of the object, whilst inaugurating space, is also connected with the beginnings of time. The simplest narrative contains the story of an object that left and then came back. Is the dimension of loss, enquires Laplanche, 'co-extensive with temporalisation itself?' (1999: 241). The centrality of the notion of absence and waiting in the structuring of the mind cannot be underestimated. In the analytic process this will find its echoes in the silence and the waiting of the analytic attitude.

These ideas are central to Bion's thinking, and he indicates the way in which the maternal function of containing thoughts and feelings is internalized and enables the creation of mental space. Using a mathematical metaphor, he pointed out that the geometrical concept of space derives from an experience of 'the place where something was'. If this concept is to be used to characterize mental phenomena, the concept of space in dreams designates the place where the lost object was, or the space where some form of emotion used to be (Bion, 1970: 10). It thus implies that an object's place has been lost. This mental space as a thing in itself is unknowable, although it can be represented by thoughts. Bion links the existence of this space to the experience of a container that is receptive to projections and thus allows for the realization of mental space as well as the development of thought. According to Bion, thoughts lead to emotional development, and are to be contrasted with acting out, when the space left for thinking is felt to be intolerable and there is pressure for the apparent, immediate gratification that is felt to lie in action. As Hanna Segal (1980: 101) suggested, '. . . only what can be adequately mourned can be adequately symbolised'.

In a paper on Borges and mourning, Ogden (2000) suggests that successful mourning involves a demand for the individual to create something – whether it be a memory, a dream, a story, a poem, or a response to a poem – that begins to meet, and to be equal to, the full complexity of the relationship to what has been lost and to the experience of loss itself. Paradoxically, in this process one is enlivened by the experience of loss and death, even when what is given up or taken from us is an aspect of oneself.

In the French psychoanalytic literature the concept of desire is also related to an object that was known and then lost. Desire thus refers to an absence, and belongs to the same field as phantasy and dream (Mannoni, 1968: 111). That which is longed for 'only comes into existence *as an object* when it is lost to the baby or infant' (Mitchell, 1982: 6). 'Desire persists as an effect of a primordial absence and it therefore indicates that, in this area, there is something fundamentally impossible about satisfaction itself' (Mitchell, 1982: 6). In a paper on the universal tendency of debasement in the sphere of love, Freud (1912a) says: 'It is my belief that, however strange it may sound, we must reckon with the possibility that something in the nature of the sexual instinct itself is unfavourable to the realisation of complete satisfaction'.

This may be linked to what Britton (1999: 117) has defined as 'imagination': 'This is the idea that the imagination as a place in the mind where unwitnessed events take place is in origin the phantasised primal scene'. He calls this mental space 'the other room', in which parental existence continues during parental absence. These thoughts introduce a relationship between a three-dimensional space and the Oedipal situation.

Serge Viderman, in France, has suggested the notion of 'analytic space'. Meaning reached in the consulting room is not just an expression of a repetition of the past, but a construction that comes into existence for the first time in the analytic space (Viderman, 1970). What takes place in the analysis is happening there for the first time, and it is not a recapitulation of the past. Donnet (1995) has also put forward the notion of the 'analytic site', the site of an 'analysing situation', where transference, process, interpretation and counter-transference all manifest themselves and find a formulation in the transference interpretation. This last notion of the transference interpretation is one where space and time are articulated.

These ideas are crucial to the issues discussed in the following chapters of this book, from a theoretical as well as a clinical perspective. The capacity for mental space is ultimately connected to the capacity to bear the separation from the internal parents, which is inserted in the dimensions of absence, of waiting and of time. The constitution of the individual takes place in the context of the time–space created in the relationship with the mother (and her body), who, on the one hand, is the first seductress but also, on the other hand, institutes a certain rhythm in the tolerance of displeasure. The loss of the object is at the origin of pain, but also of anxiety and desire (Pontalis, 1977: 262). These ideas relate the notions of space and time to the individual's existence.

Kristeva (1996) has pointed out that Proust's first notebook for *Recherches*, dating from 1908, is part of his work of mourning the death of his mother in 1905, a process of morning that slowly makes use of substitutes, through a process of displacement. The search for the past connotes 'a *poiesis*, a creation of that which does not yet exist and must be guided towards the light' (1996: 19). Time itself becomes a process of creation.

Norbert Elias has suggested that the concept of time is a 'man-made' idea, a relatively recent invention of modern society. As a universal dimension, time is a 'social symbol', a symbolic expression of the experience that everything that exists is part of an incessant sequence of events (1992: 40). Different societies construct different myths and answers to resolve the question of the passage of time. The struggle with the enigma of one's origins, the sexual relationship between the parents and the distinctions between the genders and between the generations find their expressions in a range of rituals, ranging from birth to funerary rituals. Chapter 9 demonstrates that these are questions present in some of the great literary works.

Anthropologists have suggested that many traditional societies do not have such abstract notions of time, but utilize concepts more closely related to their daily activities. Evans-Pritchard (1940), for instance, in his study of the Nuer of the Sudan, discovered that there was no abstract notion of time, but that they thought in terms of succession and sequences of human activities. Their points of reference are the activities themselves (1940: 103–104). Similarly Bourdieu refers to the Kabyle of Algeria: 'Time cannot be dissociated from the experience of activity and of the space in which that activity takes place. Duration and space are described by reference to the performance of a concrete task: e.g. the unit of duration is the time one needs to do a job, to work a piece of land with a pair of oxen. Equally, space is evaluated in terms of duration, or better, by reference to the activity occupying a definite lapse of time, for example, a day at the plough or a day's walk' (1963: 60).

Hallpike notes, in relation to the Kaguru of Tanzania: 'Kaguru time concepts are concerned simply with the succession of events and their duration and the relation of these successions of events with the present; and this is not evidence of an abstract awareness of time as a dimension in relation to which several processes can be co-ordinated' (1979: 346).

Gell (1992) took a different position, and argued that even cultures that apparently ignore a more abstract notion of time implicitly have a concept of time-dimension. His universalistic position was the subject of heated debate in the Friday morning seminars at the Department of Social Anthropology at the London School of Economics in the late 1970s. Stern has more recently argued that time itself is not a 'real' empirical experience, but only a generalized abstraction (2003: 18).

While anthropologists have debated the variation of notions of time in traditional societies, psychoanalysts have examined distortions of the notion of time within individuals. Hartocollis (1983) has suggested that the different psychopathologies are articulated with different distortions of the notion of time within the individual. These ideas are developed by Rose (1997) and Williams (2007). Thus, the obsessional patient suppresses the awareness of the passage of time; the borderline person is forever concerned with the here and now of the present, and has affects devoid of the time perspective. For the schizophrenic patient time stands still, whereas psychotic depressed patients feel that time moves along for ever while they themselves 'stand still' (Hartocollis, 1983: 119). Since the discussion of the case of Emma (Breuer and Freud, 1895), Freud indicated the two temporalities present in the hysteric, that of the registration of events and a second moment when they acquire psychic meaning as a result of a process of (sexual) maturation. He returned to the two temporalities in the analysis of Dora (1905) – the time of the symptom and the time of dreaming (the paper on Dora was initially called 'Dream and Hysteria'), where the theories of infantile sexuality can be identified with the phantasy of seduction by an adult, and the alternation between the reality and the pleasure principles.

The perception that patients in the analytic setting reproduce their internal experiences of time in the relationship with their analyst has been discussed in a recent collection of papers by Rose (1997), Bell (2007), Williams (2007), Davies (2007) and Bronstein (2002) (see also Perelberg, 2007). A common theme that emerges from their writings is the notion that the realization of the passage of time is an achievement in the process of development that requires a capacity to both recognize the other and be able to separate from the primary objects. It inserts the individual in the process of exchange with the other.

In psychoanalytic terms, the acceptance of an order based on the differentiation between the genders and the generations and on the incest taboo introduces the individual to an experience of renunciation and mourning (Cosnier, 1990). This is the source of identifications and thus of the foundation of psychic reality (Freud, 1917). Freud suggested that the catastrophe of the Oedipus complex represents the victory of the human order over the individual. Through the Oedipus complex, the individual enters the symbolic order by establishing the differences between the sexes and the generations. As Lévi-Strauss (1947) has suggested, together with the incest taboo, and as a corollary of it, it is the differentiation between the sexes and the generations that inserts the person into an exogamous system of exchange. The origins of society, according to Freud (1913b), emphasize the control that mankind had to exercise over its sexuality and desire, excluding force and violence and introducing the notion of space and time.

This is very well expressed in Lévi-Strauss's words:

To this very day mankind has always dreamed of seizing and fixing that fleeting moment when it was permissible to believe that the law of exchange could be evaded, that one could gain without losing, enjoy without sharing. At either end of the earth and at both extremes of time, the Sumerian myth of the golden age and the Andaman myth of the future life correspond, the former placing the end of primitive happiness at a time when the confusion of languages made words into common property, the latter describing the bliss of the hereafter as a heaven where women will no longer be exchanged, i.e., removing to an equally unattainable past or future the joys, eternally denied to social man, a world in which one might *keep to oneself*.

(1947: 496–497).

2

Après coup and unconscious phantasy

In an essay written in 1961 the anthropologist Edmund Leach suggested that the modern Western notion of time embraces two quite different kinds of experiences that are both distinct and contradictory: the notions of repetition and of irreversible processes. He contrasted these notions with those existing in certain tribal societies, where time is experienced as discontinuous, as a sequence of oscillations between polar opposites. These three notions of time – repetition, irreversibility and oscillation – are all present in the functioning of the mind and were discussed by Freud in his formulations about the psychic apparatus.

In this chapter I suggest that the concept of après coup plays a dominant role in the complexity of the various notions of time in Freud's work, in that it is the notion of time that gives meaning to all the others. The concept of après coup is central to an understanding of Freud's formulations, and works as a 'general illumination' in his conceptual framework, as discussed by Marx in his Introduction to *A Critique of Political Economy*:

> In all forms of society, it is a determined production and its relations which assign every other production and its relations their rank and influence. It is a general illumination (*Beleuchtung*) in which all the colours are plunged and which modifies their special tonalities. It is a special ether which defines the specific weight of every existence arising in it.
>
> (Marx, 1867: 27)

This quotation points out the presence of the structure in its effects, i.e. the notion of structural causality. Althusser argues that this is contained in the notion of *Darstellung*, a key element of the Marxist

24

theory of value (Althusser, 1970: 298). It also suggests, however, that although the structure is present in its effects, it cannot be seen, so that the concept also suggests the efficacy of an absence.[1] I tend to think of après coup in this way: as a central idea in Freud; it illuminates everything else.

Freud's notions of time

Freud's conceptualization of the psychic apparatus postulates that distinct timings must be at work.[2] Experiences are registered in the psychic apparatus, which is a system that exists in both space and time, and these are re-experienced and externalized through the analytic process. Repetition, irreversibility and oscillation are all present in the functioning of the mind. Freud was always considering different notions of time at any given moment of his work, as evidenced by the complexity of both his theoretical writings and his analyses of clinical cases.

The first concept of time in Freud's formulations is that of the *evolution and development* of the individual, in terms of both the biological development of the baby and the emergence of functions

---

[1]   Althusser (1970) put forward an interpretation of Marx's work from a structuralist perspective. Marx did not see social change as the result of a single contradiction between the forces and the relations of production, but held a rather more complex view of it. Althusser suggests that Marx's concept of contradiction is inseparable from the concept of a social whole. In order to emphasize that changes in social structure relate to numerous contradictions, Althusser describes these changes as 'over-determined'. This interpretation allows us to account for the way in which many different circumstances may play a part in the course of events, and furthermore permits us to grasp how these states of affairs may combine to produce unexpected social changes, or 'ruptures'. However, Althusser does not mean to say that the events that determine social changes all have the same causal status. While a part of a complex whole, economic practice is, in his view, a *dominant structure*: it plays a major part in determining the relations between other spheres, and has a greater effect on them than they have on it. The most prominent aspect of society (the religious aspect in feudal formations and the economic aspect in capitalist ones) is called the 'dominant instance', and is in turn determined 'in the last instance' by the economy. For Althusser, the economic practice of a society determines which other aspect of it dominates the society as a whole.

When I think about the notion of après coup in connection with my clinical practice, I think of a structure in dominance in that it is through après coup that meaning can be grasped 'in the last instance'. The notion of après coup gives a specific meaning to the whole body of Freud's theory on sexuality, trauma and seduction (see also Faimberg, 2005: 2).

[2]   See Green's masterly account of Freud's work on temporality (2002b).

25

and behaviour patterns that result from exchanges between the organism and its environment. This is the genetic perspective, based on the notion of developmental continuity. This dimension of time is linked for Freud to the development of the libido through the oral, anal, phallic and genital stages, with the understanding that each phase is superimposed on the preceding one, so that they co-exist. Libidinal development is dysphasic, in that there is a separation between infantile and adult sexuality.

A second concept of time refers to the *structuring of the individual* and the distinction between the ego, the id and the superego. Freud (1923) suggested that at birth no ego exists. It is primary repression that institutes the separation between the id and the ego, between primary and secondary processes that are, hereafter, regulated by different conceptions of time. The atemporality of the unconscious can only be accessed in terms of its derivatives in the system Pcpt-Cs. This is in contrast to the ego, which has 'taken on the task of representing the external world to the id' (1923: 75). To quote Freud again: 'The relation to time, which is so hard to describe, is also introduced into the ego by the perceptual system; it can scarcely be doubted that the mode of operation of that system is what provides the origin of the idea of time' (1923: 76). When the ego enters the scene, time and history also make their first appearance.

Freud suggested that the different timings in the id and the ego are thus inaugurated by repression. But when does repression occur? Here a third notion of time must be introduced. Freud (1926a) suggested that most of the repression that we deal with in our therapeutic work is repression by deferred action (après coup). By this he meant that experiences, impressions and memory traces may be revised at a later date, when the individual reaches a new stage of maturation (Laplanche and Pontalis, 1985: 111). The notion of après coup links up with the function of *repetition*. Freud stated: '. . . what is essentially new about my theory is the thesis that memory is present not once but several times over, that it is laid down in various species of indications' (in Masson, 1985: 207; see also Perelberg, 1993; Kohon, 1999a: 126, 143).

Although the full exposition of his theory appears in *The Wolf Man* (Freud, 1918), which can be viewed as providing a mythological perspective of Freud's theories on time, one can only grasp the full extent of the complexity of Freud's models of temporality by reading many of his papers, each of which indicates a new dimension that cannot be fully comprehended without taking the others into account. It is not until the metapsychological papers of 1915 that the notion of après coup acquires full significance. I will return to this point later.

For example:

- In *Sexuality in the Aetiology of the Neuroses* (1898), Freud mentions the notion of après coup (translated as deferred action): 'I can do no more in these brief hints than mention the chief factors on which the theory of psychoneurosis is based: the deferred nature of the effect and the infantile state of the sexual apparatus and of the mental instrument . . . Since the manifestations of the psychoneuroses arise from the deferred action of unconscious psychical traces, they are accessible to psychotherapy . . .' (1898: 281).
- It is in *The Interpretation of Dreams* (Freud, 1900a) that the themes of the laying down of memory and memory traces, as well as the search for an identity of perception, are proposed: 'A young man who was a great admirer of feminine beauty was talking once – so the story went – of the good-looking wet-nurse who had suckled him when he was a baby: "I am sorry" he remarked, "that I didn't make a better use of my opportunity". I was in the habit of quoting this anecdote to explain the factor of "deferred action" in the mechanism of the psychoneurosis' (1900a: 204–205).
- In *Three Essays on the Theory of Sexuality* (1905), Freud proposes the developmental model of orality, anality, phallic phase and genitality.
- And in *Instincts and their Vicissitudes* (Freud, 1915a) the important issue of the characteristics of the drives is presented: 'The aim (Ziel) of an instinct is in every instant satisfaction, which can only be obtained by removing the state of stimulation at the source of stimuli, to control them or abolish them in the aim of restoring the previous state of the instinct' (1915a: 122).
- In his analysis of the Wolf Man (1918), Freud discussed how the neurosis was constructed along two time scales; it was the second time scale that determined the constitution of the phantasy and the choice of neurosis. It is not, therefore, a question of a linear, cumulative effect that resulted in the symptom, but a reorganization of already existing memory traces related to a new stage of maturation. Moreover, for Freud this is fundamentally related to

the role of castration, the law of the father that forbids the mother as an object of desire. This notion not only rules out linear determinism and thus emphasizes the relevance of the present when reinterpreting the past (a notion that is so fundamental to psychoanalytic work), but also places sexuality at the centre of the theoretical formulations.

To quote more extensively from *The Wolf Man* (Freud, 1918):

> We must not forget the actual situation which lies behind the abbreviated description given in the test: the patient under analysis, at an age of over twenty-five years, was putting the impressions and impulses of his fourth year into words which he would never have found at that time. If we fail to notice this, it may easily seem comic and incredible that a child of four should be capable of such technical judgements and learned notions. This is simply another instance of deferred action. At the age of one and a half the child receives an impression to which he is unable to react adequately; he is only able to understand it and to be moved by it when the impression is revived in him at the age of four; and only twenty years later during the analysis is he able to grasp with his conscious mental processes what was then going on in him. The patient justifiably disregards the three periods of time, and puts his present ego into the situation which is so long past. And in this we follow him, since with correct self-observation and interpretation the effect must be the same as though the distance between the second and the third periods of time could be neglected.
>
> (1918: 45)

[This theory of deferred action had already been put forward by Freud in *Studies on Hysteria* (Breuer and Freud, 1895) when he discussed what he then called 'retention hysteria' (Breuer and Freud, 1893: 162). He also gave a very elaborate account of its workings in hysteria in Part II of his posthumously published *Project* (1950), also written in 1895. But in these earlier statements of the theory, the effects of the primal scenes were deferred at least until the age of puberty, and the primal scenes themselves were never imagined as happening at so early an age as in the present case (1918: 45).]

- In *Repression* (1915b) Freud proposes the notion of primal repression. This constitutes the core of the unconscious, together with the primal phantasies of seduction, castration and primal scene, which are constitutional (philogenetically transmitted, although this idea has been re-worked in French psychoanalysis). I will return to the discussion of this concept later in this chapter.
- In *The Unconscious* (1915c) Freud states 'We obtain our concept of the unconscious from the theory of repression'. Importantly, the unconscious is linked to the notion of discontinuities in our mental life, which is in turn linked to the issues of time and après coup:

> If we communicate to a patient some idea which he has at one time repressed but which we have discovered in him, our telling him makes at first no change in his mental condition. Above all, it does not remove the repression nor undo its effects, as might perhaps be expected from the fact that the previously unconscious idea has now become conscious. On the contrary, all that we shall achieve at first will be a fresh rejection of the repressed idea. But now the patient has in actual fact the same idea in two forms in different places in his mental apparatus: first, he has the conscious memory of the auditory trace of the idea, conveyed in what we told him; and secondly, he also has – as we know for certain – the unconscious memory of his experience as it was in its earlier form. Actually there is no lifting of the repression until the conscious idea, after the resistances have been overcome, has entered into connection with the unconscious memory trace. It is only through the making conscious of the latter itself that success is achieved. On superficial consideration this would seem to show that conscious and unconscious ideas are distinct registrations, topographically separated, of the same content. But a moment's reflection shows that the identity of the information given to the patient with his repressed memory is only apparent. To have heard something and to have experienced something are in their psychological nature two different things, even thought the content of both is the same.
>
> (1915c: 175–176)

This is a re-elaboration of what Freud had written to Fliess in 1897: 'phantasies are derived from things that have been *heard* but understood *subsequently*' (1897a: 247).

- In *Beyond the Pleasure Principle* (1920a) Freud regards conflict between the drives as between the life and the death instincts. A central aspect of the latter is the repetition compulsion.
- In *The Psychogenesis of a Case of Homosexuality in a Woman* (1920b) Freud elaborates the important notion that the past cannot 'predict' the future.
- In *A Note upon the 'Mystic Writing-Pad'* (1925a) Freud presents the idea that memory is present not once but several times over.
- In *Inhibitions, Symptoms and Anxiety* (1926a) Freud suggests that anxiety as a signal points to a previous experience of danger. (This was later re-elaborated in Winnicott's idea that the catastrophe one dreads has already taken place.) The future contains a repetition of the past.

Après coup and metapsychology

Après coup is inscribed in Freud's metapsychology, the set of papers that can be seen as having no connection with a theory of practice but are rather an expression of an intellectual tradition, a path taken by Freud in his work that is crucial to the understanding of his formulations. In Britain and America, with rare exceptions, the metapsychological papers are regarded as a relic of the past. It is in France that these papers come alive and are part of an intellectual debate. This is the main reason I have chosen to use the concept of après coup in French, instead of the German *nachträglich* (adjective) or *Nachträglichkeit* (noun) (see footnote 1 in the Introduction).

The concept of après coup is linked to other concepts of Freud's metapsychology. As Jean-Claude Rolland has emphasized (2005), the metapsychological papers cannot be read in the same way as so many of the more clinical papers. They are pervaded by a sense of strangeness in which it is almost as if it is Freud's unconscious that speaks to the reader's unconscious, opening doors which illuminate the enigma of the unconscious. Rolland points out how these writings had to be in place before Freud could take the leap towards the even stranger text of *Beyond the Pleasure Principle* and the structural model of the mind (Rolland, 2005). He adds: 'The game, for child and man, is certainly something as grave and complex as metapsychology is for the theoretical analyst. And metapsychology should always be for the latter as enjoyable and liberating as playing is for the child: something between appropriation and discovery' (2005: 101).

Unconscious phantasy

Après coup is related to the interaction between memory and phantasy. In Freud's formulations, phantasies constantly reshape memories retrospectively. Repression establishes the rupture between conscious and unconscious, so that it is retrospectively that one can speak of unconscious phantasies in the Freudian metapsychology. From that perspective, phantasy, like time, is multi-determined. Here I am in disagreement with British and American writers such as Sandler and Nagera (1963) and Spillius (2001), who suggest that Freud's central notion of phantasy is conscious fantasies, but I am in tune with French psychoanalysts such as Green (2002a,b) and Laplanche and Pontalis (1985), who suggest that one cannot select any one of the layers in Freud's work as 'central'. What gives depth to the Freudian theory of the mind is indeed the fluidity, the dynamics between the various concepts. One only has to read the clinical papers such as *The Rat Man, The Wolf Man, Little Hans* or the paper on Leonardo to comprehend the way in which unconscious phantasies are only accessed through their derivatives, retrospectively in terms of après coup. Primal phantasies – *Urphantasien* – as discussed above, are there from the beginning, although they have to be 'reactivated' in the individual history. In *all* these unconscious phantasies, Freud seems to be concerned with the question of how sexuality comes about for human beings (Laplanche and Pontalis, 1985).

The concept of après coup raises some fundamental differences in terms of how we view the constitution of the mind. In Freud's formulations the psychic apparatus is not 'ready' at birth, but is constituted over time in the process of building up memory traces based on experiences of pleasure and pain, and the differentiation between id, ego and superego. The unconscious, for Freud, is only accessible through its derivatives, in its connections with the system Pcs-Cs (Freud, 1915b,c). Repression, in terms of après coup, structures the mind and inaugurates phantasy life. In Chapter 10, I will indicate that this means that one cannot predict in the process of development, for instance, which events will constitute trauma.

The concept of après coup is related to a theory of the mind that includes multiple temporalities. There are at least seven dimensions – development, regression, fixation, repetition compulsion, the return of the repressed, the timelessness of the unconscious and après coup – like a heptagon in movement. These different dimensions of time constitute a dominant structure (Althusser, 1970), and this dominance resides in the après coup.

3

The 'oracle' in dreams
The past and the future in the present

We are fighting this war . . . so that a person can marry his own mother.

(García Márquez, 1970: 127)

In the early stages of many analyses some patients' dreams are predictive of the future course of the analysis. These dreams contain a condensed narrative about the transference relationship and encapsulate a narrative that will unfold as the analysis progresses. Although the analyst may be aware of the crucial relevance of such dreams at the time they occur, it is only retrospectively, at a later stage in the analysis, that these dreams may be more fully comprehended. Moreover, there is a specific experience that is conveyed in the account of these dreams felt by the analyst in the counter-transference but only slowly understood as the analysis unfolds. The analytic task is to change the course anticipated by these dreams, and introduce a difference in the 'prediction' that these dreams make.

Although the psychoanalytic literature contains a few references to the first dream in a patient's analysis (e.g. Stekel, 1943; Greenacre, 1975; Beratis, 1984), there is a general paucity of papers on the subject. Stekel (1943) has suggested that first dreams in analysis may express the dreamer's whole story, and are mainly derived from real-life traumatic experiences. Bressler (1961) also linked the first dream in analysis to early childhood memories and suggested that first analytic dreams may indicate that the patient experiences entering analysis as a return to the maternal breast. Franco and Levine (1969) constructed psychological profiles of the dreamer on the basis of such first dreams. Beratis (1984) has recently discussed the relevance of first dreams in

33

analysis, although she seems to interpret this first dream directly from its manifest content, without waiting for the patients' associations or relating them to the transference situation. None of these papers relate first dreams to the transference situation and the course of the analytic process itself.

If *The Interpretation of Dreams* (Freud, 1900a,b) marks the inauguration of psychoanalysis and the discovery of the unconscious, many elaborations, such as that of infantile sexuality, repression, phantasy, transference, the Oedipus complex and castration, were still to be developed by Freud. More specifically relevant to the understanding of the thesis of this chapter is the notion of repetition compulsion. In his paper *Beyond the Pleasure Principle* (1920a), Freud pointed to the existence of 'traumatic dreams', which are 'endeavouring to master the stimulus retrospectively, by developing the anxiety whose omission was the cause of the traumatic neurosis' (1920a: 32). If the present contains a repetition of the past, this past constitutes, in the Sandlers' terminology, a template for the future (Sandler and Sandler, 1994b) upon which it is the analytic task to intervene.

From 1920 onwards, Freud confronted the limits of psychoanalytic understanding (Freud, 1920a,b, 1924a, 1937a,b). Green has suggested that in 1920 there was an important shift in Freud's model, from an emphasis on representations to acting out (Green, 2002a: 163). These ideas are specifically relevant to a modern conceptualization of dreams, and *the understanding that many patients act rather than remember* (Kohon, 1999b). Dreams themselves may be viewed not only through what they symbolize, but also in terms of what may be understood as their function. This thesis expands the understanding of dreams from meaning to the experience they induce both in the dreamer and in the analyst to whom the dream is related (see also Flanders, 1993).

The thesis about the 'predictive' relevance of dreams in analysis subsumes a number of modern ideas about dreams and their interpretation:

1   The idea that dreams are expressions of patients' current states of mind.
2   There is a connection between dreams, the transference and the analytic process.
3   It is not only the content of dreams that is addressed in an analysis, but also the *experience* brought by dreams to both the

patient and the analyst (Pontalis, 1974a,b). It is the detailed understanding of these experiences in any analysis that will lead to meaningful insight (Sedlak, 1997).

4   As a consequence of the above, my thesis takes into account theories that suggest a shift in the quality and usage of dreams by the patient during the course of an analysis (Khan, 1972; Stewart, 1973; Pontalis, 1974a,b; Segal, 1986, 1991; Quinodoz 1999).

I will now discuss some of the clinical material that led me to my formulations.

Maria and the block of cement [1]

My experience of Maria at the first consultation was bizarre. I could not understand it and the description that occurred to me was that 'a part of her is not there'. It was not that she seemed distracted, but that there was a sense of absence that impinged on me with a hypnotic quality. I experienced a deep heaviness that led me to feel as if I was going to fall asleep. I decided to pursue the idea that 'a part of her was not there', in an attempt to verify her experience of herself. Maria immediately seemed to understand what I was talking about and said that she felt that since her relationship with Alex, a boyfriend some 30 years earlier, she had disconnected herself, a part of her never 'being there' again. This response, which allowed me to think that she could connect with my experience of her, helped me to decide to accept her for treatment.

In the following weeks, this hypnotic quality was pervasive in the consulting room. I was left feeling uncomfortable about barely managing to remain awake during Maria's sessions, even if I had felt alert just before she arrived.

A month into treatment Maria had the following dream: *There were three women and a huge block of concrete suddenly fell on top of them. The women were completely flattened and then started to rush about crazily. Maria said it looked like a cartoon.* She said it was a dream but it did not feel like a dream. In this session we talked about her experience that this had

---

[1]   This clinical example will be discussed more fully in the next chapter.

not felt like a dream because it was so integral to the way she felt – that she had lost her feelings and her three-dimensionality and had become flattened. It also concerned her experience of feeling disconnected from herself in the present, and her way of relating to me, of flattening me in the sessions. I could then also understand the experience of having concrete inside my head, of feeling unable to think in her presence.

The dream that 'had not felt like a dream' took on another layer of meaning, expressing a terror that she was going to be 'hit' by the analysis and would not be able to cope. Retrospectively this was also a prognostic dream, a description of what was going to happen both to her and to the analytic process.

Four weeks after the end of the first summer break Maria had an accident at the ice rink and banged her head on the ice. She had taken some children skating in her capacity as a teacher. She said that one of the boys had bumped into her on purpose making her fall backwards and bang her head. She had gone to hospital, but they had said she was all right and could go home. She came straight to the session after that. During the following year this accident and the damage it did to her body became central to her analysis. She experienced a range of physical pains and related them to the accident. The other important theme was her rage with various people, from her GP to the 'head' at her school. Although she had expressed such rage before, it was now intensified and felt almost uncontainable in the sessions. Her repetitiveness was also relentless. My patient's sense of being misunderstood and not heard was profound. She indeed felt that a block of cement had hit her and her only way of showing me how she felt was to 'hit' me with it as well.

A year after the ice rink accident and two years after starting analysis, Maria was involved in a car crash in which a car came out of a side road and hit hers. She got out of her car and banged on the other driver's window, screaming and shouting, out of control in her fear and fury. She felt that the other driver and the passenger were laughing at her, while people gathered around to watch. She told me that her car was a 'write off'.

My hypothesis throughout her analysis was that these accidents functioned like a screen onto which Maria projected her own condensed version of her history, already contained in the dream she had told me at the beginning of her analysis. The analysis has attempted to recover the unconscious processes, which these accidents may both

36

express and mask, and so introduce a difference in Maria's way of experiencing herself and others.

The dream about the block of cement has been understood by both of us as encapsulating most of the story of her analysis and her experience of it. Both of us were trapped by a block of cement in a two-dimensional world, unable to feel or think, running around like cartoon characters. The analytical task consisted of introducing differences into this two-dimensional world.

Michael, a recurrent dream and its transformation

Michael had a recurrent dream since childhood: *There was a big white screen in front of him. Suddenly a black animal appeared and rushed through the bottom of the screen, or some kind of black spot ran through and corroded the screen.* This dream used to terrify him. He remembers having it whilst in hospital after an operation. It made him feel sick then and he still feels ill when he has the dream, although this is now rare. In the course of the analysis we were able to understand some of the meaning of this dream, although the greatest insight was reached after an event in a session that brought this dream dramatically into the transference and counter-transference.

Michael was a young German man who came to analysis after a serious suicide attempt that led to hospitalization. He was born blind and remained blind for the first couple of years of his life. A series of operations then allowed him to gain sight.

One of Michael's first statements in the very first session of his analysis was about his experience that throughout his life he had been talking to a voice in his head, and that now he was actually talking to a voice behind him. He felt as if my voice had always existed, but had now become real. This communication pointed to the idealization with which he started his relationship with me. I already had a place in his mind; indeed, I had been there for a long time.

There was, however, also another side to this coin. Michael brought another dream to his first session, a dream that he felt was one of the most disturbing he had ever had:

He was in a room, and in this room he was God. There had been a car accident and there was a baby's cot. As God he had the power to decide whether this baby was going to live or to die. He decided that the baby should live. Then the

37

whole thing repeated itself in a circle like a loop and he was at the top looking at everything happening and again he was in a position to decide whether the child was going to live or to die. In the end he decided that the child would die.

At this moment he woke up, felt really frightened and wanted to go back to the dream in order to make the child live.

In that session I talked to him about the two impossible positions contained in the dream. In one he was God, with powers of life and death over another part of him that he experienced as a helpless baby. In the other *he* was a helpless baby, whose fate was in the hands of somebody all-powerful. I thought that this was what he feared that this was all he could expect from analysis. I, too, could only be in one of these positions, as God, or a helpless baby who would meet my fate at his hand. He was terrified of what we could do to each other. The inevitability of death was there at the outset, in this narrative.

During the initial months, the right amount of contact was essential in our sessions: if I said too little Michael would become quiet and withdrawn, almost lifeless; if I said too much he felt intruded upon and disorganized. The dance between us required a certain rhythm whereby we were intensely involved with each other, and this evoked in me thoughts about a rhythm that should have been present in his interactions with his mother as a small child. What I have in mind is related to Stern's notion of the ways in which mothers 'tune in' to their babies. This was a relationship where mother and baby could not hold each other with their eyes and where bodily and sound contact appeared to me to have been intense.

Other temporal dimensions slowly emerged in Michael's material. In adolescence his mind was filled with conscious fantasies of violence and in young adulthood he engaged in violent relationships with his girlfriends and peers. Through violence he attempted to exercise mastery over a world that was experienced as frightening and senseless. Some months into the analysis I began to realize that for Michael, in the transference, there was also an enormous confusion between intimacy and sexuality. He alternated between omnipotent phantasies of having seduced me into being his analyst, on the one hand, and the terror of abandonment, on the other. Different time dimensions could be identified in these experiences: the terrorized infant being cared for by a mother he could not see but only feel and hear, and the advent of genital sexuality that was superimposed over that more primitive material.

The beginnings of Michael's analysis were characterized by his wish to control me and the demand that I should provide him with clear structures so that he would be able to see where he was. In a concrete way he used to write my interpretations down and spread them around his flat over the weekends. His fear was that of fragmentation and psychotic breakdown. He was terrified of dependence, as it brought with it the panic he had experienced in the past in relation to his mother's inability to contain his terror and prevent terrible things happening to him (images and memories of being taken away from her to undergo an eye operation).

Michael's first year of analysis was characterized by a paradox. He was compelled to attack the things that were important to him. Thus the more Michael felt attached to his analyst, the more dangerous it was for both of us. Michael became able to acknowledge his terror that I would derive pleasure from hurting him or humiliating him, especially if I knew of his need for me. This was an expression of himself since he could only find repetitions of himself in the outside world.

In one session, a few weeks before the first summer break, I felt that he was terrified of his experience that I was important to him, and said so. He responded by quoting 'Each man kills the thing he loves . . .'.[2] This was accompanied by a chilling feeling I had in the counter-transference. I briefly felt invaded by an intense, inexplicable fear. There was a long, heavy silence, which Michael finally interrupted by saying that he had had a strange feeling that his jaws were dry. This was the feeling that tended to accompany the dream of the white screen, which was being corroded, damaged. He had not had the feeling for quite some time and had even forgotten that the dream was accompanied by such a feeling. The experience of the real potential for damage, murder and suicide had come fully into the transference. This session had taken place before a holiday break and at a different level we were confronting the experience of impending blackness on the eve of a separation that left him in the dark. I put this interpretation to him.

At the next session, Michael brought the following dream:

He went into a building, where there was a library with books. It was inside a Victorian museum about murder. There was a man, a doctor, who was going to

[2]   Oscar Wilde, *The Ballad of Reading Gaol*, 1897.

perform an operation on a woman with a broken leg. The operation lasted 50 minutes, during which time he killed her. He then replaced her with another woman, also with a broken leg, so that no one would suspect what had happened. There were, however, enough clues for someone using modern investigation methods to find out what had happened. My patient was watching the scene and tried to escape. He ran to another floor. He kept trying to escape, running away, and then he woke up.

I cannot within the limits of this chapter give a full account of this session. As Michael told me the dream, I immediately remembered the fear that had invaded me at the previous session, and thought that he was about to stop the analysis out of his fear of himself and me. However, what struck me most during his account of the dream was the slow, monotonous, almost hypnotic quality of his narrative, which contrasted both with the frightening content of the dream as well as the usual intense quality of our interaction in the sessions. I waited, and after a while Michael carried on giving more and more details, describing the glass windows and the bookcases in the library, peripheral to the central events in the dream. I commented on my sense of his detachment from the dream during the session, and he agreed, although he had woken up terrorized. This detached quality had also been underlined in the content of the dream itself (for example, he had been an observer of the events, and they had taken place in a museum). I told Michael that I felt that this dream had been too frightening for him, and that he could not relate to it. He seemed to understand both this and the idea that his terror of the damage he felt that we could do to each other was now also present in the session.

The dream narrated a primal scene between a castrated, damaged woman who was also ultimately a fake, because she was just a replacement for another dead woman, and a murderer. This encounter was experienced by Michael as what took place in the sessions between us. In the dream the patient ran away, although a positive aspect of the dream could be found in the idea that there were enough clues for a modern investigation to find out what had really happened, i.e. to discover that murder and castration had taken place. Over some of the sessions that followed this dream Michael's dilemma became apparent: he was frightened that the only way of avoiding damage might be to run away, and therefore kill off the analysis.

The work we did on this dream and its underlying anxieties did not

40

prevent Michael from leaving the analysis. He did not come to his sessions in the following week, the last before the summer break. I wrote to him, saying that I understood his reasons for feeling he needed to stay away but that I was keeping his sessions open to him until a week after the end of the summer break.

Michael came back after the summer, and we were able to carry on working for another few years. As the analysis progressed, life became a bit more ordinary. Michael once remembered how as a child, whenever he hurt himself, there was a panic that something serious had happened. He was able to remember situations when friends of his would get hurt but did not necessarily run home to disinfect the wound. One friend, after scratching himself while playing football, once said to him in reply to his concern: 'Don't worry, it's nothing'. He then said to me: 'I could not believe that he didn't think straight away that his arm was going to get infected, turn green and fall off'. Whenever Michael felt that there was a scratch between us, his fear was that everything was going to turn terribly wrong.

In the first few years, therefore, analysis was marked by the possibility of damage between us in terms of psychotic breakdown or accidents, especially at weekends and holiday breaks. Progressively this was understood and inserted into the language of the transference, and words gradually became mediators for actions. Dreams became a language through which to express the relationship of the transference. I think that there is an isomorphism between some of the dreams that Michael brought to analysis. The initial dream of 'the killer god and the baby' was already a transformation of the 'dream of the white screen'. A year into analysis, the dream of 'the museum of murder' brought the issues crucially to the transference. This dream was concretely experienced as a source of danger, leading to a breakdown in the analysis from which we were able to recover.

In a session nearly a year after the dream of 'the museum of murder' Michael had a dream that *he was going to be fired because he belonged to an anarchistic organization called 'Chateaubriand'*. The associations to Chateaubriand led to thoughts about luxury and abundance, a delicious meal that he could now associate with analysis and coming to see me. He thought I was French, because of my accent, my French car and also a French book he had seen in my consulting room. He experienced me as introducing anarchy, desire, into a world that had previously been experienced as fundamentally bureaucratic and dictatorial.

Michael's treatment was successful and it allowed him to build a relationship with a woman and a deeper understanding of himself. Towards the end of it he often commented on how much he had changed and how much more he could see and understand about himself.

The theme of the dream screen was progressively experienced in the transference. Throughout his analysis we progressively understood some of the layers of this dream, which was over-determined: his experience of destroying the ecstatic idealized union with the white screen, the maternal breasts (Lewin, 1946, 1948). In the present of his analysis he was frightened that I would not be able to cope with what he regarded as his cruelty, nastiness and mess. We also understood his need for idealized images of his objects, as extensions of his wishes. His attacks became ways of punishing his objects, so that they would change into what he wanted them to be. This could easily be reversed into attacks on himself.

Michael did not attempt suicide after the beginning of his analysis. Towards the end of his analysis Michael started a relationship with a girlfriend and felt more in control of his life. The changes in him could well be mapped in the changes of the quality and narrative of his dreams.

Robert and the house surrounded by glass

Robert's first contact with me was via a letter, telling me the story of his life. He enclosed with this same letter a self-portrait, painted many years earlier. Being a painter, he had felt unable to paint during the previous 10 years. He came from an artistic, upper-middle-class Italian family, with eight children, from whom he had taken flight. His father and sister were successful artists. His mother had also been successful, prior to a series of psychotic breakdowns, which had caused her to be hospitalized several times. In reading this well-written and engrossing letter, I already had an inkling of a position he wanted to keep me in: it was not a story that he told in my presence, which might have allowed some exchanges between us. I was to read what he had written outside an actual interaction between us.

Robert then phoned me and we arranged an initial consultation. A handsome man in his early thirties, Robert entered the room full of seductive sexual vitality, but also barely able to disguise his fear of me.

I had the immediate thought that he felt confused about this encounter and that he might experience it as a scene of seduction. Indeed, for the first half of the session Robert proceeded to tell me about his intense affairs with older women, which he had only managed to sustain for brief periods of time. I thought that it was important to address his confusion at the outset, and immediately let him know that I thought he was confused about what I expected from him. He calmed down visibly, relaxing back in the chair, and was then able to tell me about his great pain at not being able to paint for such a long time, and the life full of violent encounters that he had led since he had stopped painting.

At the end of that first consultation he wanted to start analysis with me, and we began the following week. At his first session, he brought me the following dream:

There was a beautiful house, the most beautiful house one could imagine, surrounded by lush gardens, and filled with works of art and famous paintings. It was very spacious, one room leading to another. There was glass surrounding it, however, and one was not able to penetrate it. One had to admire it from the outside.

This dream and the associations that proceeded and followed it became paradigmatic of the many layers of Robert's analysis. My experience of his letter immediately came to mind: his wish to be admired like this beautiful house filled with works of art, which left himself as well as the other on the outside. There was no live communication between inside and outside, between his inner world and the external. Everything was either locked in or out. This was a dream we repeatedly came back to during our work together. The house also represented the body of a mother whom he experienced as ungiving and impenetrable. Finally, it represented his fear that whatever he produced would be trapped inside her. It was his terror of what the body and the mind of his psychotic mother contained that constituted the core of what we were to explore in his analysis.

Robert's first dream provided a map to which we turned to understand a great deal about the unfolding of the analytic relationship during the first two years of our work together. Robert's implicit demand was that I should admire him, without attempting to enter into too much contact with him. He came to the sessions full of vivid dreams and thoughts, associations and interpretations about them. He worked very hard himself, both in the sessions and outside them, on his many thoughts, experiences and impressions. His fundamental requirement was that I should simply admire him and his work, without intervening. I was left outside the house. The interesting point of technique for me in my work with Robert is that this is what I fundamentally did for quite some time, aware that I was doing so. My interpretations and comments, especially at the beginning, were indeed sparse although I felt intensely present with him in the sessions. I was aware that interaction was unbearable to him. Slowly, Robert's fear of relating to me shifted and it was possible to have a different way of interacting with him in the sessions, a sense of a dialogue that could more easily be put into words that he could tolerate.

Some two years after the beginning of his analysis Robert started painting again. The conflict he had been struggling with was given vivid expression when he wanted to give me the first painting he was able to paint after such a long time. My refusal to accept it and his utter surprise allowed him to believe fully, perhaps for the first time, that our work together was fundamentally for his benefit. He started to participate in exhibitions and competitions, and won a prestigious prize in Italy. The quality of his dreams progressively changed.

In one of the last dreams he brought, *he was in the kitchen cooking with his girlfriend, and they went for a long walk in a beautiful garden, full of rare and exotic flowers.* At that time, Robert had a relationship with a girlfriend and had been offered work teaching art in a small town in Italy, which was going to give him time to develop his own painting. His girlfriend went with him. Some aspect of the relationship with me was still idealized, but as he left there was a sense that he would be able to carry on the work we had started.

The tradition of dreams as oracles

In his monumental review of existing theories on dreams, Freud distinguished between those authors who thought that only the trivial is expressed in dreams, those who viewed dreams as somatic experiences, and yet others who thought that it is only that which is not dealt with that is presented in dreams. Already in 1891 Delae suggested that dreams were unrecognized reproductions (*souvenir inconscient*) of material already experienced (in Freud, 1900a: 81). By naming his work *The Interpretation of Dreams*, Freud was joining a long tradition that emphasized the intrinsic value of dreams and their *interpretation* (see Anzieu, 1987).

In surveying the scientific literature on dreams, Freud remarked on the attitude toward dreams that prevailed during classical antiquity: 'They took it as axiomatic that dreams were connected with the world of superhuman beings in whom they believed and that they were revelations from gods and daemons' (Lorand, 1957).

The ideas that oracles predicted the future and that the future was often expressed in dreams are not new. In classical Greece, Isis, Osiris and Serapis delivered their oracles by means of dreams (see Devereux, 1976). Socrates thought of dreams as originating from the gods, and thus ascribed a prophetic meaning to them. In referring to the Hebrew sources of dream interpretations, Freud mentions the biblical dream of Joseph.

In general, ancient peoples believed that dreams were sent by the gods to guide human beings in their decisions and actions. Moreover, they regarded dreams as either favourable or hostile manifestations. This belief was held by the Phoenicians, Egyptians and especially the Babylonians, with whom the Hebrews had much contact and from whose culture they borrowed extensively.

Breton (1969) suggested that Freud had been mistaken in not believing in the prophetic nature of dreams, and their engagement with the immediate future, when he emphasized dreams as revealing the past. As a consequence he denied dreams the quality of movement. The question of prophetic dreams was a matter for scientific debate throughout the 19th century, and was discussed by philosophers such as Schopenhauer, Vashide and Pieron.

On the atemporality of dreams: the repetition compulsion

The association between dreams and earlier experiences, between the present and the past, lies at the core of Freud's thinking about dreams: 'On this view a dream might be described *as a substitute for an infantile scene modified by being transferred onto a recent experience*. The infantile scene is unable to bring about its own revival and has to be content with returning as a dream' (1900b: 546). Dreaming, he adds later '*is a piece of infantile life that has been superseded*' (1900b:567).The connections between the present and the past are thus established and understood. But what about the future?

The notion of the compulsion to repeat was to be developed many years after he wrote *The Interpretation of Dreams*. In 1909, however, when discussing the case of *Little Hans*, Freud had already proposed: '. . . a thing which has not been understood inevitably reappears; like an unlaid ghost, it cannot rest until the mystery has been solved and the spell broken' (1909a: 122). The notion of repetition compulsion was further discussed in *Remembering, Repeating and Working Through* (1914a). These ideas open the way for us to understand not only repetitive dreams – like Michael's dream from childhood – but also patterns that one can identify in the dreams of most patients. That which has not been understood or worked through is repeated in dreams. In the dreams, which are dreamt for the analyst in an analysis, patients are also bringing that which they want to work on in the analysis, so that these experiences are not repeated, unmodified, into the future.[3]

Maria brings her experience of the loss of her three-dimensionality, and repeats in the transference a relationship with a dead mother 'who is not there' or available to think about her little girl. Robert brings the experience of his internal space with which he cannot communicate, in relation to which he either feels excluded or locked in. His dilemma is between his desire for creative work and his terror of feeling trapped in the unimaginable relation with a psychotic mother. Represented in his initial dream is his inability to be in contact with himself and his desires. Michael's dream expresses the terror of his aggression and fear of the damage that can take place between people.

Pontalis has suggested that 'the dream is what makes things visible, what gives its visible place to déjà vu, which has become invisible' (1974a: 127).

An important aspect of the sequence narrated in Michael's analysis lies in the fact that an experience in the consulting room (the dry jaw, his fear and mine), followed by an interpretation, allowed a dream to be dreamt. Money-Kyrle has suggested a theory of stages in representational thought that goes from a stage of concrete representation (where no distinction is made between the representation and the object represented), through ideographic representation, as in dreams,

---

[3] Ferenczi (1923) thought of repetitive dreams as the oneiric compulsive repetition of a traumatic event.

to a stage of conscious and predominantly verbal thought (1968: 422). In Michael's case the experience in the consulting room, which included the analyst's counter-transference, took place before it could be represented in dreams. The interpretations functioned as mediator in this process. This observation is in agreement with Sedlak's (1997) on the analyst's function in the transformation of patients' dilemmas into those that can be thought and dreamt about. In his paper Sedlak also addresses the role of the counter-transference in the process.

Pontalis has suggested that to Freud dreams represented a displaced maternal body, and in interpreting dreams Freud commits incest with the body of his dreams, penetrating their secrets. In the process, Freud emerged as Oedipus (1974a: 26):

> My hypothesis is that every dream, as an object in analysis, refers to the maternal body . . . It is not the dream's contents, but the subject's 'use' of it that reveals his true pathology. The dream-object is caught up secondarily in an oral, anal, phallic organisation, but the dream process is originally linked to the mother: the variety of scripts represented in it, and even the range of meanings he invests in the therapy (faeces, present, work of art, 'imaginary child', hidden treasure, 'interesting organ', fetish) unfold against the background of this exclusive relationship. Dreaming is above all the attempt to maintain an impossible union with the mother, to preserve an undivided whole, *to move in a space prior to time.* This is why some patients implicitly ask one not to get too close to their dreams, neither to touch nor to manipulate the body of the dream, not to change the 'thing presentation' to a 'verbal presentation'.
>
> (Pontalis, 1974a: 29)

In dreaming, therefore, one is effecting this eternal return to the primitive relationship with the mother. The incest prohibition is characterized by Freud as perhaps the 'most maiming wound ever inflicted . . . on the erotic life of man' (Freud, 1930: 74).

'We are fighting this war', Aureliano José is told in García Márquez's seminal novel *One Hundred Years of Solitude*, 'so that a person can marry his own mother' (1970: 127).

In a letter to Fliess on 15 October 1897, Freud stated:

> I have found love of the mother and jealousy of the father in my own case too, and now believe it to be a general phenomenon of

47

early childhood . . . The Greek myth seizes on a compulsion which everyone recognises because he has felt traces of it in himself.

(1897b: 272)

At the end of Chapter VII in *The Interpretation of Dreams*, Freud asks 'And the value of dreams for giving us knowledge of the future?' He answers his question thus: 'There is of course no question of that. It would be truer to say instead that they give us knowledge of the past' (1900b: 621).

Dreams that bring knowledge of the past in his formulation may also be interpreted as foretelling the future. Freud himself continues:

> Nevertheless the ancient belief that dreams foretell the future is not wholly devoid of truth. By picturing our wishes as fulfilled, dreams are after all leading us into the future. But this future, which the dreamer pictures as the present, has been moulded by his indestructible wish into a perfect likeness of the past.
>
> (1900b: 622)

For the patients I presented in this chapter, the body of the mother, as expressed in their dreams and the beginnings of their analysis, was not experienced as a home, a safe place that allowed for exploration and creativity. In each of their analyses there was a search for a mental space where they could explore, think about and transform the relationships with their internal objects.

Their dreams at the beginnings of their analysis conveyed some of the crucial dilemmas that they had brought to work through in their treatment. Although these dreams anticipated the work that was to be done, it was only retrospectively that the many layers of meaning already contained in the dreams could be understood. These dreams anticipated the course of the analytic work but could only be fully understood retrospectively, thus expressing the bi-directional meaning of the term après coup, which will be discussed in Chapter 7.

4

'To be – or not to be' – here
A woman's denial of time and memory

... her experience of the accidents may be conceptualized as an attempt to emphasize a sequence of bodily experienced traumas instead of hystoricization.

(From this chapter)

Introduction

It was in the middle of the fourth year of her analysis that Maria raised the question of 'to be or not to be here'. It followed an interpretation I had formulated addressing what I felt was the central dilemma for her at that time. I had said that as she allowed herself to get more in touch with her murderous and violent feelings towards me, she had to paralyse her body and experience it as incapacitated, because she was terrified of getting out of control. I said that she felt tortured by this conflict. To be here in the session with me was to get in touch with feelings that she felt could have dangerous consequences for both of us since she feared she would feel like committing murder; not to be here, however, was to condemn herself to feeling trapped by these feelings and beliefs about herself for ever.

From the very beginning of this analysis, which lasted many years, I was consistently struck by the two-dimensionality that followed my patient into the consulting room. In her two-dimensionality the past is eradicated and a sense of time and history, which is so central for the constitution of the subject, is also lost. My patient's world has to be repetitive so that the experience of differences is avoided: differences between past and present, male and female, inside and outside, love and hate, her and me. The past was privileged as opposed to the present and future. This past, however, was presented in a reified, stilted way, through repetitive and predictable accounts that contained no enlargement or new information. It had no depth and was simply presented as the opposite of now; events and sequences of events had no place. From that perspective I would like to suggest that my patient has 'screen memories', as opposed to memories (Freud, 1899). What differentiates the two is the process of condensation and over-determination that is present in the selection of these memories. Strachey indicated that Freud refers to this notion as 'an earlier memory [which] is used as a screen for a later event' (in Freud, 1899: 302), as well as one in which an earlier event is screened by a later memory. My patient makes use of her screen memories to cover both the past and the present, holding on to an experience of time that stresses trauma instead of history.

When my patient came to analysis there was a specific moment in her life – an unhappy love relationship in her early twenties – to which she repeatedly returned. If, on the one hand, this process represented an attempt to understand something that had until then been unintelligible, it also had a defensive function. The account of her history was reduced to this point, the underlying phantasy being that there was no past that had preceded it and that 30 years had not gone by since then. Her stereotyped accounts surrounding this event served both as a screen for later events, including her experience of her analysis, and as elaborations of early childhood experiences. On the first anniversary of beginning her analysis Maria had an accident whilst on a skiing holiday where she banged her head badly; on the second anniversary she had a crash in which her car was completely destroyed.

It is within this lack of historicity, where events have to be presented as frozen and encapsulated in a stilted way, that Maria's two accidents could be understood.

Granel (1987) has discussed the unconscious processes that precede, accompany and follow accidents. These processes show that 'in many cases the situation preceding the accident is characterised by an unbearable state that cannot be worked over in the form of a representation. The unsolvable drama of the internal world is replaced by real drama (accident)'. Having an accident is an attempt to 'give form to the unformable'.

Since the accidents Maria consistently attempted to relate her various feelings and experiences to them. The accidents became another screen onto which her beliefs about her life were projected. Granel has contrasted repetitive traumatophilia with analytic hystoricization, which introduces a different perspective of temporality. The accidents expressed Maria's experience of the analysis itself as a major catastrophe in her life.

Bion (1970) considers that all processes of development inevitably involve catastrophic change. Such change is a configuration of circumstances linked together by violence, disorder and invariance. A 'new configuration' or a 'new idea' can only appear with disruptive force. The analytic attempt has been that of creating a narrative, a story, out of the enclosed and ritualized presentation of sameness.

The tension in this analysis was that of engaging in a conversation in which it was very important for Maria to adhere to a specific version of reality – one that emphasizes accidents and processes in her body as opposed to her mind – and still have a sense of a working alliance that allows the therapeutic task to be carried out. The analyst has had to undertake a double task. Whilst formulating interpretations that powerfully challenge Maria's views of herself, I had, at the same time, to understand that for her to stick to her views was akin to being able to remain alive. She was terrified that to experience herself in a relationship with me was to submit to my version of reality. As her mode of relating was so basically dominated by projections, she could only find in the other repetitions of herself. The tension in the analysis was thus between my acceptance of her experiences, necessary for containment, whilst retaining my own experience as an analyst. Sometimes this has proved almost impossible as interpretations would be followed by an attack of fury, an experience of a crash taking place in the consulting room in which I would feel as crushed as her car had been. It has been our endurance of this contradiction between our views that has allowed her analysis to take place. The analysis was thus, paradoxically, able to contain the unbearable, which was for her the traumatic experience of differences and the faint beginnings of an experience of becoming. Whilst I progressively attempted to formulate to myself my own thoughts about Maria, I also consistently had to communicate to her my understanding of how unbearable the process was for her. I will illustrate how these experiences have been manifested in the history of the analysis and how patterns have developed in the transference.

51

Background information

Maria was in her early fifties when she came for her first consultation. She had a basic problem in establishing relationships and felt analysis could help her with that. In the previous five years she had experienced many physical ailments, which included back pain, a stiff neck and stiffness in the jaws and legs. She had also had bleeding colitis.

Maria was an attractive woman, with blonde hair and dark eyes, and appeared much younger than her age. She was the oldest of three children: her sister was three and a half years younger and her brother five and a half years younger. She remembered feeling jealous when her sister was born and thinking that her mother loved the new baby best. She felt that, throughout her childhood, her mother was never available to her, being a withdrawn and cold woman, unable to show affection either emotionally or physically. Progressively in her analysis we gained access to a deep terror of her mother. She had vague memories of her mother leaning towards her, screaming at her and trying to throttle her. Maria turned to her father from very early on, seeking his love and support but was bitterly hurt by the realization that her mother always came first for him.

Her rage soon turned against herself and she started to attack her own body. She remembered being 8 years old when she started to pull out great bunches of her hair. This became an expression of her rage, loneliness and feelings of being unloved. Later on she experienced various illnesses and pains in her body and found that it was a way of engaging her mother into worrying and looking after her. The psychic pain began to be more systematically bypassed and to be transformed into bodily complaints. It was also a way of battering the body that she felt was so unloved by her mother.

Her attempts to leave home when she was 18 years old failed, and she returned to live with her parents. She fell in love with Alex, a Frenchman on holiday in Britain, and told me that although she felt very attracted to him sexually, she could not let him touch her. She described herself as 'being turned on in a way from which there was no relief'. She 'turned herself inside out', feeling 'raw'. At the time she read in the newspaper about a man in the USA who had raped and killed several women and said that she could well understand that someone could feel like that. She remembers feeling that the only way out for her was to cut her genitals. Progressively in her analysis her terror emerged that she might have done something to this man she loved, and it became clear that her breakdown was also a way of protecting him.

She very much wanted to believe that this man could have saved her, but he became very angry with her and finally gave her up. She described her heart as broken. This became the point in her life she constantly returned to in her analysis, repetitively describing it in detail, almost in slow motion. Yet, very little extra content or information was given each time. My basic experience remained that fundamentally it was a most painful and terrorizing reality that Maria was trying to make sense of. Any interpretation I formulated to her about the present was immediately related back to that period in her life. She described how she then 'disconnected' herself and experienced herself as becoming like the withdrawn, cold, hated mother of her childhood.

A few years later in college she reached such a state of anxiety and neglect of herself that colleagues felt she might need psychiatric help. She cut her hair very short and walked about the campus unwashed and dressed in rags. She was given Valium but soon rebelled against the idea that she needed it. She finished college and embarked on a successful teaching career. When she started analysis she registered for a course that would give her a university degree, which she succeeded in getting.

She told me at the first consultation that during the previous winter she had stayed in bed for six weeks. Her friends had become very worried about her, thinking that she was depressed, but she said she was actually *frozen* due to the coldness in the school where she worked. This concrete bodily experience indicates my patient's emphasis on her body as the locus for her experiences. The extended descriptions of her physiological and physical states became the stuff of which the sessions were made for years to come.

The analytic process: the patient's idiom

Throughout the first year of analysis Maria had a special idiom in which she expressed herself. The first signs of her presence were her deep cough while still walking along the street, her long ring of my doorbell and her heavy steps climbing up the stairs while still coughing.

She would throw herself on the couch and then crack the bones in her legs and back. Sometimes she would turn her head 180° from side to side, cracking the bones in her neck. She was consistently five minutes late and, when in the room, embarked on long monologues that made me feel very drowsy, sleepy, almost hypnotized, sometimes possessed by intense rage that suddenly erupted inside me. At times I felt bombarded by her in ways that felt intolerable, feeling, at the same time, acutely embarrassed for experiencing such intense feelings about my patient.

An important clue that these feelings were related to something the patient was projecting onto me was expressed in the second dream she brought to analysis, a month into treatment: *There were three women and a huge block of concrete suddenly fell on top of them. The women were completely flattened and then started to rush about crazily. Maria said it looked like a cartoon.* She said it was a dream but it did not feel like a dream. She then said that perhaps this was what had happened to her when she was 18. In this session we talked about her experience that this had not felt like a dream because it was so integral to the way she felt – that she had lost her feelings and her three-dimensionality and had become flattened. It was also her experience of feeling disconnected from herself in the present, and of her way of relating to me, of flattening me in the sessions. I could then also understand the experience of having concrete inside my head.

The dream that 'had not felt like a dream' took on another layer of meaning, expressing a terror that she was going to be 'hit' by the analysis and would not be able to cope. As discussed in Chapter 2, retrospectively, I understood that this was also a prognostic dream, a description of what was going to happen both to herself and to the analytic process. Perhaps, too, the three women represented herself, her other and the analyst, all flattened out of recognition.

During the first year of analysis some important themes emerged, which we worked on very slowly in the next years. We had access to these themes primarily via dreams, which functioned as markers of what was happening for her in the analysis: her consistent lateness (which had a multitude of meanings), her rage towards her mother, her phantasy of violence in sexual intercourse, her sexual identity, her rage towards everybody (including me), her perceptions of her physical body (which included both her fear and rejection of her femininity and of the babies she might have been able to produce) and, ultimately, overriding all these previous themes, her beliefs of

54

how dangerous it was to experience any feelings (either positive or negative) towards me.[1]

In spite of a great deal of material slowly surfacing, the quality I had experienced in the first consultation remained – 'a part of her was not there'. She would not consciously remember things from one session to the next. I gradually learned to trust my experience that I could tell something about her state of mind by tracking my own feelings. I would suddenly feel more alert and we would then have a more vital exchange. This would usually last for about 5 minutes, reaching 25 minutes in only one specific session. It never lasted more than half a session in that first year. Some years later she was to refer to her memory of how, in that first year, her heavy eyes just wanted to close.

She let me know, at the end of that first year, that she was feeling more alive. She had started to buy newspapers, something she had never done before in her life, and was also starting to do jobs in her house that she had completely neglected for years.

After the first summer break we increased from four to five sessions a week. Four weeks after the end of the break she had an accident while away on a skiing holiday and banged her head on the ice. During the following year this accident and the damage it did to her body became central to her analysis. She experienced a range of physical pains and related them to the accident. Her repetitiveness was relentless. My patient's sense of being misunderstood and not heard was profound. She spent most sessions on a raging crusade against almost everybody.

The language of accidents

A year after the skiing accident and two years after starting analysis, Maria was involved in a car crash in which a van hit her car at a junction. She told me that her car was a 'write off'. It is difficult for a non-medical analyst to assess the physical impact Maria says the accident had on her. However, the accidents seemed to have functioned like a screen onto which she has projected her own condensed version

---

[1] Money-Kyrle has suggested a theory of stages in representational thought that goes from a stage of concrete representation (where no distinction is made between the representation and the object represented), through ideographic representation, as in dreams, to a stage of conscious and predominantly verbal thought (1968: 422).

of her history. The analysis has attempted to recover the unconscious processes that these accidents both express and may mask.

During the next year Maria became progressively worse, both in her state of mind and in her bodily symptoms. The GP sent her to many specialists but no one could find any evidence of physical illness. Her rage towards everybody for not being able to understand what was happening to her made her unreachable. She felt fragmented and persecuted. All the specialists consistently said that her problems were psychological in origin and she was infuriated since she said she was experiencing 'real' pain. In the sessions I was in despair about my capacity to make contact with her.

After the Easter break in the third year of her analysis, Maria came back with twitches in her body. Her body would be overtaken by a tremor, every 20 seconds or so. The atmosphere in the sessions was of absolute terror and despair. We both felt she was capable of violent behaviour either against me or herself at the time. Throughout that whole period I sat with her in the sessions, talking to her about her feelings about being with me. My experience was of profound precariousness. If I said too much, the risk was that she would actually attack me; if I left her too much on her own, she might feel so despairing and abandoned that she could kill herself.

Eventually she managed to tell me about her fear that she would have to destroy my consulting room and throw all the furniture (and me) through the window. In the next session she told me about a film that she had seen the previous day. It was about twin brothers in the East End of London. They came from a working-class background and had been very well looked after. Yet they had done terrible things, mugging people, murdering and raping. It made her feel she was like that because she too came from this sort of background and yet she had these terrible thoughts. She was shaken by violent tremors as she told me this.

She then said that similar twitching had preceded the breakdown she had 30 years ago because she had been unable to tell Alex all her thoughts about him at the time. My response was that she was telling me now how frightened she was of having violent feelings towards me. It was a precarious moment in the session. I thought that she was also feeling frightened of me – the twin brothers were *both* violent – and I said that she was perhaps frightened not only of her own violent feelings but that I might have them too. As soon as I said this she started to cry terribly, with great sobs; she gradually calmed down, but the twitches continued. She went back to talking about the pain that had preceded the twitching 30 years ago. I said I thought that she blurred emotional and physical pain and that she attempted to bypass emotional pain with physical pain.

A few weeks later she talked about her battles with her mother and how even now her mother did not accept that she (Maria) might like different things from her. I spoke to her about her experience that there was a battle with me about realities. She has a story about herself, which is the story of the pains in her body and the accidents she has suffered. She wants to tell me about the pain in her back, in her skull, her jammed head, her twitching. She feels that at least in her ailments she is alive. She said that I had said this to her before. It was on the same day as James, her osteopath, had been spot on, although he usually was spot on. She did not feel I was usually spot on about her ailments, although I was usually right about everything else. She felt I was an expert, but not on her ailments. I said that perhaps she did not feel there really was anything else, so in effect she made me an expert on nothing. The following day she came saying she had thought a lot about the previous session. It had felt clear like a maths class, Q.E.D.

This was followed by a session on a Monday to which she came very excited. She felt that her memory was starting to come back. She woke up and remembered a tune, something she had not been able to do for ages. She had gone to a party over the weekend and danced twice for the first time in many years. She was, however, twitching more. I related the twitching to her feeling excited and her anxiety about feeling *too* excited.

In the Friday session I again had a feeling of being bombarded by her, which became almost intolerable at one point. I talked to her about how she wanted to show me what it felt like to be assaulted by a woman who was so entrenched in her own reality that nothing she could say or do would make an impact on that woman. She immediately related to what I said, saying that this was what it had felt like to be with her mother. She cried, making deep sobbing noises. Later material that she brought to the session allowed me to say to her that she experienced her twitching as the concrete experience of her contact with me, where she felt both excited and attacked by me. By the next session, the twitches had stopped.

After the summer the sessions took on a different quality; she was more able to be present in the sessions. She was twitching again, although it was much less severe and there were many fewer twitches. At one session she told me about her experience with Alex 30 years before, about being overwhelmed by her sexual feelings towards him and not knowing what to do with them. She talked about her confusion at the time between emotional and sexual feelings and the tremors preceding her breakdown. I felt it was possible to say to her then that perhaps that was the reason she felt she had to retreat emotionally. She was afraid, if she became emotionally connected to me, that she would experience uncontrollable sexual feelings; perhaps her current twitching was her experience of that, of a sexual connection with me.

She came to a session telling me how much she had enjoyed the film *Cinema Paradiso*. We were able to establish in that session not only that she felt she had to keep her anger out of the sessions, but her loving feelings too, just as in the film all the kissing scenes had been censored. She started to cry, saying that she had not thought of that and I was being so understanding. She could not handle it. She could feel herself becoming angry with me. She sobbed and talked again about something she had told me a couple of years before but had subsequently been left untouched. She had to feel angry with me otherwise she would want to hurt my genitals because I had been so nice to her.

It was a painful moment in the session. She cried, saying it was very upsetting. She wanted to be nasty to me, to shake me. She felt that was what her mother used to do to her. She then had a memory of an expression on a woman's face. It was contorted and she remembered seeing a couple by a door. She did not know whether they were making love or whether it was rape. I said that for her they were the same; this made her frightened of any contact between us. I felt it was also difficult for her to talk about this because it made her feel it was so real. She was much calmer as she left.

As the fourth and fifth years of her analysis proceeded, Maria was progressively more able to be *psychically* present in the sessions. This was, however, paralleled by an increasing experience that her body was getting worse. She spent long periods in bed and only got up to come to her sessions (in the afternoon). I then addressed myself to this conflict – that as she was able to allow herself to get in touch with her thoughts she had to paralyse her body, experience it as incapacitated, because she was so terrified of getting out of control. There followed a dream where she saw herself being held down by many people as she was wild and screaming, trying to murder someone. I said that as she allowed herself to get more in touch with her murderous and violent feelings towards me, she had to incapacitate her body because she was terrified of getting out of control. I said that she felt tortured by this conflict. To be here in the session with me was to get in touch with feelings that she felt could have dangerous consequences for both of us since she feared that she would feel like committing murder; not to be here, however, was to condemn herself to feeling trapped by these feelings and beliefs about herself for ever. She replied: 'To be or not to be here, that is the question'. Then she started to cry, saying she would rather do something to herself than hurt me.

She remembered a dream, where she had stuck a knife into an adder, which she explained was the only poisonous snake in Britain. She remembered that she saw one when she went to the zoo with her parents and they spent some time together in the snake house. Other associations led me to interpret her fear of the poisonous strength of her rage and her capacity to provoke other people to attack her; she was terrified of what she could provoke in me. This was an image of a primal couple, who were both lethal. I then said that this was what she believed happened in this room, that it was like the snake house. On the following day she came back feeling very disjointed although she also said she felt it was because she wanted to forget the previous session. She then started to cry and said it was very upsetting to think about what she must have put me through all these years. How must it have been for me to be with her in this room? In a subsequent session she said she felt I had helped her to remain alive.

The following observation illustrates some progression within the analysis a few years later:

Maria arrived and told me excitedly that she had been to a performance of the opera *Turandot* on the previous evening. She spoke graphically of the cold sadistic queen and of the sacrifice of the slave girl who was tortured and then killed herself to protect her beloved prince Calaf. What was most striking in her spontaneous account, as opposed to the frozen, retentive communications in most of our sessions, was the liveliness with which she said: 'I felt that the opera was telling my story, that I was the cruel queen and that the self-sacrificing slave girl was the part of the queen that she could not acknowledge as belonging to her'. In essence, I felt that Maria was telling me that there was not just a cold sadistic part of herself but also a loving and devoted part that she was struggling to reach. My response to her was: 'You know, I think you are also telling me how frightened you are of owning that part of yourself which feels enslaved to me'. Maria's answer was: 'When you talk to me in this way I feel that I could cry for a million years'.

This, then, was the focus of our later work in the analysis: her struggle, in the transference, between sadism and revenge, as opposed to hope and even love.

Some clinical and theoretical reflections

The connections between screen memories, accidents and the avoidance of time

When Maria started her analysis she repeatedly told me about the tragic love affair that she felt had changed her life. There was not much, initially, in the factual story. He was from France, on a holiday in England. They had met, fallen in love and she had felt unable to respond to his sexual interest in her, driving him away. Her despair about it lay in the fact of not being able to let him know how much she desired him, behind the frozen facade she had presented. From then on the descriptions started to have bizarre tones: she 'fell apart', 'turned inside out', 'her body had been turned on in a way that could not be turned off'. For a long period in her analysis her accounts of the tragic story in her life were stereotyped, repetitive and monotonous (frozen, containing none of the passion she was referring to), with no new information.

Maria's narrative had a rhythm similar to the descriptions of rituals in traditional societies, where stories have to be repeated in exactly the same way and changes, by definition, cannot occur. The function of the formalized and repetitive type of communication expressed in rituals is not that of understanding the world, but that of hiding it (Bloch, 1977). Maria's way of communicating helped me to understand that this was, fundamentally, her attempt to freeze something about her life that she had not understood. She presented herself with an internal world that was repetitive and timeless, where the repeated accounts functioned as a screen for experiences. The analytic task was that of re-introducing a historical dimension – a dimension that allows the individual to have a sense of herself over time. In a session

Maria commented that many people had told her that she looked younger than her age but that *somewhere* she knew that she was growing old. Then she added: 'It is like the portrait of Dorian Gray! In my attic I am growing old!'

In *Beyond the Pleasure Principle* (1920a) Freud interpreted his grandson's game with the cotton reel as the child's attempt at mastery of his mother's absence. Terry Eagleton suggests that the 'fort-da' game can be understood as the first glimmerings of a narrative, 'the shortest story one can imagine: an object is lost and then recovered. But then even the most complex narratives can be read as variants on this model: the pattern of classical narrative is that of an original settlement which is disrupted and ultimately restored' (in Dirmeik, 1992: 13). In her discussion of the same paper *Negation*, Tonnesmann (1992) also stressed Freud's formulation that thinking begins 'when the omnipotent control over the subjective object is shattered'.

The absence of a narrative is, by implication, an attempt to deny separation, the comings and goings and diachronical time, and to reify synchrony. A disruption of this framework is experienced as a catastrophe that has characterized Maria's analytic encounter with me – an encounter that threatens to interrupt the sense of timelessness and leads to fragmentation. My attempts to introduce organization (via the work of interpretation and construction) were experienced as terrifying and had to be defended against through thoughts and phantasies of violence. The analytic work, by the very constitution of a sequence of sessions, weeks and holidays, becomes an attempt to introduce a series of narratives incorporated into a broader one.

For much of the time, Maria attempted to deny the relevance of the analytic process for her. Thus, especially during the first few years, she would not remember what we had talked about in sessions. Interpretations would either be confirmed in terms of her saying: 'this was exactly what had happened when I met Alex, 30 years before' or 'this was exactly what I had been thinking on my way to the session today'. Such responses had a number of functions. It was an attempt, continuously and firmly, to expel me from her field of experiences, to disavow the analytic process and the passage of time. I had, at the same time, an awareness that what she said was also true. Bollas (1987) has coined the term 'transformational object' for the analyst's role in gaining access to and transforming that which is known but the patient has never been able to think or talk about. I have found Bollas's work relevant, specially in the process of understanding this patient's reaction when I thought I was saying something new to her. Her reply that she already 'knew' what I was talking about was true, and was not just a wish to undermine the analyst.

In any analysis one is bound to find layers of material pointing to different stages of the patient's development. It is fundamental to distinguish between these different layers otherwise the analysis may be hindered by a lack of historicization for the patient. In the case of Maria this seemed to be of particular importance, as the patient herself tended to crush and condense her history. I think that at least two dimensions of time unfolded during her analysis: at the beginning of her treatment, the moment in her life she returned to repeatedly was the love affair in her late teens. She remembered that her mind *then* became filled with violent and frightening thoughts and she was afraid she would end up by harming her boyfriend. In the analytic process, Maria struggled with the terror that this was also what was going to happen between us. The two accidents Maria suffered during her treatment became the concrete representation of the damage that can happen in the encounter between two people, of the destructive violence of the couple. As the analysis progressed, however, it also become clear that this was her belief about her early relationship with her mother. These different time dimensions – pre-genital relationship with the mother and primal scene – not only became condensed into one but later crystallized into a specific content in the relationship with her boyfriend. Essentially this is an example of après coup, as discussed in the previous chapters, in that later events retranslated earlier ones.

In the analytic process, my patient 'actualized' her earlier experiences. Sandler (1976) has coined this term to indicate the patient's attempts to re-establish with the analyst an early object relationship. This approach combines an experience of the transference as actualized in the consulting room as well as a comprehension of the unconscious phantasies. This actualization is not only of wished-for patterns of relationships but also of experiences that were not previously understood.

The language of the body: hysterical symptoms or traumatic events

Since Breuer and Freud's statement that hysterics suffer mainly from reminiscences (1893) and Freud's work *Remembering, Repeating and*

Working Through (1914a), the idea that psychic conflicts can be expressed in ways other than words has been familiar in psycho-analysis. Originally, Breuer and Freud related hysteria to the re-experience of the original psychic trauma. Freud was still, however, emphasizing the importance of having access to the past in the psychoanalytic process, whereas psychoanalysts today would also emphasize the communicative role of that which cannot be put into words, such as symptoms and actions present in the psychoanalytic process (see, for example, Limentani, 1966). The importance of that which is beyond verbalization, either through somatization or in enactments, was thus suggested very early in the psychoanalytic litera-ture and has been discussed by most analysts dealing with a variety of symptomatic presentations present in hysterical, psychosomatic and psychotic patients. Verbal processes are bypassed and conflicts are expressed in non–verbal ways: *memories are represented in symptoms.*

Some psychoanalysts have dealt with specific kinds of symptomatic presentation in their patient. McDougall (1974, 1982, 1989), for instance, distinguished between hysteria and psychosomatic illness, suggesting that whilst in hysteria the body 'lends itself' to the mind, in psychosomatic illness 'the body does its own thinking' (1974: 441). The symptoms in the latter function as signs rather than symbols and follow somatic rather than psychic processes. Rosenfeld (1978) has pointed to psychotic islands present in the psychosomatic illness. The lack of the capacity to experience psychic pain in such patients has been noted by Sifneos (1977), De M'uzan (1974) and Fain and Marty (1965). In hysterics, McDougall suggested, the symptom tells a story. She thus follows Freud's suggestion in the *Project* (1950) that hyster-ical symptoms follow primary process mechanisms because they are created by ideas and memories.

In Maria's analysis, what has allowed me to formulate my under-standing of her has been the transference framework and my attempt to trace her thoughts, behaviour and symptoms in the relational con-text in which they were expressed (Marty *et al.*, 1963). The analytic task has consisted of the expansion of the chains of associations that insert the various phenomena in the context in which they occurred. This also implies that, for a long time, the emphasis of the analyses is on the form and *functions* of the patient's communications rather than on the content of the material. The relevant material to be understood thus included all the various symptomatic manifesta-tions that Maria brought to the analysis, from the various pains she complained of, to her twitches and the dramatic centrality of her accidents.

Maria fears that to experience herself in relation to me is to become imprisoned in a violent world and to succumb to what she experiences as my wish to take her over and tear her to pieces. The dilemmas for the transference are obvious, and she attempts to deal with her terror of me by carefully watching and regulating how much she can actually interact with me at each session. If there is an obvious sado-masochism implied in frequently keeping me waiting, and in the process of relentlessly letting me know of the minutiae of the functioning of her body and of the various other professionals she has seen, the main function of all this is not to attack me, but to defend her very survival.

My patient's thoughts of violence were attempts to deal with an object that is experienced as terrifying and dangerous, and as an attempt to create an equilibrium where she neither feels too separate from nor too overwhelmed by this object. When the analyst formulates interpretations – of whatever kind – she is *inaugurating* something for the patient, independently of the content of the interpretation. The analyst introduces differentiations and separations into a territory previously more chaotic and undifferentiated. The theories present in the analyst's formulations are thus not there – present in the mind of the patient, available to be uncovered – but become constructions made by both the analyst and the patient in the analytical process. In metapsychological terms, the analyst is, in this process, helping to construct the patient's preconscious. The understanding of the analytic process as a process of construction cuts across the dichotomy of whether one is dealing with a deficiency or lack or a disruption related to trauma: 'all are dysfunctions of the preconscious system' (see Aisenstein, 1993).

In her analysis my patient has relentlessly and sadistically projected onto me her rage at feeling unloved, as well as her terror of me. At the same time, she cannot experience differentiation because this means being in touch with an inner reality where the stress is on violence and murderous encounters between two separate people. She has attempted either to contain these contradictory experiences in a relationship with her own body, which has thus been characterized by violence and fragmentation, or to project them outside, as in her experience of the two accidents (which are also violent encounters). She has persisted in encountering an external world that she feels is dangerous and violent towards her. Her analysis has consisted of a slow process through which we have attempted to understand her profound terror of both fusion with and differentiation from me, since she feared she could only find in me a mirror of her self.

It is because any encounter between two people is potentially violent, sexual and murderous that Maria had to retreat into a timeless world where people did not exist as whole persons and thus were unable to differentiate from each other. They were maintained as part objects, in the same way as she felt herself to be a collection of bits that are in pain and suffer. Thus the various parts of her own body become the containers of profound and prolonged pain, stripped of psychological meaning. The analytic process has presented her with an impossible dilemma: to be in a relationship with me implied the risk of this violent and dangerous encounter; not to be, however, would condemn her to remaining trapped in a two-dimensional, timeless world. I have suggested that it has been the endurance of this paradox in her analysis that has allowed the analytic process to take place. The analysis has thus been able to contain the most unbearable: the progressive experience of differences.

5

The interplay between identification and identity in the analysis of a violent young man

Issues of technique

There were three men, a weak man, a bodyguard and a violent man who was able to overcome the bodyguard.

(From one of Karl's dreams)

The ego is an imaginary function which intervenes in psychic life as a symbol. We use the notion of self as the Bororo (a Brazilian tribal society) uses the parrot (a totemic symbol). The Bororo says 'I am the parrot' and we say 'I am I'.

(Lacan, 1978: 52)

In the previous chapter, I discussed a patient who, at the beginning of her analysis, and for many years of her treatment, retreated into a space in her mind where time and differences were avoided: between self and other, male and female, past and present.

In this chapter, through the account of the treatment of a violent young man, I will suggest that violence could also be used as a way of obliterating the fluidity of identificatory processes, and paradoxically represented an attempt to create a space between himself and the other. This analysis indicates the process through which time and difference were progressively inserted into the language of the transference. This was a long process, as the five times a week analysis lasted for 10 years.

Introduction

In his letter of May 1897 to Fliess, Freud described identification as *a mode of thinking* about objects (in Masson, 1985). This mode of thinking lies at the origin of the constitution of the individual, through a series of modifications of the ego. It is an *unconscious* process that takes place in *phantasy*. In the early modalities of identification, mental processes are experienced in bodily terms such as ingesting or devouring. It is through the process of internalization and the progressive modification of the ego, the differentiation between ego, superego and id each ruled by different timings, that the individual is constituted. These identifications, by definition unconscious, are in conflict with a sense of 'I' as the centre of the subject and is one of the several revolutions introduced by psychoanalysis in terms of its thinking about the individual. The individual is not the 'I', or in the poet's Rimbaud's formula: 'Je est un autre' (in Lacan, 1978:17). This postulation itself institutes a division within the individual, which therefore cannot be viewed as a whole or as being a single, coherent system. There are conflicting identifications within the individual that are diverse and disorderly.

Freud's papers *On Narcissism: An Introduction* (1914b) and *Mourning and Melancholia* (1915d) introduced this major shift in his work away from a theory that predominantly accounted for the vicissitudes of the drives towards a theory concerned with the internal world and identifications (see also Abraham, 1924). Freud had already discussed the role of incorporation whereby the individual would identify in the oral mode with the lost object; the constitution of the internal world was made through identifications. This path, however, can be traced in his discussion of *Leonardo* (1910), *The Schreber Case* (1911a) and *The Wolf Man* (1918). In *The Wolf Man* (1918; see also Wolheim, 1984) Freud discussed the shifting identifications in the primal scene, which have an impact on the constitution of the individual's character. Thus, whilst remembering the scene of his parents' intercourse, the Wolf Man's identification shifted from identifying himself with his mother as being beaten by his father (in a passive role), to identifying with his father doing the beating (in the active role). In his discussion of *The Rat Man*, Freud (1909b) understands the origin of his patient's persecutory feelings to lie in the denial of the differentiation between the sexes and in the undifferentiation between love and hate.

In this chapter I develop the distinction between 'identification' and 'identity'. Identification, as a mode of thinking, presupposes a fluidity between different positions and ideas, which is present in all individuals. Freud's fundamental thinking about sexuality throughout his work concerns the fluidity between masculinity and femininity: 'psychoanalysis cannot elucidate the intrinsic nature of what in conventional or in biological phraseology is termed "masculine" and "feminine": it simply takes over these two concepts and makes them the foundation of its work. When we attempt to reduce them further, we find masculinity vanishing into activity and femininity into passivity, and that does not tell us enough' (Freud, 1920b: 171). It is only in certain conditions that one might become more aware of one's shifting identifications, like, for instance, in dreams, when one may dream of being in a variety of different positions, or of possessing characteristics usually attributed to others.

'Identity', in contrast, is an attempt that each individual makes to organize these (by definition) conflicting identifications in order to achieve an illusion of unity. It is only this illusion that allows an individual to make the statement 'I am this' (and not that). Characteristics associated with the notion of 'identity' include 'constancy', 'unity' and 'recognition of the same' (Green, 1977: 82).

My distinction between identification and identity parallels that between the individual and the person (Perelberg, 1981). The *individual*, as formulated by Freud, is de-centred, constituted in the structure of the ego, id and superego. The emphasis is therefore not on conscious but on unconscious processes that are fluid and mobile by definition. The *person* is defined in terms of the ideas one has about oneself, which include images one has about one's body, one's characteristics and the group or groups one belongs to (I am a Johnson or I am British). It is the personality, the mask, that is presented in terms of 'I am this' (and not that).

This chapter discusses these distinctions between 'identification' and 'identity', the 'individual' and the 'person', and suggests some implications they have brought to the understanding of material derived from my clinical practice.

Firstly, in certain individuals the fluidity of identificatory processes becomes overwhelming for the mind, because of the lack of distinction between phantasy and reality. There may then be an attempt to immobilize a specific aspect of the whole range of identificatory attributes in order to say 'this is me'. This is a fundamental characteristic of violence, in other words it is an attempt by an individual, potentially overwhelmed by the extreme mobility of their identificatory processes, to rigidify it and establish a *persona*, an *identity*.

Secondly, the violent behaviour may be an attempt to prevent the extreme fluidity *between masculine and feminine identificatory processes and avoid the recognition of the profound sense of entrapment inside a female figure*. The physical act of violence is an attempt to create a mental space in relation to confusing internal primary objects, locked in a violent primal scene, but specially in relation to the mother.[1]

Thirdly, these ideas are to be understood in terms of the narcissistic structures of the violent patient, who attempts to evade the experience of relating. Green (1983) defines narcissism as fundamental resistance to analysis: 'Does not the defence of the One imply the refusal of the unconscious, just as the unconscious implies the existence of a part of the psychic apparatus that has a life of its own, which defeats the empire of the Self?'[2]

Fourthly, in the violent patient there seems to be a passage from an 'unconscious phantasy' to a 'delusional system' in response to a need to separate from internal objects through external violence. If we accept Freud's formulation that phantasies of violence in the primal scene are universal, in the violent patient these phantasies acquire the status of actual beliefs.

Fifthly, the violent patient attempts to immobilize the experience of an extreme mobility of internal identificatory processes. A technical challenge in the analysis of these patients is for the analyst to identify and keep in mind the *shifts between the identificatory processes* and formulate them in terms of interpretations to the patients.

Finally, as the analyst is progressively more able to identify the patient's internal movement between different states and identificatory processes and is able to integrate these into interpretations to the patient, the patient is himself more able to tolerate the internal fluidity between identificatory processes.

I will now examine material from the five times a week analysis of a violent young man, from which some of these thoughts are derived.

---

[1] This hypothesis has been more fully discussed in Perelberg (1995).

[2] 'La défence de l'Un n'entraine-t-elle pas *ipso facto* le refus de l'inconscient, puisque celui-ci implique l'existence d'une part du psychisme qui agit pour son propre compte, mettant en echec l'empire du Moi?' (Green, 1983: 9).

Karl, a violent young man

The main information Karl brought about himself at his first consultation was his special relationship to his mother. Karl was in his
early twenties and his father left his mother when she was pregnant
with him. His mother married when he was still a baby, and this
man adopted Karl as his son. Three years later the couple had a baby
girl. Karl felt, however, that his mother always let him know that he
was the most important person in the family for her. At the same
time, he experienced his mother as unable to tolerate his sexuality or,
even less, him being a man. He said that his mother used to tell him
that she wished he was gay, because gay people never leave their
mothers.

His father was violent towards him throughout his childhood, hitting him frequently around the head. He recalled being frightened of
his father. When he was 18, Karl decided to study martial arts and felt
that his father then became frightened of him and stopped hitting
him.

The analytic process: the patterns
of the transference

In his first consultation Karl presented me with a question that he felt
had become an obsession for him and that expressed his concern about
the nature of his parents' sexuality. He told me that his parents were
involved in 'sado-masochistic games'. He had known this since his
childhood because he and his sister had listened to them through their
bedroom door. In this same consultation, Karl started to let me know
about the extent of the violence in which he had been engaged. At
university, he had got involved in seriously violent situations with
other young men (an example was that of a fight where he and other
youths had used broken bottles, which had left him in hospital with
15 stitches in his head) and in escalating violence in his sexual relationship with a girlfriend. At that first consultation I noted the possible unconscious association between his question about the nature
of his parents' sexuality and his own relationships with male and
female friends.

In tracking the way in which Karl related to me in his analysis, it
was progressively possible to understand that he attempted to escape

from an experience of having a mind each time his analyst understood him. He then had to disappear by not coming to his sessions for a time. At the beginning of the analysis this was expressed basically in the states of sleep Karl would get into, from which he could not be awakened, either by several alarm clocks or by his mother shouting at him. He could disappear from the sessions for a week, for instance, without realizing that this time had passed since his last session. The interpretations, during this period, consistently pointed to this complete retreat both from the encounter with the analyst and from the obstacles Karl inevitably experienced in his relationship with me. At these times Karl's sleep was dreamless, and this was also interpreted as a flight not only from me, but also from the experience of having a mind. Karl also spent a great deal of time compulsively playing computer games where violence was expressed in a robotic way against dehumanized enemies.

Karl gradually revealed how difficult it was for him to maintain contact with real living people since this involved levels of frustration, violence and terror that he simply could not tolerate. Yet as his confidence in the analytic relationship grew, his thoughts and aggressive interactions outside the sessions became more vividly present in his accounts during the sessions. At times he started to inundate me with descriptions of extremely violent behaviour that left me disgusted, frightened and hopeless about the possibility of my having any impact on him. It became progressively clear, however, that my main function seemed to be that of simply receiving this massive projection of his anxieties and containing them, before we could even begin to understand their unconscious meaning. Obviously the existence of the Anna Freud Young Adults' Research Group was crucial at that point, as a point of reference in my mind – and his – as I often experienced despair when alone with him in my consulting room.[3] I

---

[3] The Anna Freud Research group has undertaken analysis of young adults as part of a subsidized scheme and has been meeting twice monthly since November 1990. The initial chairmanship of Dr George Moran was followed, after his death, by the clinical direction of Mrs Anne-Marie Sandler. The aims of the research, whose director was Professor Peter Fonagy, included the study of the efficacy of psychoanalysis with this age group. In addition to Anne-Marie Sandler, Peter Fonagy and myself, the participants of the group were Anthony Bateman, Marion Burgner (who died prematurely in October 1996), Luigi Caparrotta, Rosemary Davies, Rose Edgecumbe, Julia Fabricius, Anne Harrison, Hansi Kennedy, Brian Martindale, Duncan McLean, Joan Schachter, Maria Tallandini, Sally Weintrobe and Anne Zachary.

often also wondered if he had any idea of the impact he was having on me.

At this stage I felt able to say no more than that his violence seemed to follow on from his fear of my intrusiveness in the transference. He responded by telling me that he possessed a gun and bullets that he kept at home. As he talked about this, it seemed that he was keeping a part of both himself and myself hostage, terrorized by his potential destructiveness.

Inevitably my interpretations were rooted in my counter-transference: Karl needed to know that he could terrify me as a way of protecting himself from his own fear of me.[4] My interpretations allowed him to get rid of the gun but this left him without the power to terrorize me and he felt lost, abandoned and deeply depressed. To counteract his depression, he intensified his accounts of criminal activities. After I interpreted to him the function of his criminal activities as a means of creating a distance from me and the analysis, he was able to understand and acknowledge that it was easier for him to come to the sessions after dangerous criminal encounters, such as obtaining and selling stolen diamonds, which gave him a sense of omnipotence. I also suggested that this was because he felt less frightened of my power over him. His criminal activities thus served to distance him from me and although they had many determinants, one transferential aspect was undoubtedly the wish to avoid a meaningful emotional relationship.

As he found himself more interested in relating to a woman, Karl was in a state of terror of the woman's poison, of her trickiness and perversion. His reaction was that of flight from the woman/analyst/girl, which left him feeling ashamed, humiliated and confused. He engaged in criminal activities with his male friends but was then overtaken by an extreme state of anxiety about his homosexual feelings. He attempted to deal with these feelings through violence, which again left him frightened and persecuted. This configuration of primitive Oedipal anxieties and the oscillations, from which there was no escape, was present in many of his sessions.

---

[4] Being able to detect fear in me had the function of reassuring Karl that the fear was no longer in himself, so allowing him to feel safer. Sandler (1959) has suggested that in order to preserve its feelings for safety, the ego will make use of whatever techniques it has at its disposal. He gives examples of the way in which defence mechanisms can operate in the service of this 'safety principle'.

The alternation between presence and absence, life and death, love and hate

At the beginning of his analysis Karl had many dreams that portrayed his experience of himself as inhuman, machine-like and deprived of feelings and thoughts. He dreamt that he was a computer or of being different kinds of monsters; once in particular he was a monster that was disintegrating. In the more detailed clinical material that follows, one can identify a trajectory whereby Karl is able to bring to the analysis images that express his terror of losing himself and becoming imprisoned and manipulated by a lethal couple. We will see a progression in his analysis towards a capacity to experience himself in a more humane way.

At the beginning of the third year of analysis, though, the image he spoke about was that of a disembodied head that did not belong to himself. This image was derived from a play by Denis Potter that had been shown on television and had made an impression on him.

In one particular session Karl came in and threw himself on the couch. He started telling me about watching *Cold Lazarus* by Dennis Potter on TV. He said he was not sure what had caught his attention so much about the play. He had been unable to sleep through the night thinking about it. He had watched it on both Sunday and Monday and explained that the play is being shown on both channels. He told me the story, saying that it was science fiction and thus something that he would be immediately attracted to. In the story a man has his brain cryogenically preserved in the hope that it could be revived in the future. In the play, the man's memory was being revived 400 years later by two scientists. Karl said that it had been something in the quality of the language that had arrested his attention. It was like a language without a link with anything else, coming straight from the head. It reminded him of himself when his mental state was not good: 'The thing about this man is that he is just a head so that his memories in a way do not belong to him. *He does not have an identity*. He is just what this couple of scientists do with him'. (Karl then explained that they were a man and a woman.)

I said that he was describing a quality he could identify in himself when he was avoiding having any feelings and was talking from his head only. He is now saying that when he was in that state of mind – without feelings – *he felt that he did not have an identity*. His identity had then been taken over by another part of him – the 'scientist' – who he felt was in control of him.

He said that there was a connection between that play and *Karaoke*, another play by Potter in which a character, who is an author, felt that people around him were repeating lines from his plays, which were being fed back to him about his own life. I then spoke to Karl about his experience of relating to another person, and suggested that he felt he could only re-find his own lines.

Later in the session I pointed out that there was also the issue of possession: was he a possession of mine or was I a possession of his? Could either of us have a life of their own, a 'real identity' (using his terms)? Violence became his solution.

Karl then told me about a dream: *There were three men, a weak man, a bodyguard and a violent man who was able to overcome the bodyguard.* In his associations Karl spoke of 'great men', such as Rabin or Kennedy, who were nevertheless in a very fragile position. We understood this dream as expressing the various experiences he had of himself. Underneath the bodyguard there was a fragile man, who was afraid of being hit by the violent aspect of himself.

A more three-dimensional experience of himself had, however, started to emerge in his analysis, as we also identified that it was the bodyguard – the man 'in between' – who tended to come to the sessions. Karl was, however, afraid of being left with a perception of himself as a weak and unprotected man who was bound to get killed. In the transference I was at the time acutely aware that I needed to keep all three aspects of him in mind.[5]

There was in this material, however, also an emphasis on the inevitability of death, as I could not avoid pointing out at the time. Karl then disappeared from a few sessions and when he came back he brought

---

[5] Accounts of films he had seen were an important ingredient in Karl's analysis. At times, as in the sequence above, an account of a film, followed by an interpretation, was then followed by a dream. Money-Kyrle has suggested a theory of stages in representational thought that goes from a stage of concrete representation (where no distinction is made between the representation and the object represented), through a stage of ideographic representation, as in dreams, to a stage of conscious and predominantly verbal thought (1968: 422). I think that films in Karl's accounts served to contain projections of experiences before they could be represented in dreams. The interpretations function as mediatory in this process. This observation is in agreement with Sedlak's (1997) observation on the analyst's function in the transformation of patient's dilemmas into ones that can be thought and dreamt about, although in his paper Sedlak is addressing the role of the counter-transference in the process.

another dream: *He was inside a tomb and a panther was approaching him. He was terrified as the panther came closer and closer and he woke up terrified.* In his associations Karl remembered first seeing a panther during a trip to the West Indies with his mother, who had taken him on a visit to a friend who kept a panther as a pet. In the session we were able to understand that the tomb was where he felt he had been for the week he had been absent from the sessions, and that he was now afraid of me, a panther, which posed a danger to him as representative of the outside world. He was, however, also afraid that, like his mother's friend and his own mother, I would want to keep the panther in him as my pet.

This opened up his memory of a film called *The Vanishing*, which he told me was the most terrifying film he had ever seen in his life. In the film a man called Hoffman had lost his girlfriend. She had vanished in a petrol station and he spent three years looking for her. Throughout this period he kept getting letters from a man saying that he had made her disappear. This man tortured Hoffman in this way for three years; when they finally met, he told him that he, Hoffman, could take him to the police if he wanted because there were no traces whatsoever of what he had done. The only way Hoffman could find out what had happened to his girlfriend was to go through the same thing as her. Hoffman thought long and hard; in the end he decided that he had to find out what had happened. He took the tranquillizer this man gave him and at that moment he was sealing his fate. He fell asleep and woke up in a coffin, buried under the earth. It was the most terrifying experience anyone could think of, to be buried alive.

He then said that a scene that he could not forget was in a car, when Hoffman became friendly with the fascist psychopathic kidnapper. Hoffman laughed with him and said that all his life he had done what was expected of him. Karl could not forget this scene. He said that one knows that people who are kidnapped sometimes become friends with their kidnappers, like people who are kidnapped by Muslim extremists and then return to the West mad, holding the Koran and saying their kidnappers were in fact good people. Karl told me about an American, Hollywood version of the same story made by the same director, with Jeff Bridges in the leading role, which had been a disaster. They had changed the ending so that Hoffman is saved by – he laughed – *John Wayne!* Later Karl added that in fact it had been this man's girlfriend who saved him just as he was being buried.

I said to him: 'You know I think that it was terrifying for you to see in this film the way you bury yourself alive in your bed/coffin. You are terrified of experiencing yourself either like Hoffman, who takes the sedative, or the psychopath/murderer who gets a kick out of it and out of having killed the girlfriend three years ago (the analysis). I also feel, however, that it is terrifying for you to wake up and find yourself in the coffin.' (I also thought that he was also terrified that trusting me was like taking the sedative that led him to feel buried in my couch and thus converted to radical Islam, my mad version of things.)

He was very struck by all this. He said that he could understand what I was saying but he was not really afraid of me now.

I added something about his misgivings about the ending. He thought that the version of the movie with a happy ending had been a disaster, in contrast with the terrifying one. He had also pointed out the fact that it was the man's girlfriend who had saved him, not John Wayne. I felt that this showed his mixed feelings about the idea of a girlfriend/woman analyst saving him.

This was an important session. Karl had himself found a narrative and an image that referred to his own experience of his two states, of being dead and the terrifying waking up: the wish to be 'saved' but also the terror of being saved by another entrapping/not-birth-giving woman/mother/analyst. Ultimately it was the fear of a couple made up of the murderer and the coffin, a couple that was not life-giving and, ultimately, lived inside him. What I felt was so important in this session was the way in which we were able to identify these various positions within himself: the murderous couple and the victim who was being murdered.

Karl missed the next session and on the Friday session he said that he had not been able to wake up on Thursday. He could not understand why. He talked about his relationship with his girlfriend, the first real relationship in his life, which he felt had changed him. Then he talked about a film called *A Matter of Life and Death*, which was one of the most beautiful films he had seen. David Niven played a pilot in the Air Force during the war whose plane had been attacked. He was falling through the air and Death was coming to fetch him. It was, however, very misty so that Death could not find him. In the meantime, a woman had heard David Niven on the radio when he was hit and she had fallen in love with him. She went to find him in the hospital and they fell in love with each other. Then Death caught up with him and the rest of the film was about the tribunal at which David Niven defended himself. He said that because of these two days, he had fallen in love and that it was not his fault they had missed him, but now he needed his life extended. The judge, who had the power to decide whether to let his life be extended or not, in the end decided to let him live. It was really a most striking film, Karl added. The title was most appropriate, 'a matter of life and death'.

I said that he felt that his analysis and his analyst had changed the course of his life but that this put him, at the same time, in the hands of a judge who had to decide whether or not he could carry on living (or having his analysis). He was not sure if the judge was going to be benign or not. Karl said that he was not used to meeting benign people in his life. I pointed out the contrast between *A Matter of Life and Death* and *The Vanishing*, the former expressing the capacity for love he now felt he had and the latter expressing the destructive/ fascist forces inside him. I said I thought it was difficult to find connections between these two films, these two experiences within himself. He was quiet for a moment (a rare experience) and then said that he could not understand why Hoffman had to take the sedative, *what did he want to find out?*

This reminded me of his first session with me, when he said his parents had read a sado-masochistic book by David Niven. He and his sister had stayed behind the door listening, to find out if his parents were playing sado-masochistic games.

I said that perhaps Hoffman wanted to know if his girlfriend and the fascist had engaged in sado-masochistic games. This perhaps expressed the way in which he was still caught up in what went on in his parents' bedroom, which he feared was a scene of death, as opposed to *A Matter of Life and Death* when David Niven is actually able to find himself a girlfriend to fall in love with. The problem, however, was that this put him in the hands of the heavenly judge. In this case it was a benign one, in contrast with the psychopathic kidnapper/killer that Hoffman had faced. I added: 'You know, I think that today you want me to know that there is a loving, devoted part of you as well'.

He said this session had been really amazing!

Discussion: phantasy and beliefs

In Letter 57 to Fliess (in Bonaparte *et al.*, 1954), Freud indicated that the myths elaborated by children about their origin have a special relationship with paranoia. In Letter 91 (*ibid*), Freud proposed that this myth is common to all psychoneurosis, but that it has a special connection with paranoia because of its immediate presence in consciousness. Its function would be that of flattening megalomania and introducing a barrier against incest.

The study of *The Rat Man* (Freud, 1909b) introduces other elements to the understanding of paranoia: the origin of the feelings of persecution lies in the lack of differentiation between the sexes, and between love and hate. Karl's analysis brings the understanding that a lack of differentiation between life and death may also be present in some patients, as well as a terror of finding out that they are establishing this identity between the two.

While he is asleep in the coffin, Hoffman is not aware of his predicament, which includes the question of whether he is submitting to a man (Hoffman) or to a woman (or a woman's womb = the coffin). It is only when he wakes up that he is terrified by the fact that he is trapped inside the coffin, which can ultimately be experienced as the combination of a parental couple who are not life-giving: the psychopathic father who commits murder by burying him, and the entrapping mother who does not allow him to be born or to live outside her body and her mind. The coffin was also the couch, the 'bedrock' of Karl's analysis, where he was afraid of waking up to find out that he had submitted to a couple who had committed murder in the primal scene. In a state of ultimate sleep without any dreams Karl attempted to remove all representations from his mind. The counterpart to that is the violence, where all this gains representation (as expressed in the derivatives of his unconscious phantasies in his analysis) and has to be expressed in action.[6]

---

[6] Britton has proposed a distinction between phantasy, belief and knowledge. He suggests that '*belief* is an ego activity which confers the status of psychic reality on to existing mental productions (phantasies) thus creating *beliefs*. These beliefs may be conscious or unconscious, but cannot be relinquished without becoming conscious. Whether they are conscious or unconscious they have *psychic consequences*; conversely, unless a phantasy has the status of belief, it does not have consequences' (1995: 19–20). I think these distinctions are useful in that for my patients, especially for Karl, his unconscious phantasies about the primal scene have the status of beliefs.

78

I have suggested in another paper that for Karl the terror of the image of a violent couple in the primal scene is that it has the status of an actual belief (Perelberg, 1995). Examples from two other sessions indicate Karl's confusion between phantasy and belief. In one session Karl told me about a series of programmes made by someone who had been sacked from the BBC. He was someone who faked events and then interviewed people about them. Karl gave me the example of how this man 'invented' a drug, described its effects and then interviewed important politicians about it. People were even considering now suing him for tricking them. This man's programmes were so well made that nobody could ever guess that the situations were faked. I said that I thought that this addressed an important issue for him, the boundary between what is real and what is fake. I thought that in some way we had had an experience of that earlier in the same session, when Karl had attempted to have an intellectual discussion about what psychoanalysis thinks about the symbolism attached to sports cars. This had been a fake conversation, in contrast to what were his own thoughts and fears about a specific stolen car – this confusion between what is real and what is fake made him feel confused about what was real and what was fake in his own analysis.

In another series of sessions Karl told me about a book he was writing about a man who had many dreams and, when he woke up, met characters from his dreams in reality. They started to have a life independent from his dreams, until one of them committed a murder. This was their attempt to become real characters and not just a piece of fiction, to have their own identity. In the session we understood the murder as that of his thinking self, an expression of his imprisonment in his own mind so that he could not understand somebody – himself – as having an independent mind of his own. The murder became, paradoxically, a representation of his *identity*, which meant, for Karl (and his fictional character), '*I am this*'. The paradox was that Karl was now able to write this story, although the risk, at the same time, was that he might experience himself as disengaged from the story that was, in fact, his own. The real drama for Karl was his struggle to become real, and not just a computer, a pet, a disembodied head, a fictional character in the hands of writers, scientists, parents or his analyst.

In my introduction to a collection of papers (Perelberg, 1997) I identified confusion between phantasy and belief in patients who commit violence or attempt suicide. This is, for instance, present in

Campbell's analysis of a suicidal patient, for whom an unconscious phantasy – which in the case study was the patient's identification between his body and that of his mother – became a *'delusional conviction'* in the pre-suicidal state (1995). These acts constituted *a mode of thinking*. Internal phantasies and external facts become confused with each other. This theme will find echoes in my own patient's 'beliefs' that he had been conceived through an act of violence and allows the suggestion that a 'delusional' quality in the relationship with the internal object is present in violence against the self or others.

This observation places the studies on violence at the centre of psychoanalytic investigations of phenomena that are potentially at the limits of symbolic representation, not only due to mechanisms of repression, splitting, denial and negation but also because they relate, at the same time, to something profoundly destructive in the psychic sphere that breaks through the capacity of the mind to contain it. Such a suggestion raises questions about the processes present in thinking, and the capacity of the mind to know itself (see Fonagy, 1991; Fonagy and Target, 1995).

Masculinity, femininity and the phallus

In order to counteract feelings of helplessness and precariousness ('I am not weak, but strong', 'I am Me'), Karl activated feelings and acts of violence that allowed him to believe that he had, by himself, created another version of himself. He gained an omnipotent phallic identity. But what is the phallus?

In *Totem and Taboo* Freud (1913b) described the primal patricide committed by the original horde, who killed and devoured their father. This was followed by remorse and guilt (as they both hated and loved their father) and the dead father became more powerful than he had been while alive. The *dead father* is thus the possessor of the phallus. I find it interesting to link this myth in Freud's work to the notion, present in so many traditional societies, that the individual only becomes a full person when dead and transformed into a (phallic) ancestor (Perelberg, 1997); see, for instance, the Tallensi (Fortes, 1970). The phallus appears as an important symbol in many funerary rituals.

What does it represent in these contexts? Why should the phallus be an important symbol in funerary rites? Bachofen has suggested that the funeral rite 'glorifies nature as a whole, with its twofold life and death giving principle ... That is why the symbols of life are so frequent in the tomb ...' (1967: 39). Does this also account for the fact that the themes of sexuality and fertility dominate the symbolism of funerals (e.g. amongst the Lugbara of Uganda: Middleton, 1960; the Trobriand Islanders of the Western Pacific: Malinowski, 1948; and the Kashi: Parry, 1982)? What is being emphasized in the contexts of these rites is both separation and integration, part and whole, masculinity and femininity, and life and death. I would further suggest that it is the finite, limited quality of the facts of culture that is ultimately denied in the symbol of the phallus. From this perspective the phallus is the signifier not only of a power structure but also of universal fears, beliefs and wished-for states of completeness and plenitude.

Thus in this myth of origins the phallus, unlike the penis, is possessed by nobody (male or female) and *represents the combination of both sexes, where neither is given up.*[7] In Karl's personal mythology, however, the mother is the possessor of the phallus, becoming a combination of both sexes as she eliminated the father in the primal scene. (An example of this was one of Karl's dreams where there was a woman whose nose was shaped like a penis.)

Freud's myth, in which the father needs to be murdered, seems to me to be a mythical account of the process of growing up, where the parents need to be destroyed by the adolescent in order for him to mature. This perspective is perhaps the counterpart of Serge Leclaire's (1975) suggestion that a real child can only be born when the parental couple are able to give up the idea of an idealized child. This implies the existence of real parents who can help first the child and later the adolescent cope with feelings of frustration and progressively emphasize the reality principle. The counterpart is that the young adult too must be able to give up and mourn the wish for idealized parents so that the real parents can be accepted and the young adult can be born.

The acceptance of an order that involves a differentiation between the sexes and the generations introduces the individual to an experience of renunciation and mourning. The individual must renounce his own parents, take them as sources of identification, develop his own sense of temporality and history and thus acquire an individual

---

[7] Birksted-Breen has proposed the distinction between phallus and 'penis-as-link' (1996a). Whilst the former is 'representative of omnipotence and completion' (p. 651), *of narcissistic organization*, the latter represents the 'mental function of linking and structuring' *and the internalization of the parental relationship.*

'project'. This would indicate a distinction between those who have been able to inaugurate their own individual project and those patients who have become immobilized in another's temporality, as happened with Karl.

The individual and the person

Freud pointed out the fluidity that is the hallmark of identificatory processes. This fluidity contrasts with the individual quest for a *coherent* identity, a sense of cohesiveness that is denied him by the very nature of the psychic apparatus. It is, however, only the feelings of security engendered by attachments to objects of both sexes that prevent the individual from feeling overwhelmed by the pressure of the phantasies and desires of the pre-genital sphere, because they may then be anchored in a set of secure object relationships.

From very early on this became a problematic issue for Karl, when he became confused about his experiences of his biological father's absence, his stepfather's violence towards him and his mother's collusion with his phantasy that he did not have a father (Perelberg, 1995). Karl attempted to deal with his stepfather's violence by studying martial arts and creating fear so that he would no longer be abused. In his phantasy, however, he is also defending himself against his wish for fusion with the dangerous pre-Oedipal mother.[8]

However, Karl's longing for his stepfather was even more conflictual than his feelings of hatred and hostility. Only after several years

---

[8] This conflict has been identified and discussed in different ways in the psychoanalytic literature. Some examples are as follows: Ferenczi (1923) suggested that adult sexuality is at some level a symbolic return to the womb and thus a symbolic merging with the mother. Erikson (1950) also pointed out the fear of ego-loss in situations that call for self abandonment: 'in orgasms and sexual unions, in close friendships and in physical combat, in experiences of inspiration by teachers and of intuition from the recesses of the self'. Loewald (1951) argued that the fear of loss of ego through regression to the 'primary narcissistic identity with the mother' is one of the deepest dreads – the dread of the 'engulfing, overpowering womb'. Guntrip (1968) suggested that the schizoid person hovers between two opposite fears: the fear of isolation in independence with loss of ego on the one hand and the fear of bondage to or imprisonment on the other. Glasser (1979) addressed the conflict implied between the longing for and the terror of fusion with the mother as being the 'core complex' in perversions. Rey (1994) described the claustro-agoraphobic dilemma present in borderline patients who feel trapped inside their objects. They try to escape but then are afraid of losing the object on whom they depend, and feel agoraphobic. See also the recent contribution by Kohon, 2007.

was he able to tell me about his longing for his father's love and admiration.[9] Karl remembered looking at pictures of his stepfather climbing, when he was young, in an admiring way and having conscious thoughts of wanting to be like him, so that his stepfather too could admire him. This was confusing for Karl, as it was mixed up with memories of the utter humiliation he suffered. Karl told me of a fight with his father when his father hit him and Karl's pyjama trousers fell down, leaving him naked and extremely humiliated in front of both his father and mother, who had witnessed the scene. He felt confused by the idea that his father got a 'kick out of it', that this violence towards him excited his stepfather, and this thought became blurred in an expression of his own desire to submit to his stepfather. Thus he felt a mixture of hate and love, since the person who was his persecutor was also the person he loved. Karl, in this way, experienced himself as the child/victim of mad parents, a reminder of Lepastier's observation of how often adolescents present themselves as the children of mad fathers (1991).

Violence for Karl represented both an attempt to give birth to another person who was disconnected from the lethal parental couple *and, at the same time*, a repetition of the relationship he attributed to this couple. Violence for him had a defensive function and was an attempt to create a persona detached from his conflicting identifications (Mauss, 1938).

The idea of the person is linked to specific attributes that make up an identity: in many societies this identity is marked through masks, body painting or ways of dressing: I am this, a Bororo, a Kwakiutl, a parrot, I am a man, I am tough (Lévi-Strauss, 1977). Psychoanalysis, however, reminds us that this identity is by definition imaginary: 'the ego is an imaginary function which intervenes in psychic life as a symbol. We use the notion of self as the Bororo (a Brazilian tribal society) uses the parrot (a totemic symbol). The Bororo says "I am the parrot" and we say "I am I" '.[10]

The concept of identity has a tradition in psychoanalysis. In discussing adolescence Erikson believed that 'identification is a mechanism

---

[9] In a letter to Ferenczi, Freud (1960) established a link between paranoia and the detachment of the libido from its homosexual component.

[10] 'Le moi, function imaginaire, n'intervient dans la vie psychique que comme symbole. On se sert du moi comme le Bororo se sert du peroquet. le Bororo dit "je suis un perroquet", nous disons "je suis moi" ' (Lacan, 1978: 52).

of limited usefulness' (1968: 158) and that identity formation arises out of the repudiation of childhood identifications. This is the result of the process of socialization. Erikson also indicated that adolescence is a period of 'identity confusion' but although he describes the process he does not conceptualize the nature of theses processes in terms of the internal world. 'Identity diffusion' (which Erikson later replaced by 'identity confusion') becomes the result of a lack of an 'assured sense of identity'.

Kernberg (1975) uses the concept of 'identity diffusion' to designate a poorly integrated concept of the self and of significant others. These concepts in psychoanalysis tend to be attached to specific theoretical frameworks that emphasize the 'unity of the personality', which in many ways differ from the formulations I am developing in this chapter. Freud himself used the term identity 92 times in his work, mainly to emphasize the relationship with the environment. His central conceptualization about the individual, however, points out that identity is an illusion. This is my point of departure. Indeed this is a central criticism that the French school of psychoanalysis has towards the British object relations theorists, i.e. their belief that identity can be seen as stable and coherent. This idea – of the illusory nature of identity – would find support in modern anthropological writing.

In her seminal paper Kestemberg (1966) suggested that identifications and identity are part of the same movement, a dialectic between images and desires (p. 153). Identity refers to the quest for a sense of internal coherence. Yet, the human subject is elusive, to capture Kennedy's expression when addressing this issue (1998).

Issues of technique

Bateman (1997) draws on Rosenfeld's distinction between the two types of narcissism (1987b), namely thick- and thin-skinned narcissists, and suggests that narcissistic and borderline patients tend to move between these two positions. Thin-skinned narcissists are fragile and vulnerable whilst thick-skinned narcissists are inaccessible and defensively aggressive. Bateman suggests that it is the *movement* between these positions that opens an opportunity for analytic treatment.

I have found this suggestion extremely useful and would like to add here that it is extremely important that *the analyst is aware of this movement and takes it into account in her interpretations.* Karl came to his sessions at times when he was moving between positions – when he was the bodyguard between the weak man and the killer, as expressed in his dream. However, what characterized his movements in terms of their underlying phantasy was the alternation between an attempt to *retreat from a world of representations* (which he experienced as danger-ous to himself as well as to others), on the one hand, and a world of violence, on the other. In other words, a movement from a *blank space* to *violence*.

The blank page was characterized by Karl's absences from the sessions, especially when he was locked in dreamless sleep as an attempt to create a space without obstacles, a space in which he identified with an idealized mother in order to escape the terror of entrapment. In this state, Karl tried to deny access to any representa-tion, both of the internal world (of phantasies) and the external world (of thoughts, which require secondary process), in an attempt to reach a state of narcissistic closure. At the other pole there was a massive entrance to the world of representation (in violence), which ceases to act as a representation but reaches the status of a belief. The alterna-tion is thus between the blank space and the actual beliefs as expressed in violence. These two states may also reflect a massive split be-tween an all good world (blank) and an all bad world that needs to be destroyed through violence. The analytic task becomes that of enabling the patient to be more aware of this alternation.

When Karl returned after missing many sessions, sometimes over an entire week, he felt so excited about his achievement that it was as if a new life had started for him. He had survived whatever he felt he had been through. At times he was so rational and plausible in his explanations that I could see myself 'following' his reasoning, and forgetting my feelings and thoughts during his absence, that this time the analysis really had been terminated. When he came back I too felt that we had survived something. Progressively I had to keep in mind the movement between these two states, the presence and absence, the sessions and the blank pages of the sessions he had not come to, that he wanted to leave out. One has to capture the movement in between the sessions of the various identifications – and not the momentary identity – 'I am this' (and not that). 'I can't see any reason why I should not be able to carry on coming to the sessions now', he would often say. Or, 'I see no reason why Sofia and I cannot carry on relating as well as we did this weekend'.

85

He was terrified by the link between these two states, which left him confused and feeling out of control. My interpretations started to centre on this *link* between presence and absence, word and silence, masculine and feminine identifications, persecutor and persecuted, the written and the blank pages of the sessions. Time and difference were progressively inserted into the language of the transference, in the verification of the pattern, and were given shape both in the dream about the tomb and in his response to the film called *The Vanishing*. Both were his representations of the world to which he had retreated and from which waking up was so terrifying.

Karl progressively became more able to identify these oscillations himself and was, for instance, more able to relate not being able to come to sessions to something that he felt had frightened him in a specific session. He was less frightened of his oscillations between identifications and more able to talk about them, as in the example of his account of feeling ashamed in front of both his mother and father. In another account he was able to tell me about having the fleeting thought over a weekend that his girlfriend appeared to him to have some masculine traits, without feeling too persecuted by these thoughts.

Psychoanalysis is always characterized by an indeterminism, perhaps because phenomena are over-determined so that many different phantasies are necessarily attached to the patient's symptomatology. The psychoanalytic task is consistently that of 'linking' affects, images and words as they are expressed and experienced in the transference and counter-transference so that the preconscious may be constructed.

The individual is thus placed in a chain of reciprocity in relation to their internal and external objects. I have previously suggested that Karl's fundamental concern in his analysis was to regulate his distance from his analyst (Perelberg, 1995). This can be further understood as representing his conflict about entering a chain of reciprocity that is, ultimately, the force of the life instinct itself. It was Karl's inability to take part in this system of exchange that condemned him to death itself, to his coffin. In his analysis we have been able to reach representations of this enclosure, which, by definition, indicates his progressive entrance into the symbolic sphere, with its dimensions of time and space.

6

Full and empty spaces in the analytic process

Eros is not speaking and even Thanatos is more muted than usual.
(Cournut, 1975: 96)

I was one of three men. Suddenly I had lost two of them. We were in a market place and it was very crowded. I searched and searched and could not find them. I felt let down by them because they had not waited for me.
(From Simon's dream)

In this chapter I expand a distinction first proposed by Pontalis (1974b) between two categories of patients that differ in terms of the impact they have on the analyst. On the one hand there are patients who create an empty space in the analyst's mind. The response they provoke is a lack of a chain of associations, a kind of depressive feeling that remains after they leave. The patient may bring dreams and associations, but they do not reverberate in the analyst's mind. The experience is of dryness, a dearth of memory, which may – at times – leave the analyst with a sense of exclusion from the patient's internal world. In Jean Cournut's words, Eros is not speaking and even Thanatos is more muted than usual (1975).

At the other extreme there are patients who fill the consulting room not only with their emotions and their actions, but also with their words, dreams and associations. The experience is that the analyst is over-included in the patient's world. They have dreams that directly refer to the analyst and one feels consistently involved in the patient's analysis.

Both of these types of patients communicate through actions as well as words. In spite of the differences between them, I would like to

87

suggest that they share an experience of something 'un-representable' in their internal world, which is expressed in terms of either an absence or an excess of affect. The pathway through which the analyst can understand both of these types of patients is via the counter-transference or, to put it differently, the analyst's passion. Bion has indeed suggested that a psychoanalytic interpretation should illuminate an object in the domains of 'sense, myth and passion' (1984: 11).

Many patients may alternate between these two types of experiences. We are all familiar with patients who fill a session in order to empty it, or those who fill a session with their sense of emptiness. However, the two types may serve as models of thinking about the impact these patients have in the analyst's mind.

In *Analysis Terminable and Interminable*, Freud suggested that the bedrock of any analysis is the 'repudiation of femininity' (1937a: 250). This statement may be viewed as lying at the crossroads of the discussion about the limits of the theoretical and clinical psychoanalytic formulations I have been referring to. In the examples I present I will be trying to relate the repudiation of femininity in its connections to the gaps implicit in psychoanalytic understanding.

Simon

Simon was in his late twenties when he first came to see me and was in analysis for many years. At the first consultation he told me many things about himself but seemed to be emotionally out of touch with what he was saying. He wanted to embark on an analysis in order to understand more about himself and also because he felt that he could do more with his life. I was moved by his account of his psychological struggles throughout his life. I felt that he might be presenting a delayed mourning reaction to his father's death, some two years earlier.

What struck me about Simon from the beginning was not the content of the many dreams he flooded me with. These repeatedly depicted his sense of rejection, abandonment, regression and depression. What progressively did impress me most profoundly was my experience of a sense of absence in him, of a desolate being, and the semi-alive state that would also envelop me during the sessions with him, preventing any associative work from taking place in my mind. Simon presented himself as dramatically detached from himself, and seemed to have no interest in his own thoughts and/or indeed his dreams. He could easily interrupt and abandon his own train of thoughts, without any sense that I might have been following him with interest. He might indeed, at that point, have no conception that there was anybody there listening to him. I had an initial thought that he seemed to be enacting utter maternal detachment.

Simon was the youngest of six boys and came from a Mediterranean country. His mother was alive and lived in the country where Simon spent the first 20 years of his life. His father died two years prior to his starting his analysis. Simon had memories of parental rows and horrendous physical violence. His mother seems to have suffered from severe depression, with psychotic episodes throughout Simon's childhood in which she locked herself in the bathroom and threatened to set herself on fire. The father would leave the children helplessly knocking at the bathroom door, pleading with her to come out. He was experienced as indifferent and absent, preoccupied with his career ('He treated me like a bastard!'). In the same way, the father became a bastard, an illegitimate part of Simon's mind.

Simon remembered always being a withdrawn child. He did reasonably well at school until adolescence, when he started failing. He did manage, however, to get into and finish university, after which he came to the UK with little money, but with the support of his family. Simon's sexual life was marred by inhibitions, and he lived a relatively abstinent life.

In the first dream Simon brought to analysis *he was in the sea and he felt a movement whereby he was being swallowed by deep waters and then expelled upwards*. This dream and the associations that followed vividly provide images of the way in which Simon plunged into a primitive transference, marked by a fear of psychotic breakdown. Another image present in this first dream seemed to be his experience of his whole body as a penis. Simon depicted his experience of losing himself and feeling dissociated.

There were many dreams during these initial few years that emphasized the experience of feeling stuck or imprisoned, in water or in muddy ground, or caught up in fire. Simon's fear of being swallowed up continued to be expressed in the way he flooded me with his speech and dreams. I quickly learned that I should not concentrate primarily on attempting to analyse the content of these dreams, but look rather at their function and what they brought to the feel of the session.

Simon's presentation as a passive, gentle man was disturbed in the counter-transference by some irritation towards him. Gradually, I came to understand my experience of being immobilized and of feeling controlled by the pace he set, as the first three years of his analysis were marked by a sense of immobility and *lack of reciprocity*. He seemed to have a strange capacity to respond to me in a way that immobilized me.

I also felt watched. My attempts to verbalize these experiences and formulate them into interpretations led Simon to reveal that he had, on occasions, parked his car in front of my house to watch me and my family, although he had consistently fallen asleep before he saw any of us. He secretly attempted to control his objects just by being there, perhaps related to his experience that he could not have an impact on his mother. This opened up the space for a whole new area, where he could tell me more about his phantasy life, and its sado-masochistic quality.

Another central theme that was gradually openly expressed was of the violence of his inner world. He consistently brought to the sessions his experience of vulnerability in the face of a severe and violent superego that contained his projected rage towards his parents, unmodified by any kind of loving figure. Thus his fragile state was greatly exacerbated over weekends and breaks when he had an unconscious fear of abandonment, which he reacted against with hatred, often turned against himself. For instance, there were many accounts of accidents that took place in his house over the weekend, such as his pullover or the tea towel catching fire. These accidents also indicated the profound identification with his psychotic mother.

Simon was consistently attracted to scenes of violence. For instance, after a bomb exploded in the City of London he spent hours watching a building that had been destroyed. Books and films about the Holocaust fascinated him, thus creating in external reality a scene of murder where he would identify with *both* the victims and the murderers.

During the earlier years of analysis, his phantasies about a crippled and abandoned part of himself that needed care but provoked revulsion in the other were expressed in many dreams. On a Monday session, for instance, he brought the following dream: *I was one of three men. Suddenly I had lost two of them. We were in a market place and it was very crowded. I searched and searched and could not find them. I felt let down by them because they had not waited for me.*

Simon was quiet for a moment. Then he said that on a journey he had made to Belize he had taken a taxi to go to a market place and that there were so many people the taxi could not move. A beggar put his arm through the window. His hands were deformed with leprosy. They were repellent. The beggar would not take his hands out of the window for some time, until somebody pulled him away. Simon said that another incident was when he was two years old his mother lost him in a street, which might have also been a market. He was found by the police, who took him home. He had no memory of this event but had been told about it several times.

I said that I felt that he was telling me how difficult it was for him because on the one hand he felt desperate to be found by me, but on the other hand he was afraid that I would think he was so unaccept- able (sick and repellent like the leper on his trip) that the only solu- tion would be for him to lose himself. He then felt desperately alone and lost. Beyond the castration imagery in the 'two men' who disap- pear and the deformed hands, I also thought that the dream expressed his loss of contact with these experiences, and that this left him feeling flat and one-dimensional (as opposed to three-dimensional).

Once he had a dream about *a man dressed in white standing against a white wall. He was so still that he could not be seen.* The familiar theme of him disappearing re-emerges, like in the first dream of his analysis of disappearing into the sea. This dream followed a session where I had felt we had made some contact. The invisibility and stillness was a reversal of the violence he feared in any contact, reverberations of the violent primal scene he feels he witnessed between his parents when they hit each other. He consistently expressed this conflict between the wish to be seen and not to be seen, between wanting to know and not to know, a reminder of the Wolf Man's wish to know nothing, to foreclose (see Green, 1986b: 230). When Simon had parked his car in front of my house, the aim was to observe in order to eliminate the object, the third (negative hallucination) – in this case, knowledge of the existence of my family and my life independent from him.

It is this aspect of his analysis, this consistent elimination of himself and his objects so that they cease to exist, that is so difficult to under- stand and interpret. One is left with blankness and empty spaces. Over the years this was expressed in many different ways. For instance, a peculiarity of his way of talking was that he could develop a line of reasoning expressing the advantages of one point of view about some- thing, only to follow that by an exposition of the opposite point of view. He could also start his discourse with a phrase, and then introduce so many other sub-phrases that the line of his thinking would be lost. This would correspond to a lack of thoughts and associative working by myself. Or he might be absent from one session through oversleeping, often after a session when we had a more lively interaction, or preceding a holiday break.

Although the theme of damage both to self and object was consistently at the threshold of being present in Simon's analysis, he avoided persecutory anxiety. I think that one of the risks in such an analysis is for the analysis itself to become a substitute for life. It becomes an enclave (O'Shaughnessy, 1992) not of cosiness, but of stillness and immobility: white against white. This can potentially happen as a result of either too much interpretation or too little. If the analyst interprets too much – which I think I tended to do in the early years of Simon's analysis – the patient lives through the analyst. If he/ she interprets too little, the sessions are invaded by the silence of death.

The analytic work centred on Simon's essentially passive attitude, which aims to control his objects. This passivity also expressed masked aggression, and his wish to control the object had a pathologically narcissistic aspect to it. There was a considerable degree of exhibitionism involved in his passivity, which aimed to expose himself and his suffering (a martyr) and ill treatment by his objects (his grievances).

I would like to present some clinical material that illustrates Simon's struggle in relation to contact with the analyst. I will also provide some material about the preceding Monday session.

On Monday Simon presented the following dream: *Some people were taking fish out of the water and dealing with them with gloves. I kept shouting they should wet their hands otherwise the fish would get dry.*

Simon: I read in an article that people who go fishing and handle fish with dry hands, by the time they put them back in water they have removed the protective layer. [He is quiet again.]

Analyst: Perhaps you yourself felt left without a protective layer for the weekend. [Simon protested, saying that he had felt that the Friday session had been really helpful, that he had really liked what I had said, etc. I was quiet and after a while he commented on himself.]

Simon: I am digging my heels in. But I did not go away feeling you left me without protection. Maybe I was feeling deskilled this weekend . . . I feel that the dream about the fish is about my own bloody cruelty . . . In a strange way this weekend I was not so disorganized . . . It wasn't all gloomy. On Friday I gave a seminar that went very well, the students were excited. I was pleased with the way I did it.

Analyst: [I think about what he had said about his cruelty, which we have seen before is also his experience of leaving behind a depressed, blind mother/analyst. His mother always needed him next to her, for her own needs.] Perhaps it is also what you feel is possible to tell me, what you feel I can tolerate. Can I tolerate you giving an exciting seminar?

Simon: This reminds me how I could never tell my mother I had had a good day . . .

On Tuesday Simon arrived on time.

Simon: I managed to work on the chapter yesterday evening. [He talks a bit about the chapter of the book he was writing.] I felt better during the day. Then I had this image of my father's office. He had such a tidy office, everything organized. A bit like your room.

Analyst: Yesterday you felt more organized inside, which felt like being in your father's room, or my room.

Simon: I was thinking about what you said yesterday, when you mentioned that the week felt containing to me . . . You also told me, when I said that he treated me like a bastard, about the difficulty of giving my father a place in my mind. I think that's right. I can begin to function properly if give him a place. I have to reconcile that with the fact that I didn't have a space in his thoughts. [Cries.] There was a typing school near my house and my brother encouraged me to go there when I was 12 or 13. I used to go at six in the morning . . . As I was talking I remembered his type-writer. I never touched it . . . My father asked me, some time before he died, if I could send him an electric one from London. I never did it. I thought that I would take it with me when I went home.

Analyst: When you feel able to work, you feel that you are touching your father's typewriter. [He cries. There is a long silence, which is unusual.]

Simon: Sometimes when I write I feel like I am a thief, because this chapter I am now writing is for a textbook, and I took what I wrote from so many sources, adding statistics . . . [He is quiet again.] My father used to write in longhand before he typed. He had a Parker pen for some 30 years. On one occasion I took it and I lost it. I was already at university. I was careless; I just left it there. I came ten minutes later and it was gone. He didn't say anything. In a way I wished he had. [Silence.]

Analyst: You know, I think that you are saying that when you want to have contact with your father inside or with me, you feel that you are stealing, and this makes it so difficult for you. Can you use a pencil or a typewriter, or are you then stealing from your father, your mother, or from me? [The reference to castration anxiety was obvious here, but I did not say anything.]

Simon: [In a stronger voice.] I have been organizing the whole new programme for the postgraduate course. I have never been involved in anything like this. I feel that it is quite an interesting thing to do. I was interested in the way this other professor found me.

Analyst: You wonder if you can feel like you have been found.

Simon: Funny you saying that. On Friday I discovered an article written by Anna Freud 'On losing and being found'. [Silence.] As I feel more capable, I feel less angry with my father, but I feel sadder. When I started to write the chapter, I couldn't get the beginning in hand. Once I got it, I began to be able to do it. It became enjoyable. [There was a long silence, which lasted to the end of the session.]

The experience of losing himself in water over the weekend, of merging with the idealized mother/analyst, was followed by the painful experience, which is the contact, which is also potentially life-taking. If I treated him delicately, with gloves, he was in danger and felt that I was killing him. If he got into the water he was also lost, as he was terrified of emerging from the water. I thought that progressively, during the week, he was able to experience more contact, although by the end of the week he felt that he was thrown back into the water for the weekend. Sexual imagery was also present, in that he was terrified of losing himself inside a woman.

Simon's analysis consistently pointed to his sense of isolation. If he was above water, he was alone, isolated or endangered. If he was under water, he was lost and could not be found. I think there was some progression in this analysis, and on the whole Simon became more able to be active in terms of his internal objects and in relation to his external ones. However, one of the technical dilemmas for the analyst is to avoid becoming too active, in an attempt to organize the patient's internal experiences, or too passive.

Some way into his analysis Simon recounted the following dream: *He was on a roundabout and there was a rock in the middle. He was reversing into a woman and in his attempt to avoid her he almost ran over a man and fell over a precipice.*

This was a dream brought to a session for which he had been late. He had expressed feelings of guilt both about being late and for not stopping to help a man whose car had broken down on his way to the session, in the same way that he had not stopped to help a woman a few weeks before. He had been stuck in traffic. The 'reversal into the woman' expressed his experience that men and women appear symmetrical and interchangeable. His wish to both be a woman and to eliminate her (run her over) led him to feel stuck, endangered, unable to relate to either the feminine or the masculine side of him.

Simon once told me about a teenager who had run away from home at 16 and was sexually abused, and who used to cut herself. He felt very sympathetic towards her and felt that he understood her destructiveness. He described how she cut herself making criss-cross patterns, as if these were 'no go' areas, like saying 'no, don't trespass', 'don't come inside'.

The bedrock of Simon's analysis was the repudiation of the feminine, of the possibility of a (positive) passive attitude towards his analysis inside him (*passivité de vie*, as suggested by Denys Ribas, 1999). However, there was also the wish 'to run the man over', which left him feeling as if he had no choice, an experience of disorientation and danger, in a universe where he did not know the difference between men and women, and was unable to submit (positive passivity) in a receptive way to either a man or a woman.

Patricia

At the beginning of her analysis Patricia also struggled about taking a feminine position. I would like to stress that although I will be underlining one aspect of this patient's way of relating to me – her passion – at other times Patricia related to me in a friendly manner. She was, however, able to get into states of mind where she would communicate through a display of passion, excesses and repeated enactments that were progressively understood as her attempts to include the analyst in her internal dramas.

Patricia was born in a Spanish-speaking country, and her analysis with me was to be her third. The first analyses had been carried out in her country of origin, in her own language. She was in her late thirties, married and had three children. Patricia brought explosiveness into the consulting room from the second consultation onwards, and embarked on a relentless attack that lasted for the first couple of years of analysis. Nothing escaped her criticisms, from the various elements of my settings – the horrible curtains and couch cover – to the obviousness of my interpretations. Patricia also consistently threatened to walk out of the analysis, giving me repeated ultimata, especially if she felt that a specific session had not been worth the money she paid me. These onslaughts, where contempt and hatred were expressed with great intensity, contrasted with a sense of coldness that was not clearly expressed but only alluded to in dreams, and in her reported lack of mourning and crying at the death of her mother some years prior to her starting her analysis with me. It was my sense of her fragility, vulnerability and terror, which was barely perceptible but nevertheless present, that helped me to endure these long and repeated onslaughts.

With this dramatic presentation, Patricia kept me engaged, thinking and challenged. The main point for her was to keep me engaged and interested, to *fill* the space of the session with a sense of interaction between us. So long as I was engaged, we would both survive. Indeed, at the first consultation she had brought me a dream, in which *she was being taken on a frightening trip inside a plane/elevator, towards death. Then somehow this elevator stopped and she was able to step out. She had survived.* Her associations were to the trains to the concentration camps, and that she somehow managed to escape. The issue of survival was, therefore, at the core of this analysis, which was experienced not only as her salvation, but also as a plane/elevator taking her on a frightening trip. I often thought of this dream during Patricia's outbursts, and experienced that she was trying to defend our very survival. The sado-masochistic dimension she brought to the consulting room was aimed at reviving the dead mother/analyst.

The understanding of this struggle for survival involved many layers of meaning throughout her analysis, in the work of construction and reconstruction. On the eve of coming to the first session she had a 'horrible dream about her mother', the first since her mother died. *Her mother was sitting behind a desk with a commode behind it. Her mother was wet and there was urine under her chair.* Somehow it made her think about the analyst's position behind the couch. She was very upset. I said that I thought that she was feeling anxious about flooding me with her thoughts and feelings. The significance of this mother who had died also indicated her anxiety about an analyst who would not be able to contain her because she was a dead analyst. Progressively in the analysis of the transference, Patricia's mother emerged as not in touch with her little girl's anxieties.

There was, however, another dimension to this dream. The mother sitting behind her desk was also a representation of herself, removed from her own experiences. The urine under the chair was that which flooded, and could not have access to representation.

These considerations paved the way for the following nightmare, which woke her up:

Everything was frozen, covered with ice. There was a great deal of snow everywhere. A piece of the land where she had been standing broke off, as if it was an iceberg, only underneath the ice there was ground, which was covered. It was very frightening until a van came to her rescue. This man came to her rescue. He threw her a piece of rope, which she had to tie around both her hands.

(And she lifted up her hands to show me how the rope would have been tied around them. She laughed nervously, saying it was peculiar.) Then she woke up really frightened and it took a few seconds for her to realize where she was.

She had some thoughts about the man who rescued her, whom she thought might be her son. She also talked about her relationship with her three children, and how enslaved she had felt when they were young.

I thought that the dream depicted her frozen internal world of thoughts and feelings and the danger she might face if this ice broke off, although she also thought that there was land underneath the ice. The problem about being rescued was the risk of becoming enslaved by her rescuer (in a masochistic way, although I did not say that at the time). This frozen world could also be seen as a place where she took refuge from both her melancholic state and her paranoid anxieties.

If the relationship with a mother who was not aware and absent was only accessible via the transference and enactment in the consulting room, what was more accessible to consciousness were her feelings and experiences towards her first daughter when she was born. It took some years before she was able to acknowledge, full of shame and guilt, how she had felt towards her baby daughter in her first year of life. She had experienced the baby as so demanding that she had been terrified that she might have harmed her. It was that raging, crying baby that I often experienced coming into the consulting room.

There was, however, also an erotic charge to her relationship to me, from the orgiastic way she relished the freedom of her sadistic attacks, to the sensuality of her bodily movements on the couch. She would come in, sit down on the couch and take her shoes off with great sensuality, like a woman seducing her lover.

Progressively Patricia alternated between critical and sadistic attacks on me, and idealization. She came to one session after a holiday saying she had had many dreams. She remembered them but she was also wary because she did not want me to be just like her 'dream analyst'. I repeated the expression 'dream analyst', pointing out its ambiguous meaning. She laughed and said that I was indeed her dream analyst.

After some six years of analysis Patricia decided to leave. She had been in analysis for most of her life and she felt she had now gained enough from me to allow her to leave. We decided to set the finishing date for a year later. A few weeks before we finished she had the following dream:

There was a tiny crippled woman in a wheelchair. A man named her. We were all smoking. I thought that we should eat and drink. The atmosphere was dirty, depraved. Then I was going to marry her. I sucked her penis to get her hard. I looked for her vagina but there wasn't one. I got myself someone I did not want to marry. Then I was looking for a man who would be on duty. He'd be away on holiday. Would there be anyone there?

Patricia's associations were to a very difficult time in her marriage – her husband went to see a therapist, who told him to leave her. He told Patricia all about it 10 minutes before she had to go out to work, saying he was going to leave her.

Patricia: I was furious with him and with her. I did not know whether he would leave me or whether I should leave him. But I was so attached to him . . . I also think about a friend. She has two red setters. We met walking in the fields. She is terribly thin. She is always happy, full of beans. Her husband is such a misery; they are like chalk and cheese.

Analyst: You know, you are telling me that this is a terrible time for you. You feel that this is like a marriage coming to an end. Who is leaving whom? Perhaps you feel that you have to show me your cheerful side in order not to let me know about the anguished, attached one.

Patricia: I can understand what you are saying with my head. In many ways I don't want to leave you. I dread this coming May.

Analyst: I think that you relate feeling vulnerable to having a vagina. You feel that if, perhaps, you had a hard penis, you would not feel so vulnerable. But this leaves you feeling disabled. You fear I am like that too. I cannot offer food or drink, just cigarettes, and the two of us are the same. Neither of us have vaginas, but we can't have hard penises either . . . This leaves you feeling despairing . . .[1]

Patricia: [Silence.] There was a depraved horrible atmosphere in the dream. It reminds me of not crying at my mother's funeral. I thought that I should be crying. I was sad, but cut off. I adored her. Yet I was unable to cry. I know now how capable I am of being angry.

Analyst: Sometimes it is difficult to cry. [There was a silence.]

---

[1] Patricia's dream indicates how towards the end of her analysis she was still in a conflict about her psychic experience of having an inner space, a vagina, as an expression of femininity and receptivity. The French analysts have indicated the relevance of the construction of inner space in the sequence of women's development, from being in the womb, handled in the mother's arms, to the construction of the potential inner space from the mouth to the anus and finally to the vagina, leading eventually to the actual inner space of a woman's womb in pregnancy and its externalization during childbirth (Kristeva, 1995; Cournut, 1998; see also Brierley, 1932). The three orifices (mouth, anus and vagina) as well as the sensory surface of the skin, working as a boundary, are the main ways that women progressively experience inner space (see also Chasseguet-Smirgel, 1976).

The following is from the penultimate session of her analysis.

Patricia: [Silence.] I have to trust that if you are letting me go it has to be all right. [Silence.] I value and have always valued what you have given me. Even when I was so angry with you, I always said I thought you were admirable in that you never attacked me back.

Analyst: Perhaps you find it difficult to make a link between the you who is speaking now and another you that can still feel so enraged with me. [A reference to the session on Friday when she slammed the door in utter fury as she left.]

Patricia: I know that I am leaving with an enormous capacity for rage. It is very difficult for me to recognize it. Friday's session was so disturbing, that I can move so quickly from one feeling to the next. There is no other relationship out there in the world where I can experience and express it, so much aggression. There are times recently I have been really upset with what I have said to you in the past.

Towards the end of her analysis there was guilt, a wish to repair and less persecution.

Discussion

From 1920 onwards, Freud confronted the limits of psychoanalytic understanding through the elaboration of the concepts of the death drive, primary masochism and the repudiation of femininity (1920a,b, 1924a,b, 1937a,b). If the topographical model of the mind suggested an intrinsic link between drives and their representations, then the structural model of the mind and the concept of the death drive postulated a drive that did not correspond to a representation, but expressed itself through repetition compulsion. The topographical model of the mind emphasized a psychic world 'full of representa-tions', whereas the structural model of the mind pointed out the 'radical heterogeneity of psychic life' (Green, 1999: 83). Freud became progressively more interested in understanding phenomena that are potentially at the limits of symbolic representation, not only due to mechanisms of repression, splitting, denial and negation, but also because they relate at the same time to something profoundly destructive in the psychic sphere that breaks through the capacity of the mind to contain it.

Both Simon and Patricia present either a lack or an excess of affect that has not been mentalized and cannot be expressed through words alone, but is enacted in the consulting room in the transference to the analyst. Patient and analyst enact aspects of the patient's internal world so that this world is actualized (Joseph, 1975, 1985; Sandler, 1976; Feldman, 1997). One of the most significant changes in the analytic process in recent decades has been the way in which we all focus less on analysing detailed content and more on the way in which the internal world is actualized in the transference and counter-transference. We are within the domain of drives and desires, not only of words and their representations.

Simon's internal world of objects is expressed negatively in terms of lacks and absences; Patricia's is expressed in terms of her passion, her excesses and her symptoms. She brought to her analysis a mother who could not contain or metabolize. The dead mother/analyst who is urinating, in the first dream she brought, left her knowledge of herself frozen. However, cold and heat, sadism and masochism, also alternated in her presentation, all expressed through the compulsion to repeat and enact with the analyst in the consulting room.

I have identified several layers of temporality in both of these patients' analyses. In Simon's case, these relate to the phantasies about the scenes of beating as the primal scene, and the advent of genital sexuality that was superimposed over that more primitive material. However, beyond (or before) all this there is the silence, the emptiness, which is an expression of the compulsion to repeat the unimaginable relationship with a psychotic mother. It represents not only his only way of withdrawing from this psychotic mother, but also a state of fusion with her.

In Patricia's analysis, the enactments in the consulting room gave us access to a terrified baby, unable to be contained by a mother who was represented as having no internal space for thinking and, concretely, as not having a vagina.

Both patients struggled with unresolved issues of mourning and guilt that led to feelings of emptiness. Patricia took a phallic position and Simon took a schizoid one: both struggled with their capacity for receptivity. Neither could trust the mother. For Simon, the psychotic mother was dealt with by withdrawal, silence and an evasion of any pain or suffering. For Patricia, the mother who was unable to contain the little girl's primitive anxiety took precedence. The first patient dealt with the mother through a lack of words and feelings, and the second by an excess of emotions and actions.

The bedrock

The analyses of both patients discussed in this chapter concern a battle for survival and express archaic modes of relating to the object. For Patricia, love and hate flood crucially, passionately, to the fore in a battle for the exclusive *possession* of the object. Simon, in his silence and withdrawal, attempted to live *inside* the object in order to feel alive. Their relationship with their internal objects had to be enacted in the consulting room. It is this, both the excess of the dramatic and the sense of emptiness created by the absence of words and emotions, that I suggest as pointing to the domain of the drives, the *pulsional*, as the expression of something at the border.

For both patients, trust in the object and separation from the object might, perhaps, be the most unattainable task. Both also express this difficulty in their passivation, a repudiation of the feminine. Freud's work is evidence of the struggle to identify what is specifically feminine. Already in a letter to Fliess of 25 May 1897 (in Freud, E.L, 1960, manuscript M) he stated: 'The essential element, which is repressed, is always the feminine element'. There is, thus, identification between the feminine and the unconscious, throughout a path that links the feminine and the object of psychoanalytic investigation (Green, 1999). Sexuality is created through division and discontinuity and femininity has been equated with that which is missing, which, however, is ultimately characteristic of both sexes.

A Child is Being Beaten is central to Freud's theoretical development (1919a). This phantasy links masochism and femininity and expresses the guilt feelings for incestuous desires towards the father, desires that are repressed and reconstructed in the analytic process.

Is this seduction by the father, however, not a second one, following a first seduction by the mother? The paper was written before Freud's reformulation of his theory of femininity and the discovery of the pre-Oedipal phase (see Perelberg, 1998). The mother, according to Freud himself, is the first seductress: 'The first sexual or sexually coloured experiences which the child has in relation to his mother are naturally of a passive character' (1931: 236).

At the end of his life, Freud offered the suggestion that the repudiation of femininity is the bedrock of analysis. Green has interpreted this suggestion in terms of the repudiation of the mother and the position of passivity facing her: 'Now the psychoanalytic cure is not possible without this confident passivation, where the analysand gives himself to the analyst's care' (1986b: 248),[2] in a transformation of the way the baby trusts the mother's care.

Throughout his work, Freud equated femininity with passivity, although he was careful to consistently point out that he was referring to femininity in both sexes. 'Passivity' is linked (in terms of après coup) to a 'phantasy' of a specific position in a scene of seduction in the primal scene. 'Receptivity', in contrast, implies activity on the side of Eros and is to be contrasted with what I have designated as 'lack of reciprocity',[3] which represents a withdrawal from the object. I suggest that the refusal of femininity ultimately represents the rejection of differences between the sexes and generations, in an attempt to retain a phallic position.

Pulsions and representations

At this point I would like to discuss two epistemological issues. The first is, perhaps, more conceptual, whereas the other is more clinical. Both have implications for a theory of technique.

The theoretical question requires a preliminary, epistemological, formulation. I would like to postulate that there is a necessary disjunction between theory and the clinical phenomena that it aims to describe. Freud himself reflected on the theoretical impossibility of establishing a rigorous causal link between clinical cases and theoretical formulations. He pointed to the 'gap' between the drive and its representation in the psychic structure (1920b). This formulation

---

[2] Chasseguet-Smirgel has suggested that femininity stands for receptivity (1970). Egle Laufer, in numerous unpublished and published papers (1993), has addressed the active and passive identification and the relationship to the body in adolescence. Dana Birksted-Breen also addressed the issue of the repudiation of receptivity in her paper read at a Scientific Meeting of the British Society in March 1999.

[3] Lévi-Strauss has suggested that 'reciprocity' is the hallmark of the cultural order (1947, 1969). The incest taboo, by forbidding families to enter into endogamous marriages, inaugurates a system of exchange and reciprocity, instituting the distinction between gender, generations and the contacts with the external world. In psychoanalytic terms one would be referring to the distinction between narcissistic structures and structures that contain a triadic, Oedipal constellation.

emphasizes an *a priori* theoretical acceptance of the limits of psycho-analytic understanding. I suggest that this finds its ultimate expression in the concept of drive (*pulsion*) at the border between the somatic and the psychic – a concept that emphasizes the limits of any concept in itself.

The second point of departure for this chapter was clinical. In the last few years one cannot avoid being struck, when thinking about one's own clinical practice, or reading reports by colleagues, by the patients who come to analysis and yet seem to be able to retain an exteriority in relation to it. At times one is able to comprehend the way these patients relish attacking the analysis and the analytic setting, their inability to mourn and therefore to tolerate guilt and the object's separateness. On the other hand, at times one is also left with the impression *that the analysis has just not reached the patient*. These analyses raise questions about the limits of our theories and formulations. Aulagnier (1975) has used the analysis of psychotic patients to hypothesize about a psychic nucleus that, by definition, evades attempts to understand it. McDougall (1986, 1989) has suggested that somatization, as a response to psychic conflict and mental pain, is a monumental challenge to psychoanalytic understanding in that pre-symbolic disorders express an incapacity to contain an excess of affective experience.

These two points – disjunction between theory and clinical practice and the treatment of borderline organizations – raise important questions for a theory of technique. On the one hand, one should be aware that interpretations that *fill* the analytic space might give an illusion of full understanding but, paradoxically, create enclosures and erase any notion of time. On the other hand, interpretations that leave too much space might exacerbate feelings of fragmentation and the experience of death. A Zen proverb states that the wheel is made of wood, but it is the *relationship* between the wood and the emptiness around the wheel that allows it to move. I think that the balance between 'closed' and 'open' interpretations is a current challenge for psychoanalysis.[4]

---

[4] The contrast between 'closed' and 'open' is derived from Lévi-Strauss's (1947) distinction between societies without history, where time is circular and repetitive, and societies with history, where time is seen as continuous and irreversible. The beginnings of the story of Macondo, in *One Hundred Years of Solitude* (García Márquez, 1970), are a reminder of a society without history: '[Macondo] was a truly happy village where no one was over thirty years of age and where no one had died . . . For José Arcadio it is always March and always Monday'.

In this chapter, I have pointed to 'the modernity of the concept of *pulsion*', as a concept-limit that is still powerful and relevant, in that it refers to that which is at the limit of conceptualization. A substantial part of psychic phenomena remains opaque and seems to escape all causalities. This implies a view of the mind that is not unitary, either in terms of content or structure (Green, 1998: 83; 2000b). The concept of 'border' pushes for the notion of 'movement', of something that always lies beyond full understanding. It reintroduces Freud's notion of a disjunction between drives and phantasies. The theory of 'drives' is the theoretical support for the presence of a force in psychic life, which resists both evolution and taming (Green, 1998: 71).

The Controversial Discussions and après coup

Introduction

I first read the texts of the Controversial Discussions while I was still in training. At the time, they were unpublished, but accessible in the internal bulletin of the British Society. Having been brought up in Rio de Janeiro, before coming to England I belonged to a tradition that had strong links with French psychoanalysis. Whilst reading through these papers and discussions I noticed that the concept of après coup had not once been mentioned. And yet, I also thought that it might have been crucial in clarifying some fundamental conceptual differences. Descriptively some of the authors were very close to outlining some key aspects of the concept. Furthermore, the issues were more clearly discussed then than they have been since in the British Society.

In this chapter I would like to establish a distinction between what is *descriptively named après coup*, and what is *dynamically identified as après coup*. This parallels Freud's distinction between the descriptive unconscious and the dynamic unconscious in the topographical model of the mind. *Descriptive après coup* refers to the way in which the concept has found a use, especially but not only in the French literature, where it means retrospective signification in the moment to moment progress of a session. What I am interested in discussing here is *dynamic après coup*, which is at the core of Freudian metapsychology.

Korzybski (1941) quoted Bateson's statement (1973) that '*the map is not the territory*', whilst at the same time asking the question '*What is it in the territory that gets onto the map?*' His response was: 'What gets onto the map *is difference*', be it a difference in altitude, a difference in vegetation, a difference in population structure, or whatever. One selects a very limited number from an infinite number of facts, and these *become information*. In fact, what we mean by information – the elementary unit of information – *is the difference that makes a difference.*

Four papers were discussed in the Controversial Discussions, over a series of 10 meetings between January 1943 and July 1944. For the discussion in this chapter, I will concentrate on two of the papers discussed during six of the meetings. The first was written by Susan Isaacs on 'unconscious phantasies' (1948) and was discussed over five meetings. The other was written by Susan Isaacs and Paula Heimann on 'regression' (in King and Steiner, 1990: 687–709). Pearl King has suggested that the discussion of this latter paper took place in only one meeting because there was so much consensus about the issues (King and Steiner, 1990: 686). My impression is different. I think that regression was an issue that had permeated most of the discussions and some of the crucial points of difference had already been established, as I will outline below.

These two papers and the discussions that followed them contain core issues central to psychoanalysis not only at the time, but also subsequently. In fact, they have been central to discussions in the British Society on the nature of unconscious phantasies in their connection with the issues of temporality and sexuality. Green has suggested, in the French translation of the Controversial Discussions, that 'These controversies are the most important document of the history of psychoanalysis' (King and Steiner, 1996: xi, my translation). Furthermore, I wish to discuss these issues in the light of the concept of après coup.

Freud and après coup

Thomä and Cheshire (1991) have pointed out that the adjective/ adverb *nachträglich* and the noun *Nachträglichkeit* are frequently used by Freud in connection with his concept of temporality and psychic causality. They compare the entries in the English 'Freud Concordance' (based on the *Standard Edition*) relating to 'deferred' and Freud's German usage of these key words. There is no official concordance to Freud's correspondence and clinical-theoretical works in German. The value of some of these comparisons in any case is limited by the facts that *Gesammelte Werke* and *Standard Edition* cover somewhat different textual ground and the 'Wednesday protocols' upon which we also draw may sometimes have been recorded by someone other than Freud himself. Faimberg has suggested that the choice of translation involves a 'particular way of conceiving temporalisation and psychic causality' (2005: 1). She argues that the word 'deferred action' suggests, in addition, *a linear conception of time*. It also expresses the direction of the arrow of time, in a sense opposite to that suggested by *après coup* – which is 'retroactivity'.

Après coup and unconscious phantasy

Après coup acquires meaning in the context of a structure that contains many other concepts and includes multiple temporalities – progressive and regressive movements take place together and reciprocally influence each other. These include development, regression, repression, fixation, repetition compulsion, the return of the repressed and the timelessness of the unconscious. This creates a complex structure that gives Freud's concepts of time a multi-dimensional perspective. *My image is that of a heptagon in motion*, rather than a linear perspective, even a bi-directional one, in that it contains multiple notions of time, the diachronic heterogeneity of the psychic apparatus (Green, 1998, 2000a). As discussed in Chapter 2, the concept of après coup in Freud is intrinsically linked to the notion of trauma, memory and unconscious phantasy.

The Controversial Discussions

Questions of time, life and death, as well as beginnings, were certainly present at the time of the Controversial Discussions. Freud had died in England, away from his country of origin, as a Jewish refugee from Nazi persecution, saved by the generosity and concern of his friends. The presence of the Second World War surrounded the discussions, and at times the participants had to take refuge in the basement of the Institute in the middle of a debate. A decision even had to be made allowing those with families to leave, as if it was not obvious that personal survival might at times take priority over the survival of ideas.

London and the bombings were the backcloth of these controversies. It is not surprising that temporality was indeed at the core of the discussions, and that it seemed that one was attempting to separate the present from both the past and the future, when the present had such enormous and tragic dimensions. Trauma, repetition and unpleasure refer us to *Beyond The Pleasure Principle* (Freud, 1920a).

Previous examinations of the Controversial Discussions have concentrated on the debates surrounding disagreements over timing and the nature of phantasy, as well as disputes over whether the earliest months display vivid, complex oral-cannibalistic phantasies involving internal objects and massive introjection and projection, or whether they are mainly narcissistic and auto-erotic (see Hayman, 1989, 1994; King and Steiner, 1990). In examining the debates in the Controversial Discussions in this chapter, I would like to concentrate on key differences expressed in the discussions in relation to temporality. In the process, I will focus on the concepts of regression, the Oedipus complex and unconscious phantasy in its connection with sexuality. Although the concept of après coup was not once mentioned during the controversies, it will be helpful in order to illuminate the depth of differences between the ideas expressed at the time in important ways. Furthermore, these key differences still exist today.

There is an 'official' version of the debates in the British Society, which works almost like a 'founding myth' and goes more or less like this: This was a time when two (immigrant) factions (Freudians and Kleinians) were in conflict with each other, each trying to prove that the other one was wrong. In the middle there were the natives of the island, who had a balanced view, in that they agreed with most of the new ideas, but not with all of them. They were the moderates, who became known as the middle group.

Closer examination of the discussions, and the concentration on the issues of temporality and metapsychology, indicates that some of the most crucial criticisms came in fact from this 'middle group', and from the views expressed by Glover, Ella Sharpe, M. Brierley and Sylvia Payne, as well as Hoffer and Friedlander.

The papers in the Controversial Discussions

The first paper was presented by Susan Isaacs, on the nature of unconscious phantasy. It put forward the idea that unconscious phantasies are 'the primary content of unconscious mental processes' and 'the mental corollary, the psychic representative of instinct'

(Isaacs, 1948). These ideas are consistent with Freud's ideas about primal phantasies, although the two formulations are different in terms of both content and structure. For Freud these primal phantasies are castration, seduction and primal scene. For Klein, unconscious phantasies are particularly derived from the death instinct.

In reading through the five discussions that followed this paper, one notices that regression became a key concept around which questions concerned with temporality were debated.

Regression

Freud had distinguished three levels of regression: topographical, temporal and formal. He gave a fuller definition in a note added to *The Interpretation of Dreams* in 1914:

> Three kinds of regression are thus to be distinguished: a. topographical regression, in the sense of the schematic picture [of the psychical apparatus]; b. temporal regression, in so far as what is in question is harking back to older psychical structures; and c. formal regression, where primitive methods of expression and representation take the place of the usual ones.
>
> (1900b: 548)

Laplanche and Pontalis (1973) have indicated that the term regression is descriptive, and that Freud did not provide a 'rigorous theoretical basis' for the term. An examination of how this concept was thought about in the Controversial Discussions enables one to pinpoint differences in relation to issues of temporality.

Backward and forward movement

In the commentary below, delivered in the first of the 10 discussions, which was dedicated to the paper on unconscious phantasy, Jones equated phantasy with hallucinatory wish fulfilment. There are two central ideas expressed in relation to his understanding of regression.

Firstly, he believes that one reaches early expressions of fantasies through regression. Here 'early' means 'early on in time'. Green has pointed out that 'the term is untranslatable in French, as neither "précoces" nor "primitives" encompasses what should each time be designated as happening early in life'. Melanie Klein argues that what is linked to the most ancient past is necessarily what is 'most determining and more fundamental to the psyche' (Green, in King and Steiner, 1996: xii, my translation).

Secondly, according to Jones there is continuity between later manifestations and earlier ones. This is related to the notion of *genetic continuity*, an idea much emphasized at the time of the Controversial Discussions by the supporters of Melanie Klein. These two points were at the centre of many of the 10 discussions, although challenged by several participants, such as Brierley, Payne, Hoffer and Friedlander.

There is, however, another idea, namely that later manifestations may reactivate earlier ones, in other words the notion of a double movement, forwards and backwards. Is this idea of a bi-directional temporal movement equivalent to après coup?

Thomä and Cheshire (1991) have indeed pointed out the two directions implied in the concept of *Nachträglichkeit*. Reactivation of predispositions, or of these schemata and clichés as defined by Freud (1912b, 1918), might stimulate associations to, and memories of, similar situations in the past. Freud in fact described a disposition with regard to *Nachträglichkeit* as follows:

> Our view is that infantile sexual experiences are the fundamental precondition for hysteria, are, as it were, the disposition for it, and that it is they which create the hysterical symptoms, but that they do not do so immediately, but remain without effect to begin with and only exercise a pathogenic action later, when they have been aroused after puberty in the form of unconscious memories.
>
> (Freud, 1896c: 212)

Thomä and Cheshire suggest that the concept operates in two different directions:

> On different occasions and for different purposes (for example, explanatory as opposed to therapeutic), Freud approaches his concept from two different standpoints in time: sometimes he looks backwards from the point of view of the therapist reconstructing a phenomenal-developmental sequence of events and experiences, and sometimes he is looking forward as if through the eyes of the original traumatic event which is setting off a series of potentially

pathogenic developments, and some of whose effects are going to be 'carried over' into the future.

(1991: 420)

Nachträglichkeit was usually translated by Strachey as 'deferred action'. This translation has been considered unsatisfactory by many authors because the idea of the delayed effect of an early trauma is often combined in Freud's usage with that of the retrospective reconstruction of the psychological significance of that trauma. Consequently: translators have the problem of whether or how to signal this aspect of the concept – which the German does not suggest; and it has been thought that the concept implies a kind of 'backward causality' that challenges conventional notions of temporality.[1]

Thomä and Cheshire add the following note:

The essential difference between the verbs nachtragen and 'to defer' consists in the fact that they express exactly opposite relations to time: the former is backward-looking (nach = 'after', so after what?), whereas the latter is forward-looking (defer . . . until when?). Both words have linguistic roots in verbs of motion, though different ones: in the case of 'defer', it is obviously the Latin ferre, which means 'to carry' (or tragen); while tragen seems to come from the Germanic root meaning 'to drag' or 'to draw along' (in spite of the temptation to derive it intuitively from the Latin trahere!).

(1991: 421)

However, the term does also carry a relevant metaphorical meaning, namely 'to bear a grudge':

---

[1] Faced with this issue, the translators of the new French 'standard edition' decided nevertheless to adopt a single term that has two-way connotations. Explaining that they propose to render nachträglich as 'après coup' and Nachträglichkeit as 'effet d'après coup', Bourguignon *et al.* (1989: 82–83) write that: 'Lacan is responsible for having restored this concept its full importance, which Freud forged from the time of the seduction theory and maintained throughout the whole extent of his writings. Our only innovation, for this translation, is to have rendered the noun . . . by the term effet d'après-coup (and not effet après-coup which, like the English "deferred action", conveys the impression of a simple delay in the action effected by the past on the present, whereas l'effet d'après-coup is effective along the reverse vector also: from the present toward the past)'. The distinction being signalled here, piquantly by a single letter (or maybe two) in French, is something like that between a delayed or belated effect and an 'after-effect', where the latter implies the continuing consequence of some previous event.

112

... whereas Strachey's preferred rendering calls attention to forward-looking elements of the micro-theory, Lacan by contrast focuses on its backward-looking aspects by adopting the usage 'retro-action' and cognates in his French (e.g. Lacan, 1966b: 839).

(Lacan, 1977: 48)

Can one identify these ideas – back and forth movement, polysemia of meaning, non-previous determination of meaning and retrospective re-structuring of earlier representations – in terms of their link with sexuality in Jones's comments in his first intervention in the Controversial Discussions?:

I can see no real difference between the two phrases (hallucinatory wish fulfilment and phantasy). *Behind it, however, lies a difference of opinion which becomes manifest with the word 'regression'.* It is not at first sight easy to discern the nature of the trouble over this quarrel-provoking word. I have always regarded the matter as simply one of a reciprocally complemental series. If, for example, we compare a phantasy or reaction after puberty with a corresponding one between the ages of, say, three and five, then we may surely say that either may reinforce the other. *The continued unconscious operation of the earlier one may strengthen the later one, while contrariwise an emotional event at the later age may through regression reanimate and reinvest an earlier attitude.*

(King and Steiner, 1990: 323–324)

Jones emphasizes the double movement, progressive and regressive. Later phantasies may reactivate earlier ones through the process of regression. Conversely, earlier phantasies may 'reinforce' later ones. One is not yet clear about what he means by the term 'reinforce'. Jones continues his comments by addressing an important dimension to do with directions:

What proportion of the final cathexis is derived from the earlier and what from the later source has nothing to do with a prior theory, but is to be determined by investigation of each particular case. On the whole experience definitely confirms Freud's emphatic statement, quoted by Mrs Isaacs, that the earlier impulses have an intensity greater than anything that comes later and incommensurable with any other. To the pre-Freudian world the situation of course appeared

113

otherwise, since they knew nothing about the existence of the earlier impulses which Freud revealed. The reason why the matter is to us a commonplace is just because we are familiar with the existence of these earlier ones, and it is this fact that gives the clue to the nature of the present difficulty. For myself I cannot make sense of the whole conception of regression except in so far as we have reason to think that there is something to which the regression takes place. A regression backwards into the blue has no meaning for me. Thus when Walder talks of extraordinary cannibalistic phantasies being familiar at the age of three or four, but ascribes them to regression, this conveys nothing at all to me if it does not mean a reanimating of <u>corresponding oral phantasies at the age of, say, six months;</u> why a child of four should suddenly be seized for the first time with the desire to eat breasts passes my comprehension.

(*ibid*: 324)

Jones makes several points here. Firstly, he emphasizes the relevance of the early impulses, and suggests that they have a 'greater intensity' than later ones. Secondly he suggests that there is 'something' that attracts the regression. Thirdly, he assumes that what is found in adults can retrospectively also be found earlier on. This will be related to the concept of *genetic continuity*, an idea consistently emphasized throughout the Controversial Discussions by authors such as Isaacs and Jones. The dimension that is missed out altogether in this comment is re-signification, a re-structuring of earlier events in the light of later events and, most importantly, the Oedipus complex. The notion that something is waiting to find meaning in the future that illuminates an event in the past – a crucial aspect of après coup in the way it was discussed before in this paper – is missing. This is clear in the following statement, as Jones continued:

The presence of such phantasies in older subjects had long ago led me to deduce the actual existence of them in young infants, and this inference has in my opinion been amply confirmed by the analysis of them carried out by Mrs Klein and others as well as by the observational data to which Mrs Isaacs has often drawn our attention. In saying this I am naturally not prejudging the numerous obscure problems concerning the precise nature and variety of such phantasies, their relative importance, nor the fitting-in of them into our theoretical scheme: there

114

will be much to say about all such matters once their existence is granted.

(ibid: 324)

A different emphasis is present in the following comments made by Friedlander, who suggests that through the mechanism of regression *later phantasies acquire aspects of earlier ones, so that what one has access to is a retrospective modification of early phantasies.* Thus oral phantasies expressed in later years may not be derived from the oral phase itself, but may have acquired their oral aspect through regression. One could suggest that this is a component of après coup:

I want to concentrate today on the question of regression. Some of you may remember that in the discussion after Walder's paper . . .*Jenny Walder drew attention to the fact that phantasies of oral character expressed in the third or fourth year of life need not be old phantasies formed during the oral phase but may derive their oral character from regression.* Dr Jones refers to this same occurrence when he mentions the phantasy of the child of four who wants to bite the mother's breast. This phantasy could originate (a) from the wish to bite the mother, an instinct derived from the genital and anal-sadistic phase, (b) *the wish to bite the breast may be due to regression to the oral stage, recalling the old dim wishes and frustrations concerned with feeding.* This controversy has played a role in our discussions here ever since. Mrs Isaacs when talking about regression admits the difference in Mrs Klein's view as compared with the psycho-analytical theory, but her statement does not make the significance of this difference clear. This statement rather conveys the idea as if there were an incompatibility between recognizing the importance of the psychological happenings in the first years of life and recognizing the mechanism of regression. As far as is possible in so short a space of time I want to show that the mechanism of regression is indispensable in Freud's theory of the aetiology of the neuroses and intimately bound up with the theory of libidinal development. I also want to show that Mrs Klein's view of the 'early mental development' must necessarily lead to a depreciation of the importance of the mechanism of regression because Mrs Klein has given up Freud's theory of the development of libido.

(ibid: 343)

In continuing her comments Friedlander emphasizes the notions of stages of development, fixations and developmental arrest. In the next segment, I think that Friedlander indicates the backwards and forwards movement of the libido:

> To come back to regression: certain conditions, either environ-
> mental or inner psychic or a combination of both, may at any time
> during life arouse a conflict between the instinctual drives and the
> ego. As a way out of this conflict the forward movement of the
> libido may be checked and a retrograde movement may take place.
> The whole of the libido already advanced to the phallic or even
> genital phase or only part of it may be included in that retrograde
> movement which will stop at the strongest fixation point. This
> process is described as regression of the libido to a former stage of
> development. *This former stage of development, let us say the anal-
> sadistic phase, will now be reinforced by the already further developed libido
> and it will be extremely difficult to say in any given case which amount of
> the instinctual drives is derived from the original fixation and which from
> the regressed libido.*
>
> (*ibid*: 345, my italics)

She adds that in Klein's thinking the process of development is seen in a more static form, and that the concept of regression has no place in this theory. The whole of the libido remains fixated on these early phantasies throughout life, without undergoing the biological developmental phases described by Freud.

M. Brierley, in her intervention, coins the very interesting term *retrospective sophistication*, which I think comes close to the concept of *après coup*:

> I think, personally, that some of the precocity attributed to Mrs
> Klein's infant is due to this simple fact, that an adult cannot make
> any content of infantile experience intelligible to other adults
> without subjecting the experience itself to some degree of falsifica-
> tion or *retrospective sophistication*. Where I think Mrs Klein may
> sometimes err is in forgetting that this process of retrospective
> sophistication is not limited to adults but, presumably, occurs in
> every phase of development with reference to preceding phases.
> Phantasy systems which emerge from repression in adults contain
> many elements derived from post-infantile life which, in their turn,

have succumbed to repression and have become assimilated to systems of infantile origin. These infantile systems may themselves give signs of developmental stratification. Thus, they often show a number of different versions of the same plot. One may find a primitive oral theme in an anal–oral version, and this may again be repeated in a genital version. In other words, revival of the same primitive experience assumes novel forms corresponding to the stage of development and the current life situation. This kind of experience with adults leads me to think that a phantasy which can be demonstrated in a child of two years may have unmistakable reference to suckling or weaning experiences and may, in fact, revive such experiences. But in the two-year-old this re-editing *or retrospective sophistication* will be operative. *His phantasy may have a form corresponding to his current development rather than to the stage to which its content refers.* It may well show a considerable degree of subject–object differentiation, but such differentiation may be largely *retrospective*; it need not be taken for granted that it was present during the original experience.

(*ibid*: 471, my italics)

Glover thought that regression in oral hallucinatory gratification activates the memory traces of the actual experiences at the sensory end of the apparatus. He also thought that many Freudian concepts had been left out – these include the biological progression of an instinct series, the early formation of object images, fixation points, regression, the possibility of permanent withdrawal of cathexes from pre-Oedipal fixation systems and, last but not least, the theoretical and clinical significance of the Oedipus complex.

In the eighth Controversial Discussion, on the paper on regression itself, Glover gave his most complete views on the matter. He thought that the Kleinian presentations:

. . . far from simplifying our approach to mental function, abolishes distinctions that are essential to our understanding of the mental apparatus. Two other matters must be considered before we discuss the present paper on regression by Mrs Isaacs and Dr Heimann. In the first place, so long as we were concerned with basic concepts of the mental apparatus, discussion was essentially non-clinical. There was (or rather should have been) no possibility of confusing the metapsychological and the clinical use of terms . . . the confusion existing in Kleinian metapsychology could well be attributed to lack of discrimination between the concept of psychic apparatus and clinical descriptions of mental activity.

(*ibid*: 711–712)

Glover adds:

> When it comes to a subject like regression it is increasingly import-
> ant to distinguish the metapsychological from the clinical aspects of
> the subject, the more so as it is increasingly easy to confuse these
> aspects.

(*ibid*: 712)

Anna Freud early on in the discussions, also focusing on the theory of regression, seemed not to identify the profound differences implied in the discussions for the metapsychology, as she pointed out that the differences concerned the first year of life only. However, she later indicated that the discussions indicated differences for the whole theory of the unconscious.

She highlighted the following points, in connection with our present theme of temporality:

> As concerns the new *theory of regression* Mrs Isaacs herself speaks of
> divergence of opinion. But I think that *she underestimates the far-*
> *reaching consequences of her point of view, when followed to its logical end,*
> *for the theory of the neuroses. It shifts all emphasis from the later stages of*
> *development to the earliest ones*, gives secondary importance only to
> the level on which the breakdown of the personality occurs, puts
> the concept of fixation-points out of action and, incidentally, gives
> rise to nearly all the existing differences of the technique of psy-
> choanalytic treatment. This, of course, needs and, I hope, will find
> further elucidation.

(*ibid*: 329, my italics)

One of Anna Freud's criticisms of 'the new Kleinian mode' was that it used the one term, 'phantasy', for a range of early mental functioning that she would describe with different terms, such as thinking, reality-thinking, remembering, wishing, longing, and so on. Glover suggested that Isaacs confused images, ideational representatives, instinct end-presentations, reality-thinking, phantasy and memory.

Throughout most of the discussions there was an attempt to clarify the issue of temporality in psychoanalysis. At times the debates seemed to be locked in terms of whether one should emphasize earlier events or later ones. Was the manifestation of an unconscious phantasy a product of an earlier event (as the Kleinians were emphasizing) or a later one that acquired earlier aspects through regression (as the Freudians and the 'middle group' were *both* emphasizing)? My sense is that the concept of après coup solves the dichotomy of whether earlier or later events are more important as it indicates the way in which in Freudian metapsychology later events resignify earlier ones, which then emerge with a new meaning. For Freud this is centrally indicated in relation to the Oedipus complex, and I will now look at the way this concept was thought about in the discussions of the two papers.

The Oedipus complex

A crucial aspect of the discussions centred on ideas related to the Oedipus complex. The differentiation between the positions expressed in the debates is not simply a dichotomy between the positions of the Kleinians versus the Freudians, with another group in the middle. Once again, some of the crucial issues that relate to the Oedipus complex, its structural function and temporality are raised by those who were later to belong to the middle group, as well as some (Anna) Freudians objecting to the positions expressed by the Kleinians.

If, on the one hand, I am covering old ground, at the same time I do not cease to be surprised about the way in which differences between, say, the Kleinian Oedipus complex and the Freudian view tend to be blurred even today in the British Society. As Kohon suggests: 'Not only was the Oedipus complex then made to appear earlier in life (e.g. by Melanie Klein and her followers), but it was transformed into something radically different: it ceased to be the model of sexuality and meaning for the subject' (1999a: 8).

In the Freudian model there is a reorganization that takes place with the Oedipal situation, and sexuality is its motto. In the first of the Controversial Discussions, Sylvia Payne questioned the concept of unconscious phantasies as proposed by Susan Isaacs in terms of both the content and the time of phantasies:

119

In the first place I should like to say that I cannot see any reason for denying the presence of some form of primitive phantasy from the beginning of extra-uterine mental life. (However) I do not think that phantasy, using the word in the usual sense, occurs until there has been a psychic experience which involves the reception of a stimulus and a psycho-physical response.

(King and Steiner, 1990: 333–334)

She goes on to point out the relevance of the Oedipus complex in Freud's thinking:

I wish to make it clear that I am not denying that the earliest phases of psychological development influence future development and that difficulties arising in them are likely to influence the whole course of development. What I disagree with is a tendency to regard a particular group of phantasies as pathognomic of mental conflict. It can be said, of course, that Freud regarded the Oedipus complex in this way, but this is not true in the same sense. He regarded the resolution of the Oedipus complex as the most important psychological event in the attainment of mental health because it implied a successful development to genital maturity, but he recognized the fact that developmental difficulties could arise before the Oedipus conflict was fully developed.

(*ibid*: 335–336)

This is another moment at which the concept of après coup would clarify the point that she herself seems to be wishing to make, concerning the reorganization that is brought about by the Oedipus complex.

Although Ella Sharpe agreed that there was a continuity between the early phantasies and later ones (thus agreeing with the notion of genetic continuity), she criticized the new definition of unconscious phantasy proposed by Isaacs for not allowing for a clear differentiation that she thought important: that is, between early 'phantasies' and the sophisticated, classical Oedipal ones. She listed a number of differences: the classical Oedipus complex required ego development and reality recognition of frustration, repression, the use of symbolic substitutes and the superego, which was inseparable from 'Freud's Oedipus complex', which she distinguished from what she called the 'super-id' of the primitive state.

Isaacs thought Sharpe made too great a distinction between the earlier and the later Oedipus complex. She wished to stress the genetic continuity by using the same term. Payne thought that although she herself believed in genetic continuity, there should be a different word for the earlier and the later states. 'We don't call a foetus a man', she said (*ibid*: 803).

Ella Sharpe pointed out very importantly that:

> . . . the Freudian Oedipus complex is of a different nature altogether, involving ego organization and repression which is inseparable from reality adaptation. The Oedipus complex is bypassed when the wish-psychosis is retained to any strength.
>
> The term 'super-ego' is only correctly used when it designates what it says: a superego. This superego is inseparable from the Oedipus complex of Freud. Some other term should be found such as 'id-ideal' in contrast to ego-ideals for those derivatives of the incorporation of the actual object when ego differentiation has hardly begun. The superego in the Freudian sense is accessible to influence and amelioration, that which derives from the belief in actual incorporation is inaccessible and adamant, the belief in righteousness as adamant as implacable evil.
>
> (*ibid*: 339)

Barbara Louw also stressed the reorganization that takes place with the Oedipus complex, and I think that the following statement was one of the clearest on this issue, throughout the whole of the controversies:

> Does Mrs Isaacs interpret Freud's theory of phantasy as a developing situation, dependent upon new psychic situations as they arise? *For example, the phantasy of the introjected mother (good or bad) must surely be modified (and perhaps completely changed) with the onset of the Oedipus conflict.*
>
> (*ibid*: 392)

Dr K. Stephen agreed with the notion of genetic continuity, but stressed the need to distinguish between earlier and later phantasies:

> My point is just this, that although of course there would be genetic continuity between these two meanings of phantasy, which must

not be forgotten, this does not, it seems to me, exonerate us from the need to keep the distinction clear between the first description of phantasy, which may be regarded as a mere subjective misinterpretation, under the influence of the pleasure principle, of the somatic accompaniment of instinct itself, and this other way of using the word to apply to subjective misinterpretations which presuppose such more highly developed perceptual and discriminative powers.

(*ibid*: 367)

In her paper and statements, Paula Heimann emphasizes the 'early' and 'pre genital', which take the place of the Oedipal:

The significance of animal phobias was discussed by Melanie Klein in her book *The Psychoanalysis of Children* (Klein 1932:178 et seq.). In her view, they are a mode of defence against the anxieties relating to the cannibalistic phantasies and to the earliest stages in the formation of the superego. Such projection is characteristic of the earlier anal stage. They provide a means for modifying the child's fears of his threatening superego as well as of his dangerous id.

(*ibid*: 694)

The first move is to thrust out these two institutions into the external world and assimilate the superego to the real object. The second move is familiar to us as the displacement on to an animal of the fear felt of the real father. . . . Regarded in this light, an animal phobia would be much more than a distortion of the idea of being castrated by the father into one of being bitten by a horse or eaten by a wolf. Underlying it would be not only the fear of being castrated but a still earlier fear of being devoured by the superego, so the phobia would actually be a modification of anxiety belonging to the earlier stages.

(*ibid*: 723)

Willi Hoffer, to my mind, made the most clarifying comments on the issue of the Oedipus complex as retrospectively reorganizing the psychic apparatus. Moreover, he pointed out the different emphases in the Freudian and the Kleinian perspectives. He said that 'according to Freud, neuroses are the specific diseases of the sexual function; according to Klein's theory, the neuroses might be called the specific diseases of the destructive function' (*ibid*: 723).

Hoffer pointed to three main characteristics of the Freudian Oedipus complex. Firstly, the attainment of the phallic phase implies an important distinction between the penis as an organ and the penis as an erotogenic zone. The second characteristic is the ability to choose an object; the third is the castration complex:

> The final outcome of the Oedipus conflict is the castration-complex. It signifies that the boy's wishes for contact with the mother have been frustrated. From now on he uses or may use this experience to combat instinctual desires by developing castration fear or by being threatened with castration by his superego. In the combination of the two facts, the acquisition of castration fear and the postponement of maturity until puberty (dichronous onset of sexuality) Freud saw the most direct aetiology and one of the three basic causes of neurosis.
>
> (*ibid*: 722)

Thus he emphasizes that it is only retrospectively that one can decide if an earlier event may be pathogenic or not. It is the later event that transforms and gives meaning to the earlier one. Is this not the concept of après coup? The following emphasis on the role of sexuality seems to me to complete the essential component in the concept. Hoffer thinks that Klein proposed a new theory of neurosis:

> According to Freud's view it is the happenings of this stage which decide about the onset of infantile neurosis. Under the strain of the Oedipus conflict the phallic organization may break down; due to anxiety caused by the intervention of the ego and superego the phallic aims are renounced and regression takes place to fixation points on former pre-genital levels. *Thus it is impossible to decide whether a given pre-genital phase will prove pathogenetic or not before the phallic phase has given evidence of either its stability or instability.*
>
> (*ibid*: 722)

A second and equally important point of divergence then concerns the pathogenic role of the sexual instinct as compared with the pathogenic role of the destructive instinct. As exemplified in the paper on Regression, the sexual significance of an action does not give rise to conflict with consequent neurotic development; such development is in Kleinian theory always taken to be due to the destructive admixture to the libidinal tendencies. According to Freud, the neuroses are the specific diseases of the sexual function, according to Mrs Klein's theory, the neuroses might be called the specific diseases of the destructive functions. Since on all pre-genital levels and also on the genital level destructiveness and libido appear fused, this differentiation may be of minor practical value: it merely points to the specific element in the mixture which is mainly responsible for pathological development. But where theoretical considerations are concerned, this new point of view has the most far-reaching consequences. To name only one problem: is it to be understood that incest is forbidden and incestuous wishes become repressed because of the pre-genital destructive element contained in them and not because of the forbidden wishes for possession of the mother which bring the boy in conflict with the father (Oedipus complex)?

(*ibid*: 723)

Thus he points out the dominant element in each model: anxiety in the Kleinian model and sexuality in the Freudian model.

In the case of Emma (see Masson, 1985), Freud had already wished to underline the centrality of sexuality in the process of signification. For him it is not possible to separate the question of time from infantile sexuality, its origins and transformations.

In summarizing the complexity of views expressed throughout the Controversial Discussions on the issue of temporality, there was overall support for the idea of genetic continuity. Some important differences were also expressed, however.

The concept of regression was a key concept throughout the discussions. I have pointed out that although only one evening was formally dedicated to the discussion of Isaacs and Heimann's paper on regression, the concept had in fact been discussed at most of the evenings.

Jones, Riviere and Heimann in particular supported the idea that what was early was more important for the psyche. Jones expressed the idea that one reaches 'early' phantasies through regression, and that there is continuity between later manifestations and earlier ones. This is related to the notion of *genetic continuity*.

Thirdly, Jones believes that there is a double movement, in that later manifestations may reactivate earlier ones, as well as the other way round.

Friedlander, in contrast, suggested that through the mechanism of regression, *later phantasies acquire aspects of earlier ones, so that what one has access to is a retrospective modification of early phantasies.*

Brierley seemed to be in agreement with this idea when she coined the term retrospective signification. Ella Sharpe agreed that there was a continuity between the early phantasies and later ones (thus agreeing with the notion of genetic continuity), but she also criticized the new definition of unconscious phantasy proposed by Isaacs for not allowing a clear differentiation between early 'phantasies' and the sophisticated, classical Oedipal ones.

The concept of après coup might have helped to solve the dichotomy between early and later phantasies, as it indicates the way in which in Freudian metapsychology later events resignify earlier ones, which then emerge with a new meaning. For Freud this is centrally indicated in relation to the Oedipus complex.

I have examined the way in which the Oedipus complex was thought about throughout the discussions of these two papers. Sharpe made an important intervention indicating that the classical Oedipus complex required ego development and reality recognition of frustration, repression, the use of symbolic substitutes and the superego, which was inseparable from 'Freud's Oedipus complex', which she distinguished from what she called the 'super-id' of the primitive state. The reorganization that takes place with the Oedipus complex was also noted by Friedlander and Hoffer. Hoffer finally pointed out the crucial distinctions between the two models. In the one, sexuality is the dominant motto, whereas in the other it is anxiety.

I would now like to show how the dynamic concept of après coup underpins the understanding of a moment in my clinical practice.

Francis

A woman in her twenties, brunette, petite and a sculptress, Francis came into my consulting room a few years ago asking to start an analysis because of her wish to improve her relationships. She had low self-esteem and tended to put herself down in social situations. She had had an analysis in her country of origin, in her mother tongue, which she had found helpful. At the first consultation Francis walked into the consulting room with light steps, as if floating, beautiful and elegant. Francis was married, with two daughters.

125

At the time I will describe, Francis had been having dreams that involved celebrities, which indicated, her idealization of me and her narcissistic identification with me. She read avidly, and had recently read a chapter in a book of mine. She thought that I had a clear style, and that as a lay person she could understand me. She said she had a similar experience of me in the sessions. I spoke in a way that she found 'organic', which she felt was part of me.

During the session I intend to describe, Francis had been telling me about her admiration for me, her awe of me because of my writing. She also talked about colleagues whom she admired greatly. It is a source of suffering for her when she feels that there is nothing she can offer. Then she went on to tell me about a weekend trip to Salzburg, where she had seen many statues of Mozart. The whole town revered him, she said, as a 'total celebrity'.

I said: *Looking at your colleagues and me as celebrities leaves you feeling depleted, with nothing.*

There was a silence for a while. Then Francis talked about a painting that she had seen in an exhibition that morning. It portrayed a little girl of about eight years of age, and its eroticism was shocking. A woman was inclined towards the girl, kissing her on her lips. The little girl's head was tilted backwards, in a position of total surrender, and yet at the same time giving an impression of actively participating in the kiss. She wore lipstick and mascara; this make up seemed to be the marker of the woman's kiss on her. It was as if she had become this woman, Francis exclaimed.

Francis paused and there was a vibrant silence in the session. She then said that it made her think of her relationship with her mother in a new way. She recollected how passionate she felt about her mother. Yet, in a fight they once had, she had thought about saying to her mother 'You are going to fuck me to death'.

(I thought that there was a transformation from the idealization of me, which left her feeling depleted, to this other layer of erotic surrender, the repetition in each session of this experience of being fucked to death, surrendering to the kiss that is her phantasy of what takes place between the analyst and the patient in the session.)

I said: *When you surrender to me in your sessions, you not only feel depleted, but also fucked to death.* Although I had thought about what I was going to say, there was an element of surprise in my saying it, and we were both silent for quite some time.

There was a flow between different moments in time in the session:

from the present of the session, to the image of the picture, to a recollection of an experience as a young girl in her relationship with her mother (the kiss), to a moment in adolescence that illuminated her experience as a little girl, and both moments in the past illuminating and giving a further meaning to the present of the session. Conversely, in the present of the session these various moments of Francis' past story acquired new meaning, in a process of re-signification. A possibility was expressed of linking that which takes place in the session to the past, and back to the present.

Four dimensions of time were present:

1 The surrender to her analyst in the present.
2 The erotic image of the picture of a woman and a little girl seen earlier that day.
3 A souvenir of her experience of passion for her mother when she was a little girl.
4 The memory of her adolescent fight with her mother when she had wanted to tell her 'You'll fuck me to death'.

In the here and now of the session, both the past and the present are interpreted and understood après coup, in the experience of a 'temps éclaté' (shattered time: Green, 2000a).

Conclusion

Green has pointed out that *Nachträglikheit* contains two ideas:

> On the one hand, the idea of coming at a later date and, on the other, the idea of a supplement. In other words, between two psychical events, I and II, the second is recognised as having a connection with the first, to which it now gives a fuller meaning than its initial, isolated, memory trace suggested. So, retrospectively, II gives I a meaning that only existed in a state of virtuality, but which was by no means bound in advance to take this direction, among the other possibilities in a polysemic context.
>
> (Green, 2002b: 36)

Faimberg has also underlined that the concept consists of two inseparable phases: anticipation and retrospection (2005: 2).

One can pinpoint this double movement in the example discussed above. There is a scene of childhood trauma that is retrospectively understood in terms of what takes place in the here and now of the transference situation. It is indeed in relation to the transference and the transference interpretation that the après coup can be depicted and constructed. The whole process takes place in the 'analytic site', which brings together transfer, process, interpretation and counter-transference, and within which the après coup takes place (Donnet, 1995, 2005). The après coup is defined by the primacy of sexuality, the erotic passivation in the transference that evokes the traumatic childhood sexual scene. In the Freudian model, as in the way the examples were understood in this chapter, sexuality and sexual phantasies are at the centre of the re-elaboration of meaning.

Over the years, the concept of après coup has come to mean many different things in the psychoanalytic literature. The concept has been extended so that more narrowly and descriptively it has been equated with the process of thinking retrospectively about one's own thoughts and work (see, for instance, Pontalis, 1977), or the retrospective and progressive dimensions of time in given sessions. Sandler (1983) suggested that psychoanalytic concepts may be elastic and become stretched. He saw this type of flexibility as playing an important part in the development of psychoanalytic theory; but it remains a puzzle as to how it is possible for such disparate meanings to be so widely accepted as if the disparity did not actually exist.

The theoretical concern with the connections between the past and the present and the implication for a theory of technique has been relevant in the history of thinking in the British Society. Joseph and Anne-Marie Sandler, for instance, have in several papers (1984, 1992, 1994a,b, 1998) distinguished between the past unconscious and the present unconscious. In their view, the past unconscious can be regarded as acting like a dynamic 'template', a structuring organiza-tion that gives form to current wishes or wishful fantasies, which are then further modified in the present unconscious before gaining access to consciousness; it is 'the child within' that gives form to all the intrapsychic content that arises in the depths – in particular, unconscious wishes and wishful fantasies.

Gill (1984) has suggested the centrality of the transference in the psychoanalytic process and suggests that the transference is an amal-gam of past and present. Ruth Riesenberg-Malcolm (1999) has sug-gested that the 'here-and-now' of the analytic situation is indeed the expression of the patient's past in its multiple transformations. In any transference interpretation, the analyst is interpreting both the past and the present as it is present in the here and now of the analytic situation. Green (2000a) has suggested the term 'shattered time' to indicate the 'collapse' between past and present in the analytic process, and especially in the analysis of dreams.

Dana Birksted-Breen cogently argues that the 'here and now' type of interpretation in the 'British School' of psychoanalysis is never a 'pure present'. She indicates that progressive and retrospective time go inherently together, 'one being a requisite for the other' (Birksted-Breen, 2003). Ignês Sodré has indicated the many similarities between the concept of après coup and that of 'mutative interpretation' (1997).

The concept of après coup cuts across a discussion of whether one is addressing the past or the present, as it indicates clearly that one is addressing both at the same time, with a mutual process of reinterpretation: the present reinterprets the past, as the past leaves the seeds that will find their fulfilment in the present, albeit with no sense of predetermination, as discussed in this chapter.

The concept of *dynamic après coup* is profoundly embedded in Freudian metapsychology. One of the shortcomings of the process of extension of the concept of après coup is that some key aspects of Freud's metapsychology have been lost in some of the papers cited above: for example, the links between trauma, repetition and infantile sexuality. One feels echoes of some of the key issues discussed during the Controversial Discussions. At the time, concepts like the Oedipus complex and unconscious phantasies, which have a specific meaning in Freudian terminology, were expanded to mean something quite different. There is a similar process taking place now with the concept of après coup, which, if it is expanded to mean many different things, loses some of the crucial meanings that connect it to Freudian metapsychology.

In this chapter I have suggested the distinction between descriptive and dynamic après coup. Descriptive après coup refers to the way in which the concept is used in particular, but not only, in the French literature, where it means retrospective signification in the moment to moment progress of a session. I have proposed in this paper the concept of *dynamic* après coup, which I think is at the core of Freudian metapsychology.

The concept of après coup might have helped to solve the dichotomy between early and later phantasies, as it indicates the way in which in Freudian metapsychology later events re-signify earlier ones, which then emerge with a new meaning. For Freud this is central to the Oedipus complex.

In presenting my clinical example, I indicated the double movement present in the notion of après coup (prospective and retrospective), like Proust's madeleine, which encompasses at least two spaces and two periods of time and can only be recovered retrospectively.

The next chapter will provide another clinical example.

8

Space and time in psychoanalytic listening

For many years afterwards I wondered about exactly what had happened in my first consultation with Patrick, and whether I had indeed asked him 'that question'. I was also confused about whether I had imagined his answer, in the light of what he told me later in the analysis. It all felt part of a nebulous event that I was not sure had taken place. Yet, I had written up fairly detailed process notes from that consultation.

Patrick had indicated to a colleague of mine that he was eager to start analysis because of his anxiety in relationships. In that first consultation with me, however, I could sense his reluctance and even fear of embarking on an analysis with me. During that initial meeting, he told me how as a student he used to fall asleep in the library, without being able to take in what he had been reading. When things became difficult or he could not understand something, Patrick would retreat into sleep or passivity. Years later I was to understand two further dimensions that I could only begin to comprehend at that consultation: his erotization of relationships; and his longing for, and fear of, taking a passive, masochistic position. I also registered at that encounter his investment in his body: a tall dark-haired man in his middle twenties, Patrick had a lean, muscular body that suggested many hours of workout and exercise. I already had a sense of the way in which he kept himself together through this investment in his body. These observations, impressions and thoughts led me to ask him at that first consultation if he had ever had a homosexual relationship. Patrick quickly denied that he ever had.

Patrick came for a second consultation, at which some of the above themes were more clearly expressed. He was afraid that he would end up doing 'anything I wanted, even licking the pavement of my street' if he embarked on an analysis with me. I did say to him at that point

131

that I thought he was telling me both how terrified he was of that possibility and also how it represented a longing in relation to me. He was struck by this, and phoned me a week later (as we had arranged) to tell me that he had decided to start analysis with me. Patrick had to wait for two months until we started, during which time, he told me later, he did have a homosexual encounter with a man (Peter). This information sowed the seeds of doubt in my mind as to whether the dialogue I had written up in my notes had really taken place. I was also concerned that I might have suggested such an event to him through my question. Was this suggestion an example of the puzzle that Le Guen has posed: 'How is it that something that does not yet exist may provoke something that will bring it into existence?' (1982: 532).

Introduction: time and space

The analytic situation is, by definition, traumatic because it evokes the state of helplessness of the newborn infant (*Hilflosigkeit*), which is the prototype of the traumatic situation and at the origin of the experience of anxiety. By inviting the patient to lie on the couch and say whatever comes to mind, within a setting where the rules are determined by the analyst[1], the relationship with the primordial object is brought forth.[2] Within the analytic space, different dimensions of time unfold, and a tension between the old and the new is set in motion. In between the patient's presentation (his speech, pauses, narrative of the dreams and associations) and the analyst's response through his internal work (where his own free associations, responses, counter-transference and theoretical models all have a place), specific dimensions of time and space are created in the context of that relationship.

This chapter will address the chain of associations between this state of helplessness, repetition compulsion, trauma, infantile sexuality,

---

[1] The analyst is, in fact, the *guardian* of the setting, as both analyst and patient are submitted to the rules of the setting in its element of thirdness. This is the way I understand Freud's statement to the Rat Man, when the patient begs Freud to spare him of telling the details of his punishment. Freud replies: '. . . I could not grant him something which was beyond my power' (SE (1909: 166)). The setting and its 'fundamental rules' constitute the third in the relation between patient and analyst.

[2] 'The first sexual or sexually coloured experiences which the child has in relation to his mother are naturally of a passive character', suggests Freud (1931: 236).

pleasure and displeasure, which lies at the core of the transference experience and finds its ultimate expression in the analyst's listening (Rolland, 1997). Transference is by definition filled with our patients' desires, which are linked to their unconscious phantasies and infantile sexuality. Transference is also over-determined, like Proust's madeleine that emerges out of a phenomenon of metaphoric and metonimic *irradiation,* associating several moments, places and memories, ultimately expressing the infantile desire of the narrator himself (Kristeva, 1996).

Memory had been at the centre of Freud's studies on hysteria. In 1914, however, Freud introduced the notion of the compulsion to repeat (1914a: 150). The discovery of the compulsion to repeat instituted a paradigmatic shift in Freud's formulations, emphasizing the process of repetition of trauma, and instituting a link between the network of concepts I noted above.

Temporality

Whilst starting with an archaeological metaphor that underlined a certain linear conception of time, Freud developed a progressively more complex model that understood temporality along several axes. In *The Interpretation of Dreams* a link is also established between space and time, primary and secondary processes. Several authors have indicated the similarity between dream work and that of the analytic session (e.g. Khan, 1962; Bollas, 1993; Ogden, 1997). Bollas has suggested that in a session our patients' material is subjected to the same processes present in the dream work: 'The analyst makes the patient's material into his own, not simply by containing it (to use Bion's metaphor) but by distorting, displacing, substituting or condensing it. For this is the work of the unconscious' (1993: 103). It is through this process that material apparently belonging to different spaces and temporalities can be brought together in a process of construction.

For Freud, the idea of making the unconscious conscious appeared as early as *The Interpretation of Dreams.* Soon after that, in 1905, he added the overcoming of resistance as a necessary task for the analyst. By the time Freud wrote his papers on technique the analyst's interpretation of the patient's dreams and free associations was not freely imparted, but might be withheld until resistances appeared. In 1911 he asked: 'At what stage in the treatment and how rapidly should the analyst introduce the patient to the knowledge of what lies veiled in his mind?' (1911b: 95).

From this time onwards Freud distinguished between understanding the patient's unconscious conflicts and the communication of the interpretation. Thus he wrote in *The Question of Lay Analysis* (1926b: 220): 'When you have found the right interpretation, another task lies ahead. You must wait for the right moment at which you can communicate your interpretation to the patient with some prospect of success'.

Moreover, the question of what it is that moves the analyst to make an interpretation also presents a puzzle. At times it feels as if one is adapting to a rhythm derived from a specific dyad, namely that patient and that analyst at a specific moment in time. At other times there is a kind of pressure that pushes one to formulate an interpretation and convey it to the patient before one has had time to properly work it through in one's own mind. Evelyne Séchaud (1997) has called this the 'interpretative urgency', which is nevertheless an expression of the unconscious of both the analyst and the patient at work in the transference. It may be a dream, a word or an association that is made by the patient or the analyst herself that enables the analyst in some profound way to really 'catch the drift of the patient's unconscious with his own unconscious' (Freud, 1922b: 239), without being aware of doing so. Psychoanalytic listening, therefore, does not just refer to the content of the patient's words, but also, and more importantly, to the psychic force of his discourse, which expresses that which is derived from the unconscious. Temporality that is then introduced is not just manifested in the sequence of the sessions, but in the multiple over-determined layers of the psychic space that are expressed in each session.

Contrasting paradigms permeate Freud's work: the emphasis on the interpretation of dreams versus the interpretation of the transference; the emphasis on reconstructions versus constructions; and uncovering (the unconscious) versus instituting it. In some ways one can understand these different emphases in terms of an oscillation between maternal functions (dreaming and free associations) and paternal functions (interpretation). A creative analytic process alternates between the two.

Repetition compulsion, the death drive and sexuality

The profound link that is progressively established between the repetition compulsion and sexuality gains its full force with the introduction of the structural model of the mind. Laplanche has suggested that the death drive is '*itself* a deepening of sexuality in its most radical aspect' (1999: 188). What Freud discovered in 1914 with the concept of narcissism was not the death drive, 'but, on the contrary, sexuality invested in the object and in the ego – object love and love of the ego' (*ibid*: 188). In 1920, the notion of sexuality changed from being associated with love to becoming demonic and unbound, in the sense of a drive, striving for immediate satisfaction in the service of the primary processes. Hence, Laplanche (1999) understands the concept of the death drive in terms of sexuality:

> [The patient] . . . is obliged to *repeat* the repressed material as a contemporary experience instead of, as the physician would prefer to see, *remembering* it as something belonging to the past. These reproductions, which emerge with such unwished-for exactitude, always have as their subject some portion of infantile sexual life – of the Oedipus complex, that is. And its derivatives; and they are invariably acted out in the sphere of the transference, of the patient's relation to the physician.
>
> (Freud, 1920a: 18)

Beyond the Pleasure Principle brought forward a conception of infantile sexuality, which is not that of the *Three Essays*. Rolland has suggested that it is a conceptualization of infantile sexuality that is 'specifically analytical'. It is recognizable in the analytic process, through the analysis of the transference, of its pressure to repeat (Rolland, 1997: 1624). It also highlights the 'tragic, traumatic and painful' aspect of this infantile sexuality (Rolland, 1997: 1625; Rolland, 2005; Green, 2007). Freud emphasizes the demonic character of infantile sexuality at the same time as he points out the similarly demonic and destructive character of the drives. As indicated by Strachey (in Freud, 1919b: 218), Freud was working on the phenomenon of 'the constant recurrence of the same thing' when describing repetition compulsion, which he had already mentioned in *The Uncanny* (1919b: 234).

Freud's technique for stimulating this encounter with the infantile in the analytic situation is the method of free association, asking the patient not to 'hold back any idea from communication, even if . . . he feels that it is too disagreeable, nonsensical, unimportant or irrelevant to what is being looked for' (1922b: 238). The analyst must not only urge that the patient 'should communicate everything that occurs to him without criticism or selection' (1912c: 112) but Freud suggests that the analyst also 'surrender himself to his own unconscious mental activity' (1922b: 239).

The analytic situation provides the elements for psychic conflicts to repeat themselves and, at the same time, furnish them with new meanings. As Kohon has suggested, 'the unconscious meaning unfolds exclusively through the patient's discourse, revealed, as it were, by the analyst's capacity to listen' (2005a: 86).

In our practice as analysts we know that it is always the next moment of a session, the next day or the next year that will clarify something that went on earlier. In many ways there is a kind of reassurance in the process, as one realizes that by definition one cannot fully know the meaning of what is happening at the moment it is happening. Any session in this way can only anticipate what will happen in the next one.

Patrick, and the tiger in the room

Patrick was of Hispanic origins and in his late twenties when he first came to see me. He was the second of three children, the youngest being a girl, Barbara. The father died when my patient was very young and the account is that he had been violent towards the mother. The mother brought the children up, working as a teacher. The family lived in a small flat, the boys sharing a room and the girl sleeping in the mother's bedroom. My patient remembers being very close to his mother. He was a good student, did well at school and got into university. He is an academic, and has recently successfully applied for a much more senior university post.

At the beginning of this chapter, I wrote about my discomfort after the first consultation, and my confusion about what had taken place in view of subsequent events. When he started analysis, Patrick told me that he had had a homosexual encounter with Peter during the two months he had to wait before starting the analysis. I experienced profound doubts about whether this had been the result of him experiencing my question as a 'suggestion', and also whether I had misheard his answer to my question. Some time later in the analysis I was to learn that this homosexual encounter had not been the first in his life, although he had not had one for a few years. Progressively I understood that the place homosexuality had in his mind was different from heterosexuality. It belonged to a more nebulous, almost secret, domain that in some ways matched the doubts I experienced about that first dialogue. That initial question evoked another layer of meaning, as it reverberated with his longing for his (dead) father, a dimension that came to be recovered in the analytic process.

The first year of Patrick's analysis was characterized by promiscuity, and his excitement about starting the analysis could barely be processed or articulated. The sessions were filled with narratives of sexual encounters with women, through which I understood Patrick's struggle to make sense of the nature of the encounter with his analyst. This intense activity eventually subsided, to be followed by another year when Patrick's life in the external world developed in many ways. He became more efficient in his job, produced more, was promoted and bought a house. At the same time, however, sexuality was barely mentioned. This brought with it some anxiety in myself about the potentially castrating impact the analysis was having on him. Dreams, associations and silences indicated to me, at the same time, that my patient was engaged in profound work concerning the nature of his relationships with the external world, and with his internal objects: father, mother, sister, brother, friends, myself. There was also some working through his oscillations between homosexual and heterosexual desire.

The moment I wish to describe took place some years into his analysis. Patrick had started a relationship with a woman some two months prior to our increasing his sessions from four to five times a week. He had wanted to come every day from the beginning, but I had not had a vacancy earlier.

The session is a Thursday, of the first week when we increased the number of sessions to five, and after a holiday break. Patrick came in and lay down on the couch. After a couple of minutes he said that he had had a dream the previous night:

It felt like a good dream. There were different parts to it, but they were interconnected by all being in the same house. Parts of the house were furnished in an old fashioned way. There was a plant, which can take an enormous

*amount of neglect and still keep well. Some parts of the house were well
decorated, others were run down.*

*I was in a group of people. We were hiding away underneath, and were all
thirsty. We wanted to get some water and then we'd go. There was a lion about
the house, and we were hiding from it. I was drinking some water, a bit dirty,
but it did not matter. I was then walking in other parts of the house. I was still
hiding. I then passed one room, which was Peril's room* [his brother, but the
connection with my name is also there]. *I thought that I should not be
found there. But there was a route to another part of the house at the end of his
room. But I had to find another way, as I could not go through Peril's room. I
could not be found there. Then I was with a woman . . .*

*I liked this dream. I liked the house, even if I wanted to avoid detection. It
felt safe, in a funny sort of way, exciting. I was filled with curiosity. I liked the
fabrics of the house, the furniture, the carpets, the whole feeling of the house. It
was a bit run down and neglected but well . . . Coming here today I was
unsure about the time. I knew it, I think it is something about the fifth session;
it is to do with the effect of that on me.* [Silence.]

Patrick: Coming here five times a week is a privilege. I know it is a
mixed one at the same time. The house is furnished and
shabby at the same time.

Analyst: There's a contrast between your experience of a furnished
house, the five sessions this week, on the one hand, and
your feelings of neglect, on the other, during the break,
your feeling that you could not be in Peril's room. It
leaves you feeling you have to hide from the lion, in you or
perhaps also in me . . . [Silence.]

Patrick: I think that the dream is also about the house and going
there with Ellen. [This was a house he had recently bought
abroad; Ellen was his current partner.] I want red curtains in
my room. Like yours. Ellen has also a red curtain in her
room. She also has a red bedspread. My Mum had red curtains that she had made herself. They were rich, had this lush
feel to them. They were beautiful, heavy, like yours. They
closed the world outside . . . [I thought at this point that he
was referring to the whole experience of seduction in this
room. I did not say anything at this point, and waited.]

Part of this dream also felt like me. The whole world was
inside, nice parts, not so nice parts. I was this lion, or this
woman watching people in my world, like you do.

138

Last night we went swimming. We talked, Ellen talked. Then she asked me: How long will you carry on? Then she announced that she does feel threatened by you. Moreover someone told her that you are attractive. All this was said in a good way, we were lying in bed. She was asking if I know what I want.

Analyst: Perhaps the lion in the dream expressed everything that feels threatening at the moment. The attraction of the lush, red curtains.

Patrick: We knew the lion was not a threat, but it was still a lion. It had somehow passed its best. We wanted to look after it. Give it water . . . It reminds me of looking after my mother when she was sick . . . If you do not get in the way of the lion it would not hurt you . . . It is a bit excessive, a lion in a house. [A long silence.]

Patrick: [Slowly and hesitantly.] As a child, lying in bed. . . . My mother was in the other room with my sister; I shared a room with my brother. There was this first night I woke up, then Peril he was rubbing against me. It was so confusing with my Mum next door with my sister . . .

Analyst: Perhaps you thought that they were doing the same . . . [Silence.]

Patrick: I think that you are right. Maybe I thought that. Maybe we all thought that . . .

Analyst: The red curtains shutting out the world outside, your mother and sister in the other room, you and your brother in the one room. [Silence.]

(My uncertainty about the first consultation came to my mind in the silence, and I was also thinking about what had happened between the consultation and starting the analysis. Perhaps these thoughts were initially evoked by the phrases in the dream that 'they were hiding', 'that he should not be found in Peril's room' and the subsequent associations in the session that seemed to be linked to erotic feelings.)

Analyst: Thinking of this room reminds me of your sexual encounter, just before starting analysis. [A long silence.]

Patrick: It is extraordinary isn't it, how things repeat themselves . . . In the dream I am invisible, I was watching everything . . . [Silence. It was time for the session to end.]

139

In the following session Patrick was very excited:

I was so excited yesterday, to see the connections between that first session, and everything else. . . . In the bedrooms at home where I grew up, my mum and my sister; me and my older brother . . . My fear of being sucked dry here from the beginning, which we talked about the other day. Now it is all being repeated all over again with the fifth session.

One can distinguish several dimensions in the session I have described:

1 A dream reported in a session.
2 The dream was in the first instance interpreted by the analyst in terms of the here and now involving the holiday break and the increase to five sessions a week.
3 The patient expanded the field of associations to his mother. The atmosphere he described in his mother's house was almost palpable in the consulting room. There was also a reflective mood. The patient evoked all these memories but he himself came back to the here and now of the analysis. He said at that point that *his girlfriend* felt threatened by the analyst. The lush red curtains point to a condensation of the erotic longing towards the mother/sister, the girlfriend and the analyst. An interpretation by the analyst indicated these links and paved the way for the patient to carry on associating to the mother.
4 The patient then introduced the sexual relationship between the brothers, bringing new information to the analysis. This was linked retrospectively, by the analyst, to the dangerously attractive curtains. The brothers were involved in sexual activity with each other in connection with the phantasy of the mother and sister in the other room. This pointed to the conflict between progressive and regressive movements, between heterosexual and homosexual desire.
5 This scene – the other room – was then linked by the analyst to the homosexual encounter years earlier, in the period when the patient was waiting to start analysis, and imagining what was happening/would happen in the consulting room (conflict between phantasies of homosexual or heterosexual encounter with the analyst).
6 The patient himself interpreted the repetition: the present and

the past of the analysis (increase to five sessions a week) and the childhood scene.

7 Finally, in the months to come, the old lion that had 'passed its best' evoked the longing for the father, a dimension that was about to express itself more vividly in the transference.

The scene between the brothers was then understood retrospectively as an enactment of what the patient thought was happening in 'the other room' – a homosexual primal scene between mother and daughter. It represented both a longing to participate in that scene and also a wish to distance himself from it by creating an all-male world. I had sensed this conflict at the very first consultation, but without the depths of meaning that the analytic process had allowed us to discover. What happened in myself following my question and subsequent events seemed to contain in an important way a dimension of Patrick's own experience of his homosexual relationship with his brother. Had it really happened? It was something the brothers had never again talked about, which led him to often doubt whether or not it had taken place. These scenes of homosexual encounters belonged to another realm, that of the 'other room', which for Freud is connected with the otherness of the unconscious, and which Ron Britton refers to as the room of the imagined primal scene (1999).

My question at that first consultation ('Had he had a homosexual relationship?') was over-determined and contained a multitude of dimensions of meaning that I could not possibly have predicted, even though I have come to regard first consultations as often containing the crucial themes that will unfold in an analysis, the full complexity of which can only be understood in terms of après coup.

A few years into Patrick's analysis, his statement at that first consultation also acquired further layers of meaning: his wish/terror that he would do whatever I wanted (he would lick the pavement if I asked him to), the orality of the desire and the derivative of an experience of a breast that had become hard and unyielding perhaps because of its refusal to fulfil his desires were all being expressed. My very question evoked (or was activated by?) a homosexual relationship characterized by orality and the threat of castration. There was perhaps a repetition, right at the beginning of the analysis, of a trauma that is analogous to the scene with his brother. One might suggest that phantasies of (homosexual) seduction, castration and primal scene were also present.

141

What is so striking in the analytic situation is the inevitable emergence of the unconscious relationships in the context of the transference. It makes me think of Freud's paper *The Uncanny*, the idea of 'something that is secretly familiar [*Heimlich-heimisch*], which has undergone repression and then returned from it' (1919b: 245). The analyst needs only to allow enough space and time for the processes to evolve. Past and present unfold in the immediacy of the here and now with enormous intensity and pressure, and one cannot predict the repercussions of one's comments, interpretations or even movements in a session as they evoke a complex network of 'affective, ideational, memorial, somatic and cognitive workings in the analysand' (Bollas, 1993, p. 45). What takes place is not the retrieval of a memory that has been repressed but 'the creation of an experience . . . that had not previously existed in the form that it is now taking' (Ogden, 2004: 178).

Further clinical material

It took another couple of years for a fuller dimension of the hatred and violence linked to sexuality to appear in the transference. For about two weeks before a summer holiday break, there had been a progressive build-up of tension with a colleague at work. I will summarize the material of a week of analysis.

A dream Patrick brought on the Monday session allowed me to point out a double layer of his connection with me: the attachment and aggression in his wish to hold on to me in a loving way, combined with feelings of hatred. There was another association in the session connected with the longing for his father.

On the following day Patrick brought a dream in which *a female colleague at work got distracted by a personal call from her husband during working hours, leaving him furious. He turned to his male boss (the head of the department) and there was a sexual feeling between them.* He also told me about a row he had with a colleague at work (Robert), who had then had a car crash. Patrick was both furious and frightened by the idea that he could have had such an impact on his colleague. This experience was obviously related to the analytic situation and his experience of exposure and danger at the time of our forthcoming break. He was terrified of what we could do to each other. Did he need to protect me against his rage? He was furious with his self-absorbed analyst who took her holidays, probably with her husband, right in the middle of the work. There were many strands in this session, but centrally the two versions of himself: the head of department and the crushed man. Is the only way to deal with heterosexual jealousy to turn to homosexuality? Could he own up to his murderous feelings towards me, my husband, the phone call/holiday break or was there a danger that this hatred would lead to violence or a crash? Underlying all this was the fear of identification with a violent father, and the equation between potency and violence.

At the Thursday session Patrick was still expressing his rage towards his male colleague. He then told me about the very hard game of tennis he had played on the previous day with his brother, and how they had exhausted themselves in the process. (The allusion was to something that was both erotic and a battle.) He was quiet for a moment, and we were both immersed in this silence, which felt full of trepidation. He then told me about his experience of often feeling enraged with his brother in the past:

He wanted servility, the bastard, he wanted things as he wished. It is nasty, hateful stuff. . . . I can now understand my jealousy of him. It was ominous. He left school, set up his own business, made a lot of money. I worked for him for a while. I was over-involved with him. He could be very generous but then there was a price to it.

On the Friday session Patrick brought a dream in which a man was being badly beaten, perhaps being murdered. In his associations it became clear that this man was linked to his father, and my comment was 'a father is being beaten to death'. This 'open' type of interpretation suggested rather than fully spelt out the links between the internal father, the external father and myself in the here and now of the transference. In my experience in this analysis, Patrick was able to carry on working on this type of interpretation himself.[3] There followed a long silence, in which I felt a lot of processing was taking place. He then said:

---

[3] This interpretation was inspired by Julia Kristeva's paper, presented to The Dead Father conference at Columbia University in April 2006 entitled 'A father is being beaten to death',

It will be great not to come here over the break. But it will be a long, long time. I will miss here, talking to you, lying down, looking at your curtains. I feel stiff, fearful, and also enormously relieved . . . I think that this is an extraordinary process . . . To become aware of how angry I was at home with Peril, the confusion between Robert [the colleague at work], Peril and you this week . . . And now my father! I was struck about my use of the word 'ominous' about my relationship with Peril, which you pointed out. It feels like I was saying that something of the past stored up trouble for the future. . . .

I thought that a lot of work had taken place, and would continue to take place during the summer break.

Hilflosigkeit and the erotic dimension of the beginnings

Freud has suggested that *Hilflosigkeit*, the state of helplessness of the newborn infant, is the prototype of the traumatic situation and is at the origin of the experience of anxiety (1926a). Laplanche and Pontalis indicate the several lines of enquiry that this notion has led to in psychoanalytic thinking (1985: 190). Firstly, it is intrinsically linked to the crucial role played by the experience of satisfaction, the hallucinatory wish fulfilment. Secondly, the total dependence on the mother has, as its counterpart, the mother's omnipotence, which emphasizes the enormous importance that the other person has for the infant.[4] Thirdly, within the framework of the second theory of anxiety, helplessness becomes 'the prototype of the traumatic situation' (*ibid*: 190). In his second theory Freud suggests that the signal of anxiety is once connected with the fear of loss or separation that the individual cannot master and is overwhelmed by. Freud relates this state of helplessness to the 'prematurity' of the infant who is 'sent to the world in a less finished state' (1926a: 190). This biological fact 'creates the need to be loved that will accompany the child through the rest of its life'.

---

[4] Winnicott refers to the state of 'absolute dependence', where the environment 'is part of the baby' (1989: 253), which feels that he has hallucinated it. These two aspects, the hallucinatory wish fulfilment and the mother's omnipotence, according to Kohon, 'create the conditions for normal madness to develop', or, in Green's term, 'original madness' (or 'private madness which is at the core of the individual's unconscious)' (Green, 1986b: 244, 246; Kohon, 2005a: 68–69).

The loss of the object is at the origin of pain, as well as anxiety and desire (Pontalis, 1977: 262).

In *The Interpretation of Dreams*, Freud tells us that once the baby has an experience of satisfaction, such as the primary experience of feeding at the breast, a trace is laid down in the memory, which he designated as the memory trace. When the baby is hungry next time he will wish to repeat that same experience at the breast that satisfied his hunger. The object – the breast – is now sought, and provides the prototype for all further experiences, including that of love. The finding of the object is always a re-finding.

The mother is thus the source of the baby's experience of pleasure. This takes place in the intimacy of the contact with the body of the mother. The 'right' amount of eroticism is crucial, so that it is not too much, overexciting the child, or too little, without an erotic investment for the baby, which is also so crucial for its relationship with its own body. Inevitably, however, the mother oscillates between 'excess of gratification and excess of frustration' (Green, 1986b). This erotic dimension is at the basis of what Laplanche has referred to as the seduction of the child by the adult, through the enigmatic message addressed, unilaterally, by the adult to the child, and which is to be found at the very heart of the 'primal fantasies'.

There is therefore a measure of masochism in this primary relationship, which Freud calls primary erotogenic masochism, that becomes crucial for individual development (see also Rosenberg, 1991). This idea assumes the importance of integrating a measure of eroticized suffering in early life. *This masochistic, erotic dimension of the primary relationship is evoked in all relationships and, I suggest, is an intrinsic part of the analytic setting. This idea brings trauma to the centre of the analytic experience.*

It is this primary erotic dimension of the relationship with the mother that is so powerfully evoked in Patrick's analysis, already at that first consultation. The erotic longing for his mother was until now experienced from a passive position, and included only a faint representation of the father. A few more years of analysis needed to take place before the father could emerge more forcefully into the transference, not as a lion that had 'passed its best'.[5] Freud's view presents a paradox, in that if the killing of the father is the requirement

---

[5] Indeed, as we worked on the longing for his father in the transference during this period, Patrick contacted his father's brother for the first time since his childhood.

for the creation of a social and psychic order, the father, however, has to be killed metaphorically only, as the outcome of the Oedipus complex and at the origin of the superego. The phantasy of the father 'being beaten to death' becomes an important achievement of Patrick's analysis. It opens up the pathway to a stronger masculine identification, to the mobilization of feelings of rage and violence, as well as the potential for the capacity to use his aggression in a more creative way. One is reminded here of the *Rat Man*, when he knows the pleasure of sexual intercourse for the first time: 'This is glorious! One might murder one's father for this!' (1909b: 201).

Interpretation

Since Freud's first systematic presentations of his views on psycho-analytic technique in the series of papers written between 1912 and 1915, contrasting approaches to the topic have been expressed. They range from an emphasis on the formulation of interpretations on the one hand, to considerations of the analytic attitude itself on the other. Ella Sharpe and Strachey represent contrasting examples of emphases. In her seminal papers on technique Sharpe proposes that 'psycho-analysis ceases to be a living science when technique ceases to be an art' (in Whelan, 2000). She suggests: 'We must not overemphasize the conscious side of our work. We shall not if we do not overemphasize the importance of our conscious logical processes but depend upon our freed unconscious' (*ibid*: 260). Strachey stresses the 'point of urgency' in the formulation of interpretations, which should refer to an anxiety in the immediacy of the transference in the analytic situation (1934). His model is the analyst as a benign interpreter of reality, internalized as a temporary new object, helping to make the unconscious conscious, and modifying the superego (see Cooper, 1987, 1988). Classical analytic neutrality is preserved.

In the British School the inclusion of the analyst's affective states in the sessions – the understanding of the counter-transference – increasingly became part of the central analytical task.[6] It is in the

---

[6] Since Ella Sharpe (in Whelan, 2000) and Heimann (1950), this line of enquiry has been developed by Money-Kyrle (1956), Bion (1967), Racker (1968), Grinberg (1962), Sandler (1976), Joseph (1975, 1985), Segal (1997), Brenman-Pick (1985), Feldman (1997), Britton (2003) and Steiner (2006). For these authors the counter-transference became a way of

process of holding, containing and transforming feelings that cannot be elaborated by the patients themselves that the analytic work is carried out. Klein had already suggested that there are 'pre-verbal emotions . . . (which are) revived in the transference situation . . . (and which) appear . . . as memories in feelings', which are reconstructed and put into words with the help of the analyst (Klein, 1937: 316).[7] In the last 30 years the understanding of the counter-transference has come to be regarded as the main area of work from which the understanding of feeling states in the analytic session is derived.

The literature, however, seems to alternate between stressing the aspects of holding and containing by the analyst in elaborating the patients' processes (maternal?), as opposed to the paternal inter-pretation. One is talking in terms of emphases, as I would suggest that any analysis would by definition include both modalities. One could nevertheless suggest that an Oedipal conflict takes place at the level of theory itself. Chasseguet-Smirgel has pointed out that in analysis the analysand is offered a womb, a potential for regression, but in the setting itself with its framework and rules the limits are also indicated, in the same way as the father separates the mother and the child (1986). The silence of the analyst would evoke that which takes place between infant and mother, whilst interpretations evoke the paternal function instituting separation between the mother/child dyad.

Bollas (1996) has suggested that: 'The associative place would be operating within the maternal order, the interpretive within the paternal order, and the patient's participation in both worlds – indeed the patient's need for both positions – would constitute a structural use of the parental couple'.[8]

In Chapter 6, I suggested a distinction between 'open' and 'closed' types of interpretations. The first is more elusive, and refers to differ-ent layers at the same time, perhaps allowing more openly for the

---

gaining access to patients' unconscious communication. Authors such as Winnicott (1949, 1956), Bollas (1993), Duncan (1989), Casement (1985), Parsons (2000), Sedlak (1997), Kohon (1999a, 2005a, b) and Perelberg (1999, 2003, 2004) have written about the way the analyst's elaborations of his thoughts and feelings during a session are an essential part of the analytic work.

[7] Winnicott characterizes the analytic work in terms of 'giving the patient back what the patient brings' (1971: 138). This is a derivative of the mother's face that reflects to the baby that which is there to be seen.

[8] At the 2004 English Speaking Conference, Ignês Sodré presented a paper that explored some of these issues in terms of the contrast between 'Freud' and 'Florence' functions.

patient to choose the level at which to proceed. A typical type of open interpretation is the one mentioned above: 'a father is being beaten to death'. This was followed by Patrick himself referring to the various levels at which he had understood the interpretation.[9] Closed interpretations tend to present a fuller narrative of what is taking place in the session at that specific moment and to point more specifically to the interplay of identifications. In the session I presented more fully, when indicating to Patrick his identifications in the dream, I offered a 'closed' type of interpretation.[10]

The minimal ingredients of an analysis are the patient, the analyst and the analytic frame. This implies a radical asymmetry between the imaginary and the symbolic. The imaginary offers a dual perspective, interpretations centred on the person or analyst, which, O'Shaughnessy has suggested, may create 'enclaves' in an analysis (1992). The symbolic offers a triangular perspective (which refers to the structure of alliance between mother, father and child), which always brings the third into the analytic situation (see Bleger, 1967; Green, 1991, 2004; Ogden, 2004) or the analytic space (Viderman, 1970).

At one level, one can see how so many of these questions are derivatives of the Oedipal myth, of what it is that one takes from one's mother and one's father, and how one can be derived from two. In Lévi-Strauss's words, what is being addressed is the question of whether the human being is born from one or from two (1972). How is it that we do not have only one procreator, but a mother *plus* a father. If the anthropologist can find enormous variations whereby – through rituals – different societies attempt to address this problem, the psychoanalyst can identify a whole range of psychopathologies that individuals develop in their attempts to deal with this same question. The centrality that Freud attributed to the Oedipus complex in the formation of the individual brings to the forefront of his preoccupations questions about origins. It is the resolution that each individual brings to these questions, and to the nature of their internal

---

[9] See Roth's paper on levels of interpretations (2001).

[10] My distinction between *closed* and *open* interpretations has some similarities with Parson's distinctions between *the near end and the far end* types of interpretations. The first focus on the details of the session, pointing out meanings that the patient cannot see for himself. The 'further end' type of interpretation aims to 'open up the possibility of something happening, without the need to know what that something is going to be' (Parsons, 2000: 197). Parsons emphasizes how important it is for the analyst to have the freedom to move between these different types of interpretations.

relationship with their father, mother and siblings, that is to be explored in an analysis.

The elaboration of the Oedipus complex (in our patients and in our theoretical models) and the relinquishing of one's incestuous phantasies (incest with one's parents in our phantasies of being their true followers) inserts the individual in a temporal dimension. This requires facing the desire to kill the father, or 'beat the father to death', as in Patrick's dream. It initiates the process of mourning.

The key to the analytic technique is the fluidity of movement between the different positions in the triangle, from silence to the containment of the projections, to interpretation.

The considerations above do not mean that the present of the analysis is isomorphic with the past. The present reinterprets the past, as the past leaves the seeds that will find their fulfilment in the present, albeit with no sense of predetermination. This is the meaning of the *dynamic* concept of après coup, as discussed in the previous chapter, central in Freud's notion of temporality. I have suggested that the concept of dynamic après coup, profoundly embedded in Freudian metapsychology, links trauma, repetition and infantile sexuality.

It took some years for something that was barely sensed at a first consultation to find meaning in the analytic process. My question to Patrick about whether he had had a homosexual relationship, his denial and subsequent information provoked a confusion in me about which I remained silent for a few years. It was not until I felt I had understood something about its meaning, in the context of the development of the transference, that I formulated my understanding into an interpretation.

The characteristics of the analytic setting itself, with the fundamental rules of lying on the couch and free association are inherently traumatic, in that they passivate the patient (Green, 1986b: 248), who is invited to entrust himself to the care of the analyst. Any analysis will repeat in some way the traumatic infantile situation. In Patrick's analysis, there is a scene of childhood trauma (the scene between the brothers) that is retrospectively understood in terms of what takes place in two moments of the transference situation. Freud told us that whatever is discovered in the transference situation will never be forgotten.

PART TWO

Applications

9

Time and memory in *One Hundred Years of Solitude*[1]

When he was alone, José Arcadio Buendía consoled himself with the dream of the infinite rooms. He dreamed that he was getting out of bed, opening the door and going into an identical room with the same bed with a wrought-iron head, the same wicker chair and the same small picture of the Virgin of Help on the back wall. From that room he would go into another that was just the same, the door of which would open into another one just the same, and then into another exactly alike, and so on to infinity. He liked to go from room to room, as in a gallery of parallel mirrors, until Prudencio Aguilar would touch him on the shoulder. Then he would go back from room to room, walking in reverse. Going back over his trail, he would find Prudencio Aguilar in the room of reality. But one night, two weeks after they took him to his bed, Prudencio Aguilar touched his shoulder in an intermediate room and he stayed there forever, thinking that it was the room of reality.

(García Márquez, 1970: 119–120)

In this chapter we will discuss the work of a Contemporary Latin-American novelist – Gabriel García Márquez – and examine the way in which he has utilized the interplay between different notions of time to construct his narrative. We will suggest that in its use of time, the novel *Cien Años de Soledad (One Hundred Years of Solitude)* deals with major and universal problems, such as a search for one's origins,

---

[1] This chapter is derived from a paper presented at the British Psychoanalytical Society entitled 'Time and Memory in Gabriel García Márquez and Vargas Llosa', written by my mother, Professor Bella Jozef, and myself in 1998.

incest, endogamy, separation, procreation and death. More specifically we suggest that in this novel there is a relationship between time and the formation of a couple that has allowed the author to write a novel that has become a myth of origins.

One Hundred Years of Solitude contains a description of the notion of time that is present in the unconscious. The following passage also illustrates how the idea of death is not present in the 'pre-history' of Macondo. Freud had indeed emphasized that there is no notion of death in the unconscious:

> Macondo was a village of twenty adobe houses, built on the bank of a river of clear water that ran along a bed of polished stones, which were white and enormous, like prehistoric eggs. The world was so recent that many things lacked names and in order to indicate them it was necessary to point . . . [Macondo] was a truly happy village where no one was over thirty years of age and where no one had died.
>
> (García Márquez, 1970: 9 and 15)

There follows a description of the introduction of secondary process, of consciousness, as opposed to primary process and the timelessness of the unconscious. Ultimately Macondo cannot resist the outside world, which cannot promise to relieve the citizens of their sense of loss. A visiting priest, appalled by the innocent but effective pagan system of 'natural law', decides to stay and build a church. *Death introduces the beginnings of time*. In Macondo, the expectancy of death brings the establishment of a cemetery. The story relates the progressive inauguration of various institutions and the passage from magic to reason. Macondo becomes a 'city with houses having mirror walls' (the appearance of the other). 'Politics replaces the idyllic balance of José Arcadio Buendia's magical natural order' (Hedeen, 1983: 358).

In *One Hundred Years of Solitude* the reader's progressive knowledge of the present and future allows her to reinterpret the past.

Permutations in space and time

The sequence of the narrative is not simply lineal, but moves back and forth in time. In *One Hundred Years of Solitude* there is a gap between the event and the writing. *Regression* inaugurates the narrative. Someone who knows what will happen in the future of the past announces that in the future the character will return to the past. To inaugurate the narrative with this regression implies an emphasis on the past through the memory of the fictional character.

The narrative is placed in the past, even if it is still going to happen in the future (Jozef, 1974). Everything is known, however, since everything had been predicted by Melquíades the gypsy, and throughout the book one comes across the phrase 'many years later . . .', which implies a freedom for the storyteller who knows the story he is telling and who may therefore stroll back and forth across the narrative time.

One can isolate two central narrative focuses in the book. The first is the history and degeneration of six generations of Buendias, beginning with José and Úrsula and terminating with Aureliano Babilonia. There is also an account of the development of 'banana fever', the period of opulence, exploitation and violence and repeated civil wars that takes place in Macondo. The events are not narrated in a chronological order. Since all events exist at the same time, the narrator can relate them from any temporal position along the matrix (Ludmer, 1972).

One of the best and most complete analyses of time and the narrative structure of *One Hundred Years of Solitude* is that undertaken by Vargas Llosa (1971), who pointed out that the narrative moves in a circle, from undifferentiated chaos to political and social organization and back towards chaos. Frequently the narrative takes the reader to a point in the future and then back to the events as they happen. At the end, the time of the narrative and the time of the narrator coincide: 'The time of this novel is simultaneous, which means that while the events extend over 100 years, they also exist in one time. Thus it is impossible to establish distinctions between past, present and future' (Carlos Fuentes in Jozef, 1974: 62; see also Jozef, 1996).

The narrative begins with the foundation of Macondo and finishes with its extinction. The future in *One Hundred Years of Solitude* is always followed by a scene of return, of regression to the starting point, and the same happens with the time that goes ahead to the future. Facing this time that moves in a continuous flow there is a time that leaves an impression of eternity – it is what allows one to stay in the middle room of José Arcadio's dream. It is in this mythical time that José Arcadio is located when he says it is always March and always Monday (García Márquez, 1970: 283). The interchangeability between past and present is replicated in that between life and death.

Ursula, at the end of the book, spent time in her room talking to dead people and 'no-one knew for certain whether she was speaking about what she felt or what she remembered' (*ibid*: 277). It is this same interchangeability that allows Amaranta, as she is preparing to die, to offer to take letters to dead people. At the end of the book Aureliano and Amaranta Úrsula are awakened at night by the traffic of the dead. Melquíades did not place events in the order of man's conventional time, but concentrated a century of daily episodes in such a way that they co-existed in one instant.

Melquíades becomes the one who creates the distance – between Macondo and the external world – and who also makes the first attempt to institute time in Macondo. His was the first funeral. In the dream quoted at the beginning of this chapter, the attempt is to retreat from time (Steiner, J., 1992) in a room where one does not have to face external (or internal) reality (the room of reality) and thus time.

Repetition (and solitude and death)

The central theme of repetition contributes to a sense of timelessness, in terms of the progressive construction of a myth of origins.

Lévi-Strauss suggested that:

> The function of repetition is to render the structure of the myth apparent . . . Thus a myth exhibits a 'slated' structure, which comes to the surface, so to speak, through the process of repetition. However, the slates are not absolutely identical. And since the purpose of the myth is to provide a logical model capable of overcoming a contradiction . . . a theoretically infinite number of slates will be generated, each slightly different from the others. Thus a myth grows spirally until the intellectual impulse which has produced it is exhausted. Its *growth* is a continuous process, whereas its *structure* remains discontinuous.
>
> (Lévi-Strauss, 1972: 229)

But what gives myth an operational value is that it is timeless: 'it explains the present and the past, as well as the future' (*ibid*: 209).

Freud regarded the repetition compulsion as an ungovernable principle existing in the unconscious. It represents the repetition of old experiences of which the individual has no conscious recollection.

It is related to the conservative characteristic of the drives (Laplanche and Pontalis, 1973). We suggest that the repetition compulsion, which is at the basis of symptom formation, can also be seen as an attempt to grasp that which has not been properly understood by the individual about him or herself. *This quest for knowledge is, in the final analysis, a search for knowledge about one's origins.*

In the Oedipus myth, there is a concern with such a search that proves to be disastrous, leading to incest, destruction and death. A major theme in *One Hundred Years of Solitude* is such a quest for knowledge – ultimately illustrated by the story, which is written in manuscripts that cannot be deciphered. It is very interesting to note that the name Melquíades means 'the son of the king' [Melq = king; 'íades' = son, in Greek], suggesting that the novel might be understood as a transformation of the Oedipus story.

The compulsion to repeat can be viewed as an unconscious effort to break through the repression barrier, in an attempt to break the rules of endogamy and of incest. The text that is finally deciphered by Aureliano allows him and the reader to acquire knowledge about his origins and his name, as well as his destiny (his death).

There is an insistence on the theme of repetition. The duplication of the narrative lies in the prophecies and in the structuring of the novel itself. In the Buendía family, everything is repeated, and this undermines the inevitability of life and death. The characters have the same names, act in the same ways and have the same aspirations. In the names everything is repeated: there are multiple José Arcadios, Aurelianos, Remedios, Amarantas and Úrsulas. Even the signs of repetition repeat themselves. At the end of the novel the gypsies who had arrived centuries before return, bringing back the magic that had then produced astonishment and wonder.

The novel is structured around a series of narrative unities that appear to be circular. Vargas Llosa identifies 14 such sequences in the novel, each of which begins with an enigmatic statement of a future event. For example: 'Úrsula had to make a great effort to fulfil her promise to die when it cleared' (García Márquez, 1970: 271). The narrative then turns to the remote past before coming back to the point when she actually dies: 'They found her dead on the morning of Good Friday' (*ibid*: 278). This narrative sequence has been designated by William James (1957) as a 'duration block' of remembered time. It is organized in terms of significant associations around events. The emphasis is on the imaginative construction or what Vargas Llosa has termed 'episodios que muerden la cola' (1971: 545), a phrase that signifies the cyclical process of evolution and involution (birth, growth, decline and death), and is also symbolic of a return to the beginnings.

The structure of the book is symmetrical (see also Jelinski, 1984). It has 20 chapters: the first 10 tell a story and the last 10 invert that story, as a mirror. The story itself is also duplicated in Melquíades' manuscripts. With the birth of José Arcadio's two sons there is a bifurcation in the narrative. In each generation there are then two antagonistic tendencies that confront each other (the Aurelianos were introverts but had lucid minds, the José Arcadios were impulsive and entrepreneurial), even if the positions are inverted in the third generation. In each generation one of the Buendías is shot and the other escapes, one has twins and the other does not, one dedicates himself to violence and the other suffers the consequences.

The dream quoted at the beginning of this chapter illustrates the whole structure of the novel. There are several other examples of such repetitive sequences:

> Amaranta's life was spent in weaving her shroud. It might have been said that she wove during the day and unwove during the night, and not with any hope of defeating solitude in that way, but quite the contrary, in order to nurture it.
>
> (García Márquez, 1970: 212)

The same circularity is present in Aureliano's making of gold fishes: 'Since he had decided not to sell any, he kept on making two fishes a day and when he finished twenty five he would melt them down and start all over again' (*ibid*: 216). This repetition marks the circularity of Macondo. In the succession of the generations there are several attempts to enter the domain of historical change: Aureliano attempts to do it through political revolution, José Arcadio Segundo attempts to build a canal to the ocean and Aureliano Triste brings the railway to Macondo.

Myth of origins

Throughout his work, Freud was interested in myths of origins, as he interpreted the riddle of the sphinx as being where babies come from. This interpretation has been extended by several analysts (e.g. Róheim, 1954), who have suggested that the sphinx refers to parental intercourse. In 1958 Lévi-Strauss interpreted the myth of Oedipus as containing a fundamental question for human beings about their origins (Lévi-Strauss, 1972). The myth, according to Lévi-Strauss, attempts to mediate a conflict between a theory that attributes to the individual an autochthonous origin, and the know-ledge that any individual is in fact born from the union between a man and a woman. The myth is an attempt to understand and elabor-ate the question of *how one can be born from two.* This question implies the renunciation of the possession of one's mother, daughter, sister, thus facilitating the foundation of culture and exogamy. The incest prohibition is characterized by Freud as perhaps the 'most maiming wound ever inflicted . . . on the erotic life of man' (Freud, 1930: 74).

The establishment of time in myths is, in so many cultures, related to intercourse between a couple. The anthropologist Edmund Leach (1961) suggested that the myth of Cronus indicates that the creation of time institutes the world of differences. In classical Greece, the sexual act itself provided the primary image of time.

In *One Hundred Years of Solitude* it is the whole world that is re-created from its creation to its destruction, in a parody of the Adam and Eve myth. One starts with the Genesis in which José Arcadio and Úrsula, his wife, live together in a virginal way, marked by the shadow of a prohibition. Prudencio Aguilar's death and the couple's rebellion against the prohibition give rise to the Exodus and the curse that pursues the Buendías. They attempt to reach the 'enchanted' place, a 'paradise of dampness and silence, going back to before original sin' (García Márquez, 1970: 17). If the couple consummates their relation-ship they will risk having a child with the tail of a pig. The book tells the history of six generations of Buendías where the relationship between the couple is problematic, incompletely realized and thus denied.

Aureliano and Arcadio have a relationship with the same woman Pilar Ternera, with whom each has a child. Arcadio, however, marries Santa Sofía de la Piedad, who is treated by everybody as a servant. Many years later they had forgotten that she was their mother and later a grandmother in the household. In that generation, Amaranta remains single, having a secret incestuous passion for her nephew. She is sensual, but remains a virgin. In the next generation, Remedios and Arcadio remain single and Aureliano Segundo marries Fernanda –

cold, frigid, enclosed in her own world – a widow whose husband had not yet died and who spent her whole life as if it had been raining (*ibid*: 259). During the years when it rained, no one went into the streets any more. 'If it had depended on Fernanda, they would never done so . . . because she felt that doors had been invented to stay closed and that curiosity for what was going on in the street was a matter for harlots' (*ibid*: 259). Thus Aureliano Segundo has a passionate relationship with his lover Petra Cotes, who, like Pilar Ternera in the previous generation, is a symbol of sexuality and fertility. Free and loved, she is also a prostitute in contrast to the 'legitimate' wife, Fernanda. In the next generation Renata and José Arcadio remain single, and Babilonia and Amaranta Úrsula, nephew and aunt, finally consummate the passionate and incestuous relationship that had been predicted generations earlier. It is only with this last couple that a 'total relationship' is reached with a woman who, whilst being a wife, can also be a mother and a lover.

Thus the Buendías fled from Riohacha in order to escape from the sins of the past symbolized in the sad picture of the ghost of Prudencio Aguilar, killed by José Arcadio Buendía. We suggest that the beginning of the book portrays a 'screen memory': 'Many years later, as he faced the firing squad, Colonel Aureliano Buendia was to remember that distant afternoon when his father took him to discover ice' (*ibid*: 9). He remembers the time of prehistory (with the prehistoric eggs), which was also a time when many things lacked names. The image has a frozen quality in his memory. Melquíades arrives, representing the part of himself that wanted to be able to see and know: Melquíades brings with him the telescope and the magnifying glass and what Aureliano wanted to see is expressed in the following phrase: 'In a short time, man will be able to see what is happening in any place in the world without leaving his own house' (*ibid*: 10). There is a prohibition on that wish to know (what is perhaps happening in his own house), expressed in the association between that screen memory and the firing squad that he is now, or 'many years later', facing (firing squad = prohibition).

In *One Hundred Years of Solitude* the sin is incest. One can identify an account of the struggle that is created between endogamy and exogamy, knowledge and renunciation, incest and culture. The battle is present in each generation. All these battles seem to centre around the question of the formation of a couple who can legitimately unite in sexual intercourse and produce children. The last Aureliano was 'the only one in a century who had been engendered with love' (*ibid*: 333). Knowledge and death come together, constituting a simultaneous process. At the end of the book Aureliano searches in the parchments for the revelation of the instant of his own conception (*ibid*: 333) and this end *brings the book back to its beginning. Knowledge becomes associated with death.*

The dream of the empty rooms is intimately linked to solitude. The images throughout the book emphasize the fact that the characters end up isolated in empty spaces, like the empty rooms of José Arcadio's dream. They feel alone in the empty rooms, and we suggest can be understood as the rooms where the parents cannot be found together and thus the knowledge of parental intercourse is avoided. The intermediate room represents that position of psychic retreat where this reality can be denied. In the circularity of the repetitions the recognition of a three-dimensional order is avoided since the parallel mirrors can only reflect each other.

Enclosure is thus a defence against the experience of externality and a struggle against the experience of separation. When José Arcadio confuses his lover with his mother Úrsula, he has reached and is experiencing both a new and an ancient state of being. 'He is per-forming a primal act, something that for a long time he had wanted to do, that is accompanied by fear and a bewildered anxiety, and has awakened for him that fearful solitude' (*ibid*: 30); García Márquez describes Arcadio's ensuing nightly pilgrimages and sexual union as following 'her path every night through the labyrinth of the room' (*ibid*: 30). Infected with a 'virulent rancour against the world' that is a hatred of disharmony, he continues to long for the comfort of the woman who has defined, by opposition to her womb-like control, that sense of primal separation from one's mother. 'We are fighting this war', Aureliano José is told '*so that a person can marry his own mother*' (*ibid*: 127).

In the following generation José Arcadio Segundo has a dream that he is going 'into an empty house with white walls and that he was upset by the burden of being the first human being to enter it. In the dream he remembered that he had dreamed the same thing the night before and on many nights over the past years and he knew that the image would be erased from his memory when he awakened because that recurrent dream had the quality of not being remem-bered except within the dream itself' (*ibid*: 217). The empty house with the white walls became symbolic of the relationship with the

161

idealized mother–breast and of the phantasy of an incestuous relationship – what Chasseguet-Smirgel (1976) designates as the archaic
Oedipus complex. It belongs to the archaic period in the individual's
history, barred from consciousness with the repression barrier – the
dream that cannot be remembered except in the dream itself.

One Hundred Years of Solitude tells us the story of a dream encapsulated in a novel that constitutes both a myth and a longing for a return
to a primary relationship. Freud has suggested that a passionate sexual
union constitutes a re-finding of the primary object. The end of the
novel contains the passion of an incestuous relationship, which brings
with it the beginnings of time and also its end.

The process of writing itself implies the re-creation of a lost world.
Proust's Elstir cries out: 'One can only create what one loves by
renouncing it' (1913–1927). The act of creation at depth has to do
with an unconscious memory of a harmonious internal world and
the experience of its destruction . . .

'What can you possibly learn from babies?' – on psychoanalytic constructions of primal infants[1]

> The traumatic significance of an event is not fixed at the time of its occurrence. Rather it is later events which will determine which experiences may gain significance as traumatic.
>
> (Kris, 1956: 73)

Psychoanalysis has developed a number of specific formulations about the notion of the individual in his/her historical development. From very early on Freud pointed out *both* that the understanding of the past history of the individual was fundamental to the understanding of his or her present adult psychic life, *and* that the present could shed light onto the past.

The status accorded to 'empirical evidence' as confirming or refuting psychoanalytical concepts, however, has varied. Many scholars have challenged the idea that it is possible to talk about 'facts' in the domain of psychoanalysis and the status of evidence in psychoanalytic theory has been widely discussed (for some of the different positions in this debate, see, for instance: Ricoeur, 1965; Habermas, 1971; Klein, G.S., 1976; Grunbaum, 1985; Spence, 1987; D'Or, 1988).

---

[1] This chapter was the co-winner of the Cesare Sacerdoti Prize at the 37th IPA Congress in Buenos Aires. It was originally written in 1986 for a Baby Observation Seminar at the British Psychoanalytical Society. Dr Geraldine Fitzpatrick was the seminar leader and Dr Brian Jacobs and Mrs Anne Harrison were members of my group. I am grateful for their comments throughout the year. This chapter was read to the Contemporary Freudian Group meeting at the British Society on 9 March 1993.

In his Presidential Address to the Montreal Conference in 1987 Wallerstein pointed out two main perspectives current in psycho-analytic theory: the natural science perspective, strongest in America and Britain, and the hermeneutical perspective, developed principally in Germany and France (1988: 8). Freud himself oscillated, at different times, between these two approaches to psychoanalytic formulations: on the one hand he would have liked psychoanalysis to be a natural science but, on the other hand, he viewed psychoanalysis as a new way of reinterpreting the domain of culture, from dreams and art to litera-ture and religion. (See the contributions to this debate by Duncan, 1992, and Steiner, R., 1992.)

In considering the plurality of approaches recognized by the IPA, Wallerstein (1988) suggested that they all constitute metaphors, i.e. attempts to systematize and give coherence to clinical observations, and to provide them with general meaning.

Following G. S. Klein (1976), Wallerstein (1988) distinguished between clinical and general theory. For him, clinical theory can be sufficiently anchored to the observable and empirically testable, while general theory constitutes the various metaphorical systems that the analyst adopts. However, it can be suggested that these metaphorical systems also cut across the domain of the 'observable' so that they are already present in the selection of what is described in the encounter between analyst and patient.

Although analysts of all schools in the British Society regard the Baby Observation Seminars as fundamental to the training of candi-dates, their reasons for doing so differ (see Brafman, 1988). Some feel that the seminars teach candidates to sustain a specific position as observers during the observation hours, to make detailed notes and to discuss them in a group. Others value the seminars as tools for estab-lishing the validity of basic psychoanalytic assumptions by means of observational data (an example of this approach is contained in Miller *et al.*, 1989).

These different conceptual frameworks are readily identified in the varying interpretations of the baby observations (interpretations given to the same baby observation by analysts belonging to different schools of thought have been documented in two sets of commentar-ies in the *British Journal of Psychotherapy*, in 1986–1987 (Vol. 3, No. 1) and 1993 (Vol. 9, No. 4)). Observations are guided by their theoretical perspectives, which in turn are themselves present in the very way the data are described. What one observes is influenced by what one's theoretical beliefs have made one sensitive to. Thus I notice that in my own notes I concentrated heavily on the interaction between the mother and her two children, and on the way I perceived and experienced my position in relation to these interactions, rather than on descriptions of the baby only (in contrast to the emphasis implicit in the title of the seminars, i.e. 'baby observation').

The central aim of this chapter is to examine one aspect of one baby's development in his interaction with his mother. At 10 months Ben refused to put anything, including food, in his mouth on his own. He also started to bite his left thumb and to bang his head against the wall. In order to attempt to understand these phenomena I look at some aspects of the baby's early development in his interaction with his mother. I will also review some of the issues raised in the literature about the timing of the differentiation between the self and the other, and about the varying complexity attributed to the psyche of babies in the first year of life.

Ben was Mary and John Sullivan's second child. Nira, their first child, was three years old at the time of Ben's birth. Mary had a normal hospital delivery. The Sullivans were in their early thirties, and Mary's parents lived in the same area and provided emotional and practical support. Mary's position in her own family of origin was similar to Ben's. John's parents lived abroad.

Mary usually received me in what she called 'the children's room', which was next to the kitchen and contained a sofa, an armchair, the television, a toy cabinet, a round table and several chairs. It was usually very neat and tidy, with only a few toys at a time out of the cabinet.

The Sullivans seemed to be comfortably off. They had two consecutive au-pairs during the period I visited them. I never met anyone else, although Mary spoke to her mother on the telephone several times during my visits. I met John only a few times during the year in which I did my observations.

The first two months: defence against 'primary maternal preoccupation'

The first two months of visits were dominated by Mary's plan to settle Ben into a routine so that she could go back to work. Mary spoke about this a great deal. She had indeed gone back to work two weeks after Ben was born, on a part-time basis, as a business consultant. When her mother could not come to look after the children, she left them with the au-pair. During the first few weeks Mary complained that Ben cried too much during the night and sometimes referred to the fact that she had let him cry, until he had stopped by himself.

After the observation session when Ben was 2½ weeks old I wrote the following notes:

I was on my own in the sitting room. Nira had joined her mother in the kitchen. After some five minutes I heard Ben through the baby alarm. He grizzled for a few seconds, went quiet, grizzled again for longer, stopped and then erupted full scale. Mary was in the kitchen and Nira started to repeat the sounds that Ben was making. Mary finished preparing the coffee, brought it into the sitting-room, arranged some small tables, one next to me and the other next to the armchair where she was going to sit. She went back into the kitchen where she stayed for another five minutes. Ben carried on crying at full blast. She then came back into the living room saying she was going to fetch Ben. Ten minutes had gone by since Ben had started to cry. I wondered about timing and thought that different mothers might have different levels of tolerance towards crying babies. I felt that Ben had been crying for a long time.

Mary came back and sat in the armchair with Ben on her right shoulder while she arranged a nappy underneath him. She talked to me all the time. Ben did not stop moving and grizzling, his movements seemed jerky, stretching and bending his legs, and curling his back. Mary said that at this stage it was very difficult to understand what they wanted, that it would take about six weeks to understand what it was that he wanted. She also said that it would take that amount of time for him to settle into a routine.

About five minutes later, she looked down at Ben, saying 'You are not really settling down, are you?' She put him down on his back in her lap and pulled her jumper up. Ben was crying and had his arms open, moving them around. She put him to her left breast. Her left arm was around him, without fully encircling him, whereas her right hand was on her nipple. She partially helped him to find the nipple, which after one miss he did. He was immediately calm and suckled for a few minutes. She said that his pattern was erratic, for a couple of nights he had not settled at all after an hour so she left him crying. She set the baby alarm and went to sleep so he must have stopped crying at some point. She noticed Ben had stopped sucking and took him away from the breast, and put him against her right shoulder. He started to grizzle again . . .

Mary said that hers was not a child-orientated house. She liked raising children but found 'looking after them boring, not intellectually stimulating and that was why she had to go back to work'.

Throughout the first two months Mary spoke to me about her plans to put Ben on a schedule as soon as possible so that she could have time for herself. She planned to wean him at the end of three months. She spoke almost frantically about this subject, which suggested to me a state of anxiety. A contradiction seemed to exist between the content of her speech and the actual process. If Ben was at the centre of her preoccupations there was also, however, a defensive struggle against such centrality. A conflict seemed to exist between Mary's conscious desire to be a 'good enough mother' and to be involved with her baby, as opposed to her fear of being overwhelmed by him. The attempted solution seemed to lie in an appearance of competence, through pragmatic and business-like behaviour. She breastfed Ben, but did not play or engage with him while breastfeeding. She held him in her arms but her arms did not completely encircle him. She did not seem to pick him up a great deal during the first two months.

Winnicott (1958) characterized the end of pregnancy and the first few weeks after birth as a state of heightened sensitivity in the mother, which enables her to adapt to her infant's needs. By adapting sufficiently, the baby's life is disturbed very little by reactions to impingement, allowing him to 'go on being'. The environment for Winnicott is therefore not merely outside the individual but is part of the individual's own personal development (1945). Stern has called this state 'affective attunement' (1985).

I would suggest that Mary was attempting to find a *defence against 'primary maternal preoccupation'*. Defence is being defined here as a set of operations that aim to reduce and eliminate any change liable to threaten the integrity and stability of the bio-psychological individual (Freud, A., 1937: 103). The individual defends himself against any situation that is unpleasurable for the ego because it is incompatible with and might disturb his equilibrium.

At four weeks Mary put Ben 'on the clock' so that he was fed every four hours. At five weeks Mary thought that Ben was putting on weight nicely and was growing fast. She had an appointment at the clinic the following week and said that if her impressions were confirmed she was going to begin to wean him slowly. She had plans to start during the night, by giving him water when he woke and cried. She said, at the time, that Ben was not going to like it and he would learn 'that it was not worth waking up for that'. At the next observation Mary told me that Ben had spat the water at her during the night but that he would slowly learn. Mary did not feel she could rely on Ben's capacity to communicate his needs to her. Already at that stage Mary expressed the view that if it was up to him, Ben would not stop feeding. She was afraid of a greedy baby.

At six weeks a change seemed to be taking place. Mary was more relaxed and she talked less frantically during the observation hour. By eight weeks the difference was more noticeable and Mary seemed to be able to enjoy the interaction with her baby, and to feel better when her baby responded to her. Perhaps at that point he began to be able to make her feel a good mother. The following observation at eight weeks demonstrates the shift:

Ben was against his mother's right shoulder, was making jerky movements and seemed to be uncomfortable. Mary started to speak to him gently, looking at him. Ben looked in the direction of her face and seemed to be responding to her by making small noises. He seemed to want to engage her in a conversation. Mary carried on speaking to him and her talking seemed to have an effect on his discomfort.

At 9½ weeks Ben was sleeping right through the night and Mary had started to give him powdered milk twice a day in a bottle. By three months, Mary had weaned Ben. She started to describe him as a good baby, much better than Nira had ever been. But even then, at 10 weeks, she referred to the fact that on the previous day Ben had cried for three consecutive hours in his rocker but had eventually stopped. She said, 'How can you know why they are crying?' Later she said to me she did not know *what you could possibly learn from babies* because they did not do anything apart from sleeping, staying awake and feeding. She said that in the first year you really just have to provide for the baby's needs and you just feed them, bathe them and change nappies, whereas after one year you have to start teaching them how to be polite and say please and that someone's character is formed from that moment on. She said it was all in the hands of the mother and that it was a big responsibility that people did not appreciate.

In the debate about the relative importance of the psychic and the somatic in the first year of life, Mary's approach was certainly heavily biased in favour of the dominance of the soma, as if attempting to deny any emotional relationship with her baby.

It was also interesting to note that at 11 weeks Mary had forgotten the anxiety she had felt during the first two months of Ben's life. Her current feelings were taken to be the feelings she had had since he was first born. Her *defence against* 'primary maternal preoccupation' was no longer present in conscious memory. As her baby became less dependent on her, Mary seemed to be able to enjoy him more. Her physical contact with Ben also increased and she encircled him more in her arms when she bottle-fed him. She always held him with her right arm and the bottle with the left so that Ben's left side was against her body. This position seemed later to have left an imprint in Ben's relationship with his own body.

Three to six months: beginnings of a body schema

My observations during the period between three and six months suggest the beginnings of the development of a body schema (Sandler, 1962). Sandler derived this concept from both Freud, in his remark that 'the Ego is first and foremost a body ego' (Freud, 1923: 27), and Henry Head (Sandler, 1962). Henry Head suggested that 'the individual, during the course of his development, constructs an inner model or schema of his own body, based on the integration of numerous bodily experiences, particularly of sensations that relate to the body's posture' (Sandler, 1962: 48). Sandler expanded the concept of body schema into self-schema, or self representation, i.e. 'the mental model that develops on the basis of sensory experience' (1962: 50). He suggests that the infant only progressively develops an internal schematic representation of himself and of objects in the outside world.

When Ben was four months old he seemed to get more involved with external objects when they were on his right-hand side, whereas when he turned towards the left he closed his eyes and made sucking movements. The external world then seemed to disappear for him. This differential orientation towards what I, the observer, describe as right and left sides might be viewed as the beginnings of an internal body schema.

The following is an example of one of the observations where this differential orientation was noted:

The front door bell rang and Ben's body shook as if he had had a fright; he was sitting on the rocker. He held his arms open, his hands were clenched and he was still for a moment. He then carried on kicking, Mary went out of the room and Nira followed her. The caller was a builder with whom Mary started to discuss work she wanted done. For the last 15 minutes of the observation she was outside the room and I stayed with Ben. After his shock, Ben turned towards the left where Mary had been sitting and stared for a while at the place where she had been. He then turned his head past me without stopping to look at me and looked at the window outside on the far right. Next he turned his attention to the coloured plastic rings in front of him and started to bang them. He carried on paying special attention to the red plastic ring at the far right-hand side. He then turned his head round again towards the left. His eyes were wide open. His head was resting on the rocker. He started to produce sucking movements with his mouth and tongue. He did that for a few seconds, then stopped sucking and his head remained in this position. He then turned his head round to the right and again started to bang his fist on the coloured rings on the right and then repeated the movement of his head, turning it round to the left, looking at the small teddy bear next to his eyes on the rocker and making sucking movements with his mouth.

In this observation Ben only made sucking movements when his head was turned towards the left. I was struck by the persistence in the differential orientation between the parts of his visual world. Ben seemed to engage more with external objects on his right-hand side, while the left was reserved for sucking movements. Later, he started to suck his left thumb only. At this point my notes also describe Mary bottle-feeding him on her right arm. Ben's left side was therefore the side that was in contact with his mother's body at feeding times.

This differential orientation was still present a few months later, when Ben started to suck and bite his left thumb only. Obviously one could also suggest that all children progressively develop a differentiation between right and left. There is, however, also the implication that Ben's interaction with his mother, in her mothering process, had an impact on the development of his body schema and that his sucking movements to the left contain a memory of this physical and emotional process.

Eight to ten months: aggression and regression

When Ben was eight months old a series of changes took place. Mary completely stopped giving him the bottle and started to feed him from a cup. Nira started to go to school every morning and Mary took her each day, leaving Ben alone with the new au–pair. At this time, Mary pointed out to me that Ben only sucked his left thumb, so much so that it was sore. When I arrived each week, Mary was taking Nira to school and I was alone with Ben for about 15 minutes, with the au–pair in the house. Mary had insisted that I should not change my observation time. I then observed that Ben was actually biting his thumb when Mary was not there. He would bite it and grizzle softly, as if the grizzling was self-comforting.

At 10 months, I noticed that Ben rocked himself back and forth when Mary was not in the room and banged his head against the wall when she was present. During one specific observation, when Mary had not yet returned from taking Nira to school, I felt Ben was feeling specially lonely and distressed. He was sitting on the floor, biting his left thumb and rocking his body, while looking through the open door into the garden. I was in the room and he seemed not to be aware of my presence. He started to cry as soon as Mary walked into the room.

The following observation took place a week later:

10 months: Ben was standing in the kitchen, supporting himself by holding a small table and playing with a toy car. He was circling the wheel of the car with his hands and making some humming sounds. He was alone in the kitchen while the au-pair was cleaning the small room. When he saw me he looked at me and after a few seconds he smiled and extended his right arm towards me. I leaned down and touched his hands and said, 'Hello Ben', before sitting down. He smiled very broadly and stood there smiling at me. A few minutes later Mary walked into the kitchen saying, 'Hello Rosine, how are you?' She was very tanned, wore summer clothes and was smiling broadly. Ben started to cry as soon as he saw her and Mary responded by saying, 'It's alright, I'm back. It's alright, I'm here'. She was coming in and out with some shopping and

171

Ben left the car with which he had been playing, stood up and then sat down on the floor and started crawling after her. After a while she came back into the kitchen and started putting her groceries away and said to Ben 'I'll be with you in a moment. I won't give you a cuddle now otherwise I won't be able to do anything else'. She carried on putting things away and Ben looked at her. When she disappeared from sight, he started to cry again. He then crawled in the direction she had gone until she came back into the kitchen. Then he sat on the floor with his back towards the wall and looked at her with his left thumb in his mouth. He kept banging his head against the wall.

After a while Mary started to say that the fact that Ben did not put anything into his mouth concerned her. She said that he only put his left thumb in his mouth and nothing else. She said that when they were in the garden the other day a friend of hers had seen him picking up things from the floor and had been worried about it. Mary had told her not to worry because Ben would not put anything in his mouth, he had never done so. She said that he played with toys; he grabbed them, he looked at them but he would not put them in his mouth. If any food fell down on the chair while he was eating, he would not pick it up but would happily wait for someone to give it to him. He loved food, she said, and yet he was not prepared to put it in his mouth himself. She did not know what it meant and was going to ask her GP at her next visit at the end of the month. After a while I asked her what she made of it and she said that she thought perhaps Ben had a disturbance in one of his motor skills and that he was not developing properly. I asked her which one that would be and she said that she did not know, it was either his taste or his hands but she was not sure. She said that he enjoyed his food, however, so she was not sure what the reason could be. She said that he would always eat his food very happily, that he absolutely adored food and would take food from anyone but would not pick up food himself if it dropped. I think she sensed my interest in the subject and said, 'Oh I will show you' and went into the kitchen to fetch a long biscuit that she put in Ben's right hand. Ben looked at it and waved it a bit and did not do anything else with it. Mary said to me 'You see, he won't put it in his mouth and yet he knows it is food'. She took the biscuit out of Ben's hand and put it in his mouth. Ben opened his mouth and leaned his face forwards so that he could bite it. He ate a bit of it and Mary said: 'You see, he doesn't do it'.

She left the room and Ben then looked at his hand and at the biscuit.

172

Some bits of it fell on the floor. Ben looked at me as if he was going to cry and I smiled at him. He looked again at the biscuit and then, after about two minutes, very slowly, he leaned his head forward towards his hand, opened his mouth and put the biscuit inside. I kept very still and just looked at him. He did it again and chewed a bit and then did it again, By this time the biscuit was very wet and was dissolving in his hands. Mary came back into the room at that point and looked at Ben. She said, 'I can't believe it, this is a real first, he has never done it before'. She then said that she had tried a few times before to teach him how to do it but he had never done it before. When he looked at her Ben started to cry and let the biscuit fall to the floor. He picked up a bit and looked at her, crying, and Mary said 'It's ten months now, Ben, it's about time you learned to do it yourself'. She then said it was all very messy and brought a piece of cloth from the kitchen and cleaned up. Ben looked around as if he was still looking for the bits of biscuit while Mary finished cleaning.

This observation raises important issues about the role of the observer in infant observations. It seemed to be because of my presence that Mary allowed Ben to keep the biscuit in his hands for longer than usual and it was in this context that he put it in his mouth. The observer's presence here had a specific consequence for the interaction being observed. This created a delicate moment in the observation as the mother might have felt that I would not believe her. There was also the question of competition, as it was in my presence that Ben did something Mary said he had not done before.

Mary perceived the phenomenon of Ben not putting anything in his mouth on his own as faulty development. My previous observations, however, contain many examples of Ben picking up things and taking them to his mouth. These previous observations allow me to suggest that his refusal now might be a regression. After a few months during which he did put things in his mouth, Ben stopped doing so at 10 months, which was also the period when he started to bite his thumb so intensely that it was constantly sore.

Regression is being used here as a descriptive term. It simply means a return 'from a point already reached to an earlier one' (Laplanche and Pontalis, 1985: 386). By refusing to put things in his mouth, Ben had regressed to an earlier stage of development that required his mother to feed him.

However, these observations also reveal Ben's anger and his attacks on himself. Thus, his thumb biting and head banging could be identified as expressions of aggression and anger, while the rocking of his body, as well as appearing to express his loneliness and sense of loss, also seemed to provide him with some holding and delineation of his boundaries (Emde, 1983). Ben used his own body to express his frustration and anger, containing his pain himself. It is possible to hypothesize that his thumb became both a continuation of and a substitute for the nipple.

In order to understand further Ben's refusal to put things in his mouth, his rocking backwards and forwards, his head banging and thumb biting, it is necessary to identify Ben's stage of development, the specific psychic structural changes that might have taken place and the complexity of the psychic mechanisms operating at this stage.

What should one emphasize: the mother, the child or the interaction?

Psychoanalytic constructions of the relationship between the newborn baby and the environment can perhaps be viewed along a continuum ranging from those who perceive an undifferentiated state in the baby at birth to those who perceive an undifferentiated state between mother and baby (hypothesizing from the baby's side of the experience) (see Hamilton, 1982). In the centre lie those analysts who perceive the baby as having a core sense of self and distinctiveness: Freud, Mahler and Kohut are located at the first extreme of the continuum; Winnicott, with his statement that 'there is no such thing as a baby', is at the other end; and Stern occupies the middle ground. Klein suggests that the baby, at birth, has a rudimentary self and is in touch with unconscious phantasies that are largely constitutional and precede experience. In 1930 Klein said that 'the child earliest-reality is wholly phantastic' (p.221).[2]

For Freud, the object is not present from the beginning, but must be created. Within the drive model, the object is created by the drives (Greenberg and Mitchell, 1983: 42) out of the experience of drive satisfaction and frustration. It is perhaps not a contradiction to suggest that a model that postulates the undifferentiated state of the baby at birth must also postulate interaction with the environment soon after birth. This is related to the role given to experience in Freud's formu-

---

[2] It has also to be stated that the specific positions held by these authors are more complex than indicated. Winnicott, for instance, does at times suggest that the 'self' is a core that someone is born with.

lations. The organization of memory traces in the psychic apparatus results from a series of pain–pleasure experiences.

The original model postulated by Freud of the undifferentiated state of the infant is not held by psychoanalysts in the three groups in the British Society, all of whom emphasize object-seeking and not only pleasure-seeking in infancy. The contributions of Kleinian psychoanalysts, and findings in the field of developmental psychology, have consistently pointed to a more sophisticated infant than had previously been allowed by most psychoanalysts. Stern, for instance, has stated that 'infants begin to experience a sense of emergent self from birth. They are predestined to be aware of self-organising processes. They never experience a period of total self/other undifferentiation' (1985: 10). Nevertheless there are still important differences in terms of what is attributed to babies in their first year of life by the main thinkers in psychoanalysis.

Spitz has emphasized the extreme vulnerability of the child at birth and its dependence on the mother (1965). The major part of the first year, when the infant is helpless and the mother provides for all his needs, is dedicated to the effort to survive. The various structures are progressively differentiated through the process of maturation. It is in the 'dialogue' between mother and child that the latter gradually builds an image of his world (*ibid*: 42). Sandler and Rosenblatt (1962) have suggested, through their concept of the 'representational world', that in order to know what is 'outside', the child has to transform 'raw sensory data into meaningful percepts' (1962: 61). 'Initially the child's representational world contains only the crudest representations of pleasure and unpleasure . . . and it is only gradually that the infant learns to distinguish self from not self, and self from object in his representational world' (*ibid*: 63).

For Klein, in contrast, the unconscious is there from the start and has specific contents, namely the unconscious phantasies. According to Isaacs, 'Phantasy is the mental corollary, the psychic representative of instinct. And there is no impulse, no instinctual urge, which is not experienced as (Unconscious) phantasy' (1943: 11). These are perceived by her as constitutional and universal, particularly derived from the death instinct. 'I have, for many years held the view that the working of the death instinct within gives rise to the fear of annihilation and that this is the primary cause of persecutory anxiety' (Klein, 1952b: 61). The early internal objects have a harsh and primitive nature, derived from constitutional envy. 'I consider that envy is an oral-sadistic and anal-sadistic expression of destructive impulses, operative from the beginning of life, and that it has a constitutional basis' (Klein, 1957: 176). The external environment has a fundamental role in the amelioration of persecutory anxiety. Here lies its import-ance, as emphasized by Klein: 'The fact that a good relation to its mother and to the external world *helps the baby to overcome its early paranoid anxieties* throws a new light on the importance of the earliest experiences (1952b: 98, my italics).[3]

Both Klein's and Freud's work contain conceptualizations of the *primal infant*. I would like to suggest this concept to emphasize the notion of the infant as constructed by a specific psychoanalytic framework.[4]

I would argue that Klein's theory contains an inherent contradic-tion. Although she postulates that object relations are the basic stuff of human experience, because Klein's primal infant comes with a ready-made 'luggage' of phantasies, it is, in the final analysis, less dependent on the real object for the constitution of its psyche. The introjection

---

[3] Throughout the various phases of Klein's work there are numerous references to the importance of the life instincts that counteract the strength of the death instincts, and to the continual process of interaction of projection and introjection in the development of the infant. Thus, in 1946 she says: 'The introjection of the good object, first of all the mother's breast, is a precondition for normal development' (p. 9). In 1948: 'An optimum in the interaction between libido and aggression implies that the anxiety arising from the perpetual activity of the death instinct, though never eliminated, is counteracted and kept at bay by the power of the life instinct' (p. 42). In 1952: '. . . processes of introjection and projection are an essential factor in diminishing persecutory and depressive anxiety' (1952b: 88). An analysis of Klein's views on psychic life throughout all of her work, however, indicates that the death instinct is dominant. Thus, 'the struggle between life and death instincts already operates during birth and accentuates the persecutory anxiety aroused by this painful experience. It would seem that this experience has the effect of making the external world, including the first external object, the mother's breast, appear hostile' (1948: 31). In 1952: '. . . a mitigation of the fear of the bad object by the trust in the good one and depressive anxiety only arise in fleeting experiences' (1952b: 71). It is only with Bion and his concepts of the container and contained that a theory of development and the effect of the object on the mind of the infant is more explicitly formulated. In Bion's conceptual framework the environment will have a more defined role. I also think that it is only in the work of contemporary Kleinian thinkers that a different equilibrium between the two types of instincts comes to the fore (see Yorke, 1973; Spillius, 1988).

[4] Stern has suggested the distinction between the 'observed infant' and the 'clinical infant' (1985: 13–14). Whereas the former is subject to observation, the latter is the result of a process of reconstruction by the analyst. The clinical infant 'is made up of memories, present re-enactments in the transference, and theoretically guided interpretations' (*ibid*: 11). The concept of the *primal infant*, as suggested in this chapter, lies at a different level of abstraction as it refers to the infant as proposed by a specific theory, as it can be compre-hended by reading the text (e.g. what Freud and Klein say in their writings).

of the object can only modify unconscious phantasies that already exist. In Klein's framework the unconscious is there from the beginning (Bleichman, 1985). Freud's primal infant, in contrast, is more dependent on the real object for the constitution of its psyche. As I will argue in the next section, in Freud's formulations the psychic apparatus is not 'ready' at birth, but is constituted over time in the process of building up memory traces, based on the experiences of pleasure and pain, and in the differentiation between id, ego and superego. The unconscious, for Freud, is only accessible through its derivatives, in its connections with the system Pcs-Cs (Freud, 1915b,c).

There is no doubt that these differences have implications for how one explains phenomena in early infancy. We now return to the question raised at the beginning of this section: what should one emphasize, the mother, the baby or the interaction? How can we have access to Ben's experience of himself and of his relationship with his mother and others? In my attempt to understand Ben's early development, I have observed his interactions with his mother. My assumption was that through the pattern of repeated experiences, memories and affective states are created and reinforced giving rise to a representational world in the mind of the infant. I also attempted to look at Ben's mother's anxiety and conflicting feelings about him at different stages, outlining what I suggested was her defence against 'primary maternal preoccupation'. The important question thus becomes not whether it is the mother or the baby who should be emphasized, but what each contributes to the interaction. One can identify the way in which Mary had difficulties in giving her baby enough experience of 'illusion' during the first two months of his life (Winnicott, 1945: 152–153). But one can also speculate about the specific contribution that Ben brought to the interaction. This latter material seems to me to be more obviously speculative.

What is Ben's stage of psychic development when he starts biting his thumb, banging his head and refusing to put anything in his mouth on his own?

Since Freud and Abraham, psychoanalysts have discussed the paradigmatic importance of the oral phase in terms of both ego structure and character formation. Glover (1924) indicated that the oral stage moulds all subsequent object relations by fusing love and aggression

177

towards one and the same object. Similarly, Erikson (1950) regarded the mouth as the primary organ for initially conducting the crucial business of internalization. Gesell *et al.* (1949) indicated that early mouthing behaviour is a mode of comprehending the world, and Spitz (1965) suggested that the mouth is the 'cradle of perception' (see also Sandler and Dare, 1970). This view, however, has not been universally adopted. Stern (1985: 236) suggested that no organ or mode appears to have a special status in relation to the process of incorporation. The eyes and ears may perform a similar function to that of the mouth.

Hoffer (1949) argued that with the help of the hand the oral-sucking drive undergoes a transformation from an instinctual demand to an ego-controlled activity. The 'mouth-self' is the earliest form of self-organization. Indeed, as indicated earlier, at 3½ months, when his mother disappeared from his field of vision, Ben initiated sucking movements with his mouth, with his face turned towards the left. At five months this differential orientation became more established as Ben sucked only his left thumb. There was the beginning of the crystallization of a body schema (Sandler and Rosenblatt, 1962). Hoffer suggested that in the oral-sadistic phase, aggressive impulses are always drawn away from the body. It is primarily the pain barrier that protects the infant from turning his destructive instinct against his own self. Hoffer argued that the process of libidinization of the body grows into self-love. The infant who likes himself will not bite himself (1949: 54). Hoffer also stated that it is very rare for a child to bite his own hand and that the teeth are very rarely the cause of self-injury (1950).

At 10 months, however, Ben was attacking himself by biting his left thumb when his mother was absent, and banging his head in her presence. In Hoffer's term, Ben did not like himself. He was, in his attack on himself, using his own body to control his experience of frustration. There is a pattern of self-inflicted pain that alters 'normal' thresholds of pleasure and pain. What are, however, the connections between Ben's symptoms and the complexity of the psychic mechanisms in operation at this stage in his development? What could one understand about Ben's phantasy life and his inner world, and about his experience of his relationship with his mother?

Ben expressed a great deal of sadness, loneliness and even despair in the absence of his mother. His head banging and thumb biting seemed also to express anger and helplessness turned against his body, which functioned as a substitute or continuation for (not a symbol of) his mother. This behaviour represents rudimentary schemata of his previous experiences with his mother and is an expression of his internalization of these experiences.

Development, structuring and deferred action

As discussed in previous chapters in this book, Freud's conceptualization of the psychic apparatus postulates that distinct timings must be at work. The first concept of time in Freud's formulation is that of the evolution and development of the individual, both in terms of the biological development of the baby and the emergence of functions and behaviour patterns that result from exchanges between the organism and its environment. This is the notion of developmental continuity.

A second concept of time refers to the structuring of the individual and the distinction between the ego, the id and the superego. Freud (1923) suggested that at birth no ego exists. It is primary repression that institutes the separation between the id and the ego, between primary and secondary process that are, hereafter, regulated by different conceptions of time. Time in the unconscious is atemporal, and can only be accessed in terms of its derivatives in the system Pcpt-Cs.

The different timings in the id and the ego are thus inaugurated by repression. But when does repression occur? Here a third notion of time must be introduced. In 1926, Freud suggested that most of the repression that we deal with in our therapeutic work represents cases of repression by deferred action (après coup). It means that experiences, impressions and memory traces may be revised at a later date, when the individual reaches a new stage of maturation (Laplanche and Pontalis, 1985: 111). This concept implies, therefore, the notion of two different times between which there is no linear correlation (see also Lebovici and Soule, 1970; Green, 1979; Lebovici, 1985). In his analysis of the *Wolf Man*, Freud (1918) discussed how the neurosis was constructed in two time scales – it was the second time scale that determined the constitution of the phantasy and the choice of neurosis. It is not, therefore, a question of a linear, cumulative effect that could result in the symptom, but a reorganization of already existing memory traces related to a new stage of maturation (*ibid*). This notion rules out a linear determinism in Freud that would envisage nothing but the action of the past in the present, as it points out the relevance of the future in also reinterpreting the past. Moreover, in terms of the discussion in Chapter 6, what is at stake is also the role of sexuality, the erotic passivation in the relationship with the mother, which will be later evoked in an analysis. It is ultimately the evocation of the child-hood traumatic sexual scene that is at the centre of any analysis.

One can argue that there are differences in the way the psychoan-alytic literature perceives these various notions of time. The Baby Observation Seminars themselves follow the first notion of time (developmental continuity) more closely and merely speculate about the second (structuring). It is, however, only retrospectively, and at a much later stage, that one can refer to the third notion of time (après coup). Furthermore, because we are observing a baby for a period of only one year, we cannot know what the influence of future experiences will be.

The hypotheses formulated in this chapter to explain Ben's behaviour have been syntonic with the conceptual discussion. I have suggested that Ben's refusal to put anything in his mouth on his own can be conceptualized as a regression. This regression occurred at a point in his development, in the relationship with his mother, when he was able to use parts of his body actively (thumb biting, head banging). His behaviour indicated a registration of both current and earlier experiences of deprivation in the relationship with his mother. These earlier experiences were re-enacted and given meaning in the anger, pain and desolation that Ben seemed to demonstrate at this point in time. These experiences were not transformed through the relation-ship with his mother. Ben had to express and attempt to control them with his own body, in a pattern of self-inflicted pain. The thumb seemed to serve as a substitute for or continuation of the nipple, whereas the head banging also seemed to provide him with some delineation of boundaries. At this stage in his development, however, one cannot identify which elements of these experiences will be activated later in life (in terms of après coup) to become traumatic. Ben would not put anything into his mouth by himself, but what can we say about how this had become registered in his internal world and what kind of impact can one predict this might have on his capacity to libidinally invest in his internal objects? Following Kris (1956), Anna Freud (1952; 1958: 13) reaffirmed that the traumatic significance of an event is not fixed at the time of its occurrence. Rather, it is later events that will determine which experiences may gain significance as traumatic.

11

The infant and the infantile
On psychoanalytic research

Whether you can observe a thing or not depends on the theory which you use. It is the theory which decides what can be observed.

(A. Einstein)

Introduction

This chapter explores the differences between the notions of the infantile on the one hand, and the infant on the other. This distinction highlights epistemological differences about what constitutes the object of analytic investigation.

The infantile, according to Freud, is the child within the adult, which may be reached through a process of construction. In *The Rat Man*, Freud equated the infantile to the unconscious:

> The unconscious, I explained, *was* the infantile; it was that part of the self which had become separated off from it in infancy, which had not shared the later stages of its development, and which had in consequence become *repressed*.
>
> (1909b: 177)

The infant, in contrast, is observable in the process of the development of an individual. As discussed in the previous chapter, Stern proposed a distinction between the 'observed infant' and the 'clinical infant' (1985: 13–14). Whereas the former is subject to observation, the latter is the result of a process of reconstruction by the analyst. The clinical infant 'is made up of memories, present re-enactments in the transference, and theoretically guided interpretations' (*ibid*: 11).

The debates on the relationship between the infant and the infant-ile, and on what constitutes psychoanalytic research, have been heated in Britain. Two seminal encounters took place at University College London, one in 1997 between André Green and Daniel Stern, and the other in 2002 between Peter Fonagy and André Green. I was a discussant in the first of these encounters (Perelberg, 2000) and pre-sented a paper at the second. These two contributions are combined in this chapter.

When I mentioned to a friend, who is a psychoanalyst attached to the Paris Psychoanalytical Society, that a debate between Green and Stern was taking place in London, he asked me: 'Who is Stern?' It reminded me of how one of the visitors to our home after one of my husband's fieldwork trips to far away places asked us about the music we were playing. In response to our reply, he asked: 'Who is Mozart?' He was a cultivated man in his own culture but this response drew our attention once more to the fact that we can all be ethnocentric and treat our own culture as universal. Whilst the Jesuits attempted to convert the Indians in Brazil so that they could become real human beings, the Indians were drowning Jesuits in order to verify whether they had souls. Humanity ceased at the borders of the tribe. By the way, our guest had never seen olives before either. It was his first visit to the West.

What took place in the two encounters at University College London was a clash between different psychoanalytic cultures, 'differ-ent ways of thinking', in Green's terms. On the one hand, Green suggests that 'no one single major discovery for psychoanalysis has emerged from research' (2000c: 24). He adds: 'There is a neglect in most of the investigations of the specificity of what is intrapsychic and unconscious, and an underestimation of the parameters of the analytic situation related to the concept of the setting' (*ibid*: 24). On the other hand, Stern suggests throughout his work that he has been able to charter some of the uncharted territory of infancy. Green, for his part, warns us: it is important not to confuse the infantile (in all of us) with the infant (1979). In his paper 'L'enfant modèle', Green presents the idea that observation studies aim to find visible in the child what is invisible in the adult when the structure of the child has been derived from the knowledge of the structure in the adult. That which has been repressed cannot be observed (1979: 30). Green's thesis is that psychoanalysis is incompatible with observation. Observation cannot tell us anything about intrapsychic processes that characterize the true nature of subjective experience. These words are echoed by Diatkine, who also states that no new knowledge has been brought to psychoanalysis by direct observation (1979: 61).

Green also asks how one can move from the procedures of experimentation to processes of thinking (2000c). Godelier (1958), Canguilhem (1979), and D'Or (1988) all support this view that the essential difficulty is to pretend that empirical evidence is sufficient when one is enquiring into the process of thinking itself. Canguilhem reminds us that behaviourism is not a science: it is a *philosophical position*. One point seems to be clear: representations cannot be inferred by observation. They can only be inferred by other representations. In the first debate and in the subsequent discussions, the distinction was made between research on infants and the Baby Observation Seminars, a formal requirement of much of the training in Britain.

At the outset Stern (2000) claims that infant observations can never prove or disprove a clinical or theoretical tenet of psychoanalysis. This would be something that Green is in agreement with.

Stern goes on to ask whether infant observation is indirectly relevant to psychoanalysis. He suggests that infant observations add to our *common sense* view of who a baby is. His aim is that of 'imagining' the infant's subjective world and finding a way of representing his relational world. In another paper Stern (1995) affirms that one cannot know the nature of the infant's subjective experience; we can only observe the interpersonal events that transpire between infant and mother.

Stern (2000) raises the following point: can an experience be structured during the very moment in which it is being lived? He brings in the example of music, suggesting that 'the infant experiences his world in units of patterned flows of feeling that last seconds'. Stern designates these as 'vitality contours'. They are more like musical phrases or feelings in flux that cannot be captured or even imagined through a single note. 'For example, a rush of anger or joy, a sudden flooding of light, an accelerating sequence of thoughts . . . can all feel like these "rushes" ' (2000: 85–86).

The assumption is that, like musical phrases, these contours are structured as they are being experienced, just as when we listen to music we capture the form of a phrase while we hear it. It is not, Stern suggests, structured après coup, even though its perceived structure can be modified in the light of later musical phrases.

The analogy with music, however, may lead us to another view. In his monumental series of volumes on the analysis of myths in South America, Lévi-Strauss suggests that 'one cannot translate music into *anything other than itself*' (1971: 578). The significative function of music cannot be reduced to anything that might be expressed verbally. Lévi-Strauss further suggests that it is the audience that invests music with one or various virtual meanings, and it is the listener who is compelled to make up for the absent meaning. The listener attributes meaning to the music in terms of his or her own previous experiences.

Meaning is thus ultimately produced by interaction between the listener and the music. This analogy allows us to think that there is a meaning that is produced by the interaction between mother and baby that does not therefore relate to 'what is going on in the baby's mind', which is by definition unknowable and unreachable or, to use Lévi-Strauss's analogy of music, is irreducible to verbal understanding. This perspective is radically different from that which stresses the mother as the interpreter of her baby's behaviour. When the mother reinterprets the baby's feelings and thoughts this is not merely an act of translation, it also produces meaning. This view embraces the essential aspect of the mother's state of mind in the constitution of the child's sense of his own mind.

In discussing Stern's work Green points to the confusion between the *infantile* (the infantile in us) and the *infant*. Our true object as psychoanalysts is the infant in the adult, which has very little to do with the question: what really happened to the infant? The infant remains intact in the adult, it is childhood that has been interiorized and discovered by psychoanalysis in the analysis of the transference. It is characterized by the absence of the real child and, as discussed in the previous chapter, can only be comprehended après coup. Although in the account of the Wolf Man's infantile neurosis Freud (1909b) attempts to reconstruct what had *happened* in the Wolf Man's infancy and early childhood, in the progression of his work Freud emphasizes the process of construction rather than that of reconstruction. The specific object of psychoanalysis, as Green reminds us, is the unconscious, which one can reach only by approximations, this 'other thing' in Freud's formulations, forever an 'internal foreign body', in the words of Laplanche (1999). The 'real' child has been lost, and one has access in the consulting room only to memories that have been invested with phantasy. Even so, as Green also reminds us, 'mnemic reverberations' are never related to one specific situation only (Green, 2000c: 71).

Pontalis (1979) has also indicated that all the Freudian concepts (regression, fixation, repetition, repression, transference) in a sense refer to the active survival of the child within. He adds that the analysis of children cannot give any indication of the 'birth' of the unconscious or of repression (*ibid*: 8). It is later in the analytic process that the past, après coup, is appropriated as a personal history.

Derivatives of the unconscious in the psychoanalytic encounter

I would like to give two examples of what, to my mind, constitutes the 'raw data' of an analytic session, of the process whereby one gains access to the derivatives of the unconscious indirectly, through slips of the tongue, dreams and processes that are indeed not accessible to observation. The first is connected with an ordinary piece of work that nevertheless indicates the multi-layered sources of analytic understanding. The second has stronger reverberations derived from observational studies.

The first one is when Anna came in for the last session of the week. She was cheerful. After a long period in her analysis when I could not say anything that felt right to her, we had now been through a moderately good phase, and she was happy with our work.

She came in and as she sat on the couch and took off her shoes, her ring caught on her tights and she said: 'Shit'. She then proceeded to lie on the couch and to cheerfully tell me about recent events in her life. Then she told me about a dream. In the dream she was dictating a letter to a secretary, Miss Smith, and told her to 'have a slash'. A colleague of hers (I will call him John Frognal) was watching this scene in a benevolent way. My patient had the association of slash with a violent tear. Smith is a common name, the name of her cleaning lady. The associations to her colleague were that he is thoughtful and benevolent, but had recently commented that a mutual friend was going mad.

I was aware of the contrast between the cheerfulness and the 'shit', which had come from another scene. John was also the name of a comedian she had told me about during a previous session. In a comedy sketch that she had seen him perform, there was a party going on, and he kept cheerfully saying 'hello' to people as he met them and 'bastard' as he moved away from them. Two levels of experiences, the facade and the backstage, the conscious and the unconscious, the domains of reason and of the unreasonable, of madness. A binocular mode of thinking, Bion might suggest. All these thoughts and associations led to the interpretation that I formulated. Although my patient was pleased with our good work, there was a 'shit' or 'bastard' coming from another part of her mind, the very part that clamoured for our work to proceed. Concepts like reversal, projection, projective identification, repression, censorship, splitting and externalization might all come to mind now, which might account for the piece of work that related to an '*unreasonable part of her mind*', to use Peter Hobson's expression when he discussed Stern's paper in 1992 at the British Society.

My second case is Michael, a young male patient who came to analysis after a serious suicide attempt (the analysis of this patient is more fully presented in Chapter 3). He was blind for the first two years of his life, after which a series of operations enabled him to see. More than any other patient I have had in analysis, Michael made me conscious of the minute interactions between us in the consulting room. The rhythm of our contact frequently evoked in me thoughts about synchronicity and timing in interactions between mother and baby. He was as aware of my minor bodily movements as I was of his and I would often notice that in our bodily posture we were inclined towards each other.

I was often reminded of this patient when reading Stern (1985), Trevarthen (1977) and Brazelton *et al.* (1974). Their work evoked thoughts about a pace that should have been present in Michael's interactions with his mother as a small child. What I have in mind is related to what Stern has discussed in terms of the ways in which mothers 'tune in' to their babies (1985). This was a relationship where mother and baby could not hold each other with their eyes and where bodily and sound contact appeared to me to have been intense.

Some months into the analysis it became clear that for Michael there was also an enormous confusion between intimacy and sexuality. He alternated between omnipotent phantasies of having seduced me into being his analyst on the one hand and a terror of abandonment on the other. Several layers of material could be identified: the terrorized infant being cared for by a mother he could not see but could feel and hear, and the advent of genital sexuality that was superimposed onto that more primitive material. In adolescence Michael became filled with conscious phantasies of violence and in young adulthood he engaged in violent relationships with his girl-friends and peers. Through violence he attempted to exercise his mastery over a world that he experienced as frightening and senseless. Obviously I cannot go too deeply into what was a complex but rewarding treatment. My point here is that this example, to my mind, brings together contributions from the works of both Stern and Green. If some shapes and rhythms of a primitive mode of relating to the external object can be alluded to, meaning can only be derived après coup, after the emergence of symbolic representations and genital sexuality have retranslated earlier experiences.

Green reminds us that no research work on the infant has access to the complexity of the internal object and is therefore prey to the uncertainty of knowledge. For Stern it is behaviour that is at the centre of his research. Green (2000c) asks how it is that one can move to processes of thinking from the procedures of experimentation.

The kind of research that Stern is engaged in is so important because formal observations of infant behaviour may set limits on psychoanalytic speculations regarding infantile experience by specify-ing competencies possessed by the child at various stages and ruling out, as improbable, propositions that presume capacities outside the developmental timetable (Stern, 1985; Fonagy, 1996). The very few studies of outcome of babies observed in early infancy suggest that predictions only hold true in a very broad way (see Reid, 1997). The future reinterprets the past and the past has limited predictive validity. This point was reinforced by a research paper (Diem-Wille, 1997) demonstrating that most of the predictions made in the infant obser-vation seminars that the researcher looked at were not fulfilled when the 'babies' were revisited some years later.

Models of research in anthropology and psychoanalysis

At the 60th Congress of French-Speaking Societies, Widlocher pro-posed a distinction between two types of research in psychoanalysis: *psychoanalytic research* and *research about psychoanalysis* (2002; see also 1994). In the former, the clinical and theoretical psychoanalytic modes are utilized in order to establish models. In the latter, research about psychoanalysis, and other techniques are utilized, and it is the theory and practice of psychoanalysis itself that is questioned. In this line of enquiry it is the efficacy of psychoanalysis that is investigated. In the former, psychoanalysis is the *instrument of knowledge*, and in the latter it is the *object of knowledge*.

The first researcher in psychoanalysis was Freud himself. He utilized the clinical model of investigation, based on a single qualitative case study through which he constructed a theory of obsessional neurosis (based on his understanding of the Rat Man), of paranoia (based on the Schreiber case [1911]) and of hysteria. One can identify the way in which his case studies are understood through simultaneous study of structure and history. In the single case study, the aim is the understanding of the working of a functional structure. In each case, the structural approach is inseparable from the developmental approach. In this way, Freud constructed hypotheses about the successive stages that gave rise to the structure. This can be beautifully attested to through a detailed analysis of his case studies. In the process of studying several case studies, Freud constructed a 'family of cases', which led to models of psychopathologies (Perron, 1988). It was clinical investigation that allowed Freud to construct theoretical models.

> I have not always been a psychotherapist. Like other neuropathologists, I was trained to employ local diagnoses and electro-prognosis, and it still strikes me myself as strange that *the case histories I write should read like short stories* and that, as one might say, they lack the serious stamp of science. I must console myself with the reflection that the nature of the subject is evidently responsible for this, rather than any preference of my own. The fact is that local diagnosis and electrical reactions lead nowhere in the study of hysteria, whereas *a detailed description of mental processes such as we are accustomed to find in the works of imaginative writers* enables me, with the use of a few psychological formulas, to obtain at least some kind of insight into the course of that affection. Case histories of this kind are intended to be judged like psychiatric ones; they have, however, one advantage over the latter, namely an *intimate connection between the story of the patient's sufferings and the symptoms of his illness* – a connection for which we still search in vain in the biographies of other psychoses. (my italics)
>
> (Breuer and Freud, 1895: 160–161)

It is worth noting, at this point, the different ways in which this theory advanced in Freud's work. Sometimes he was led by the need to understand clinical material. Examples are the clinical discoveries of the 'negative therapeutic reaction', the 'unconscious sense of guilt' that led to the formulation of the structural model of the mind, and the analysis of his own dreams, which led to his statement (in a letter to Fliess) that he no longer believed that all the statements of his hysterical patients were necessarily related to real memories of abuse but represented wish fulfilment phantasies (in Masson, 1985).

At other moments, Freud's models were pushed 'forward' by contradictions derived from the theory itself. An example is the way in which the concept of narcissism, with its emphasis on the libidinal cathexis of the self, led to a potential collapse of the notion of conflict between the drives and required a reformulation of the theory of drives. This led to the postulation of the conflict between the life and death instincts.

In an attempt to give universal validity to his theories, Freud linked them to various aspects of culture, such as the history of ideas, Greek myths, literature, philosophy, linguistics, anthropology and neurology, in terms of the prevailing ideas of his time. The emphasis on the up-to-date knowledge of his time is not, however, strictly speaking accurate. For instance, Jones (1974) pointed out how, in spite of being familiar with Darwinism, Freud utilized Lamarckism to justify some of his ideas. This was not because of a lack of familiarity with contemporary systems of knowledge, but because Freud made selective use of existing concepts that he felt were best able to justify his own ideas. These wider aspects of culture were used as metaphors, in order to give depth or greater validity to the ideas that Freud was creating, discovering and constructing. Sometimes he allowed contradictory ideas to co-exist side by side in his own framework. He also kept returning to and revising his own expositions.

The theoretical tradition of building models on the basis of single case studies is familiar to social science, in sociology and especially in social anthropology.

Malinowski was the first anthropologist to elaborate a theory of participant observation. During the First World War he lived in the Trobriand Islands of the Pacific, studying the natives. In his book published in 1922, Malinowski stressed the importance of waiting for real events to occur in order to allow the anthropologist to discuss them with his informants, and observe their behaviour and discussions when dealing with those events. The aim — and here we are dealing with the second characteristic of anthropological work — is to reveal the points of view and opinions expressed by the natives themselves. These points of view, Malinowski stressed, are expressed by individuals as members of a specific society. They are shaped by tradition, customs and even the language itself.

Malinowski compared the subject of study to a long conversation taking place among the people with whom anthropologists live during their fieldwork. A long conversation where it is not only words that are exchanged but, from time to time, also things, animals, gestures and blows, even people. Nonetheless, language plays a dominant role.

From a collection of single case studies, anthropologists then construct ideas of structures, and similarities and differences between different types of societies, such as, differences and similarities between matrilineal and patrilineal societies, or between hunter-gatherers and agricultural societies.

Leach (1961) stated that the village he studied in Burma was not in any way 'typical' nor was it in any sense a statistically 'average' village. The numerical quantities that appear in various parts of his book are not generalized statistics, but particular figures that relate to a single place at a particular time (1961: 1). The same point has been made by many other anthropologists. Bott states: 'We should therefore like to make it clear that we are discussing only some families, not all families, or the family' (1957: 10).

Gluckman (1972, 1973) further developed the methodology of extended case studies, stressing that the anthropologist's task is to concentrate his or her attention on a series of incidents taking place among the same group of people. The analysis should focus on social dramas in which one can observe the behaviour and verbalizations of both individuals and groups. Gluckman suggested that social anthropology should perhaps abandon the idea of studying whole societies, and concentrate instead on the study of 'social fields'. He wanted to perceive how people manipulate their culture in different social situations and he was thus questioning the whole idea of a consistent and rigid cultural system. Instead, he pointed out contradictions and conflicts within that system. It is important to point out, however, that Gluckman was still interested in uncovering social morphology — i.e. both the shape in which these events took place and the shape created by these events.

In ground-breaking work as a social anthropologist, Bott (1957) interviewed 20 families in depth and distinguished between two types of conjugal roles that were associated with the network of relationships around the family. Her discovery was applicable to a range of social problems involving relationships between social groups and their environment. In the preface to her book *Family and Social Network*, Gluckman confessed guiltily how, when Dr Bott first presented her material to a seminar in anthropology in Manchester, she asked what she should do with all the material she had collected. He answered: 'Write a novel'. Her analysis of the material collected, in Gluckman's own words some 20 years later, gave rise to one of the most important studies in social anthropology. A model was derived in the process of analysis of this material collected from just 20 families. Interestingly, in her Introduction, Bott said: '*The contribution of this book must lie in its interpretations, not in the facts described. Most readers will be more or less familiar with the facts from their personal experience, and none of the things described here are very novel*' (Bott, 1957: 2).

My own doctoral fieldwork in London aimed to perceive how relationships between social roles within the family could be explored when one of its members is admitted to psychiatric hospital. I was inspired by Victor Turner's notion of 'social dramas' (1972, 1974) and suggested that the situations of crisis, when a member of a family is admitted to psychiatric hospital, could be understood as social dramas. My previous research in Brazil had led me to formulate the hypothesis that a crisis usually emerges when members of the family try to understand what is happening and decide how to cope with it (Perelberg, 1980, 1981). The idea underlying the project was that such crises provide privileged moments for studying rules that are usually submerged in the habits of everyday life. Furthermore, in the specific case of a crisis of mental illness amongst the type of population I studied, the wider society intervenes through the activities of psychiatrists, nurses and social workers. This enables us to perceive not only aspects of the articulation between the family and society but also, since these interventions may change the structure of the family itself, the patterns of expectations held by these agents towards the families.

The starting point of my research was the moment when a person entered a psychiatric ward. I then followed the process of diagnosis and conducted intensive interviews with all the members of the families that were involved in the crisis, visiting each household at least once a week. In each case my contact with the family was initiated as soon as possible after the patient was admitted to hospital. Since I spent almost all day in the hospital, I was, in most of the cases, actually present when admission occurred.

The examples above make it clear that the anthropological model of understanding is derived from case studies. Fieldwork is not an encounter between two or more subjectivities. A series of mediators appear between the anthropologist and his informants. The analysis made by the anthropologist at the end of fieldwork is not simply a description of what is 'out there' but a model built out of 'raw material'. Knowledge is a process of construction, which is not just based on the discovery of facts. The *anthropological fact* itself is constructed by the anthropologist.

Throughout this book I have indicated that Freud constructed a theoretical model derived from a family of cases. More specifically central to this book has been the Freudian model of time, which can be derived from the reading of Freud's work. My contention is that Freud constructs a complex model of time that includes both structure and development, based on his analysis of a 'family of single case studies'. It is by reading all his work that one can arrive at this complex conceptual structure (see also Perelberg, 2005). This model is not linear, but makes up a structure that includes repression, regression, repetition compulsion, return of the repressed, the timelessness of the unconscious, development and après coup.

Conclusions

In this chapter I have indicated the way in which psychoanalytic models may be viewed as part of a tradition in the social sciences and in social anthropology in particular, concerned with the case study and the derivation of models from a family of case studies. I took the example of Freud's notions of temporality to indicate how one can derive a model of time from Freud's work. The dominance of time in this model resides in the concept of après coup, taken as a 'psychoanalytic fact' (Perron, 1988; Rolland, 2005), constructed at the intersection of psychoanalytic techniques and praxis. This process of construction is familiar in the history of science.

At the November 2002 Congress at Unesco in Paris, Widlocher referred to psychoanalysis as a praxis of discovery, and conferences, publications, and seminars as playing the role of a third party, real or symbolic, to whom the psychoanalyst is accountable. This permanent dialogue with colleagues who share our vision of psychoanalysis, as well as with those who present a plurality of other perspectives, is essential to the positioning of psychoanalysis among the social sciences and humanities. In this chapter I have indicated that there are well-established models of knowledge within the social sciences, derived from single case studies, that have a great deal in common with psychoanalysis. From this perspective I examined the distinction between the infant (observable) and the infantile (in all of us).

Bachelard has described knowledge as a light that also always casts shadows (1999: 146). He adds that in scientific enquiry all knowledge is an answer to a question. If there is no question, there can be no scientific knowledge. When he took over the Chair of the History of Science at the University of Paris in 1940, until then dominated by the positivists, he put forward his revolutionary view of science, not as a phenomenon of experience, nor a process of registration, but as a process of construction. This also implies a vision of the scientist that is intrinsically related to the model that is constructed. In psycho-analysis, this vision is inextricably linked to the notion of the analyst's desire and unconscious in the process of investigation. It refers to the libidinal investment of the observer in his object of research. Kohon has suggested that 'all psychoanalytic theories are libidinal, created by the desire of the author' (1999: 156).

To write the history of a theory is to write the history of the hesitations of the scientist (Canguilhem, 1979). Bachelard suggests that the history of science is the history of thoughts; in order to derive the meaning of a concept one has to look at the context in which it is found (in Canguilhem, 1979: 177). The word is not the same as the concept. Knowledge of an object of knowledge is not achieved by the observation of this object only, but is mediated by the construction of a concept about this object (*ibid*: 184).

Psychoanalysis is firmly located in this vision of the world. Although Freud drew on contemporary knowledge, psychoanalysis is ultimately connected with his vision of human nature, establishing a substantive rupture with previous knowledge. The unconscious is fundamentally unknown and is reached through a process of construction. Freud was also permanently reviewing his own ideas, establishing epistemological ruptures within the body of his own theories (the various models of the mind that he proposed). To isolate any one aspect of his thinking is to ignore this constant process of elaboration and transformation.

References

Abraham, K. (1924) A short study of the development of the libido viewed in the light of mental disorders, in Abraham, K. (Ed.) *Selected Papers on Psychoanalysis.* London: Maresfield Reprints, 1979, pp. 303–311.

Aisenstein, M. (1993) Psychosomatic solution or somatic outcome: the man from Burma. *International Journal of Psycho-analysis* 74: 371–381.

Althusser, L. (1970) Marx's immense theoretical revolution, in Althusser, L. and Balibar, E. (Eds) *Reading Capital.* London: Verso, pp. 182–193.

Anzieu, D. (1987) *Freud's Self Analysis.* New York: International Universities Press.

Aulagnier, P. (1975) *La Violence de l'Interpretation.* Paris: Presses Universitaires de France.

Bachelard, G. (1999) *La Formation de l'Esprit Scientifique.* Paris: Libraries Philosophique J. Vrin.

Bachofen, J. J. (1967) *Myth, Religion and Mother Right.* London: Routledge & Kegan Paul.

Bateman, A. (1997) Narcissism and its relation to violence and suicide, in Perelberg, R. J. (Ed.) *Psychoanalytic Understanding of Violence and Suicide.* London: Taylor & Francis, pp. 109–123.

Bateson, G. (1973) *Steps to Ecology of the Mind.* St Albans: Paladin.

Bell, D. (2007) Existence in time: development or catastrophe? *Psychoanalytic Quarterly,* 75: 783–805. Also in Perelberg, R. J. (Ed.) (2007) *Time and Memory.* London: Karnac, pp. 65–84.

Beratis, S. (1984) The first analytic dream: mirror of the patient's neurotic conflicts and subsequent analytic process. *International Journal of Psycho-analysis,* 65: 461–469.

Bergson, H. (1990) *Matter and Memory.* New York: Zone Books.

Bion, W. R. (1967) Differentiation of the psychotic from the non-psychotic personalities, in *Second Thoughts*. London: Maresfield Library, pp. 43–62.

Bion, W. R. (1970) *Attention and Interpretation*. London: Tavistock Publications.

Bion, W. R. (1984) *Elements of Psycho-analysis*. London: Karnac.

Birksted-Breen, D. (1996a) Phallus, penis and mental space. *International Journal of Psycho-Analysis*, 77: 649–657.

Birksted-Breen, D. (1996b) *The Gender Conundrum: Contemporary Perspectives on Femininity and Masculinity*. London: Routledge/Institute of Psychoanalysis.

Birksted-Breen, D. (2003) Time and the *après-coup*. *International Journal of Psycho-Analysis*, 84: 1501–1515.

Bleger, J. (1967) Psycho-analysis of the psycho-analytic frame. *International Journal of Psycho-Analysis*, 48: 511–519.

Bleichman, S. (1985) A*ux Origines du Sujet Psychique*. Paris: Presses Universitaires de France.

Bloch, M. (1977) The past and the present in the present. *MAN*, 12: 278–292.

Bollas, C. (1987) *The Shadow of the Object: Psychoanalysis of the Unthought Known*. London: Free Association Books.

Bollas, C. (1993) *Being a Character: Psychoanalysis and Self Experience*. London: Routledge.

Bollas, C. (1996) Figures and their functions: on the oedipal structure of a psychoanalysis. *Psychoanalytic Quarterly*, 65: 1–20.

Bonaparte, M., Freud, A. and Kris, E. (1954) *The Origins of Psycho-Analysis: Letters to Wilhelm Fliess Drafts and Notes: 1887–1902*. London: Imago.

Botella, C. and Botella, S. (2005) The *Work of Psychic Figurability: Mental States without Representation*. Hove: Routledge/Institute of Psychoanalysis.

Bott, E. (1957) *Family and Social Network*. London: Tavistock Publications.

Bourdieu, P. (1963) The attitude of the Algerian peasant towards time, in Pitt Rivers, J. (Ed.) *Mediterranean Countryman*. Paris: Recherches Mediter-ranéennes, pp. 55–73.

Bourguignon, A., Cotet, P., Laplanche, J. and Robert, F. (1989) *Traduire Freud*. Paris: Presses Universitaires de France.

Brafman, A. (1988) Infant observation. *International Review of Psycho-Analysis*, 15: 45–59.

Brazelton, T. B., Koslowski, B. and Main, M. (1974) The origins of reciprocity: the early mother–infant interaction, in Lewis, M. and Rosenblum, L.A. (Eds) *The Effect of the Infant on its Caregivers*. London: Wiley Interscience.

Brenman-Pick, I. (1985) Working through in the counter-transference, in Spillius, E. (Ed.) *Melanie Klein Today: Mainly Technique*. London: Routledge/Institute of Psychoanalysis, pp. 34–47.

Bressler, B. (1961) First dream in analysis: their relationship to early memories and the pre-Oedipal mother. *Psychoanalytical Review*, 48: 60–82.

Breton, A. (1969) *Manifestoes of Surrealism*. Michigan: University of Michigan Press.

Breuer, J. and Freud, S. (1893) Studies on hysteria. *Standard Edition*, 2: 1–323.

Breuer, J. and Freud, S. (1895) Studies on hysteria (1893–1895). *Standard Edition*, 2: 1–309.

Brierley, M. (1932) Some problems of integration in women. *International Journal of Psycho-Analysis*, 13: 433–448.

Britton, R. (1995) Psychic reality and unconscious belief. *International Journal of Psycho-Analysis*, 76: 19–23.

Britton, R. (1999) *Belief and Imagination*. London: Routledge/Institute of Psychoanalysis.

Britton, R. (2003) Hysteria: the erotic countertransference, in Britton, R. (Ed.) *Sex, Death and the Superego – Experiences in Psychoanalysis*. London: Karnac, pp. 7–26.

Bronstein, C. (2002) Borges, immortality, and The Circular Ruins. *International Journal of Psycho-Analysis*, 83: 647–660. Also in Perelberg, R. J. (Ed.) (2007) *Time and Memory*. London: Karnac, pp. 129–149.

Campbell, D. (1995) The role of the father in a pre-suicide state. *International Journal of Psycho-Analysis*, 76: 315–323. Also in Perelberg, R. J. (Ed.) (1997) *Psychoanalytic Understanding of Violence and Suicide*. London: Routledge, pp. 73–86.

Canguilhem, G. (1979) *Ideologie et Rationalite dans l'Histoire des Sciences de la Vie*. Paris: Librairie Philosophique J. Vrin.

Casement, P. (1985) *On Learning from the Patient*. London: Tavistock Publications.

Chasseguet-Smirgel, J. (1970) *Female Sexuality*. London: Maresfield Library.

Chasseguet-Smirgel, J. (1976) Freud and female sexuality: the consideration of some blind spots in the exploration of the 'Dark Continent'. *International Journal of Psycho-Analysis*, 57: 275–286.

Chasseguet-Smirgel, J. (1986) *Sexuality and Mind*. London and New York: New York University Press.

Cooper, A. M. (1988) Our changing views of the therapeutic action of psychoanalysis: comparing Strachey and Loewald. *Psychoanalytic Quarterly*, 57: 15–27.

Cooper, M. (1987) Changes in psychoanalytic ideas: transference interpretation. *Journal of the American Psychoanalytic Association*, 35: 77–98.

Cosnier, J. (1990) Les vicissitudes de l'identité, in Lebovici, S., Alléon, A.-M. and Morvan, O. (Eds) *Devenir 'Adulte'?*. Paris: Presses Universitaires de France.

Cournut, J. (1975) Névrose du vide in figures du vide. *Nouvelle Revue de Psychanalyse*, 11: 79–89.

Cournut, M. (1998) *Féminin et Fémininité*. Paris: Presses Universitaires de France.

Davies, R. (2007) Regression, curiosity, and the discovery of the object, in Perelberg, R. J. (Ed.) *Time and Memory*. London: Karnac, pp. 85–102.

De M'uzan, M. (1974) Psychodynamic mechanisms in psychosomatic symptom formation. *Psychotherapy and Psychosomatics*, 23: 103–110.

Dennis, A. (1995) Temporality and modes of language. *International Journal of Psycho-Analysis*, 76: 1109–1119.

Devereux, G. (1976) *Dreams in Greek Tragedy*. Berkeley and Los Angeles: University of California Press.

Diatkine, R. (1979) Le psychanalyste et l'enfant. *Nouvelle Revue de Psychoanalyse*, 19: 49–63.

Diem-Wille, G. (1997) Observed families revisited – two years on: a follow-up study, in Reid, S. (Ed.) *Developments in Infant Observations: The Tavistock Model*. London: Routledge, pp. 182–206.

Dirmeik, F. (1992) Comments on 'Negation'. *British Psychoanalytical Society Bulletin*, 28(2).

Donnet, J.-L. (1995) *Le Divan Bien Tempéré*. Paris: Presses Universitaires de France.

Donnet, J.-L. (2005) *La Situation Analysante*. Paris: Presses Universitaires de France.

D'Or, J. (1988) *La-Scientificité de la Psychoanalyse*. Paris: Presses Universitaires de France.

Duncan, D. (1989) The flow of interpretation – the collateral interpretation, force and flow. *International Journal of Psycho-Analysis*, 70: 693–700.

Duncan, D. (1992) Hermeneutics and psychoanalysis. *British Psychoanalytical Society Bulletin*, 28(10).

Elias, N. (1992) *Time: An Essay*. Oxford: Blackwell.

Emde, R. N. (1983) *Rene Spitz: Dialogues from Infancy*. New York: International Universities Press.

Erikson, E. (1950) *Childhood and Society*. New York: Norton.

Erikson, E. (1968) *Identity, Youth and Crisis*. London: Faber & Faber.

Evans-Pritchard, E. (1940) *The Nuer*. Oxford: Clarendon Press.

Faimberg, H. (2005) Après-coup. *International Journal of Psycho-Analysis*, 86: 1–6.

Fain, M. and Marty, P. (1965) À propos du narcissisme et de sa génèse. *Revue Française de Psychanalyse*, 29: 561–572.

Feldman, M. (1997) Projective identification: the analyst's involvement. *International Journal of Psycho-Analysis*, 78: 227–241.

Ferenczi, S. (1923) *Thalassa, a Theory of Genitality* (trans. H. Alden Bunker). New York: Psychoanalytic Quarterly Press, 1938.

Flanders, S. (1993) *The Dream Discourse Today*. London: Routledge/Institute of Psychoanalysis.

Fonagy, P. (1991) Thinking about thinking: some clinical and theoretical considerations in the analysis of borderline patients. *International Journal of Psycho-Analysis*, 72: 639–656.

Fonagy, P. (1996) Discussion of Peter Wolf's paper 'Infant Observation and Psychoanalysis'. *Journal of the American Psychoanalytic Association*, 44: 404–422.

Fonagy, P. and Target, M. (1995) Understanding the violent patient: the use of the body and the role of the father. *International Journal of Psycho-Analysis*, 76: 487–501. Also in Perelberg, R. J. (Ed.) (1997) *Psychoanalytic Understanding of Violence and Suicide*. London: Routledge, pp. 51–72.

Fortes, M. (1970) *Time and Social Structure and Other Essays*. London: Monographs on Social Anthropology, University of London.

Franco, D. and Levine, A. (1969) Psychic reality and psychic structure as predicted from the manifest content of first dreams. *Proceedings of 77th Annual Convention of the American Psychological Association*, 4: 493–494.

Freud, A. (1937) *The Ego and the Mechanism of Defence*. New York: International Universities Press, 1966.

Freud, A. (1952) Some remarks on infant observation. *Psycho-Analytic Study of the Child*, 8: 9–11.

Freud, A. (1958) Child observation and prediction of development – a memorial lecture. *Psychoanalytic Study of the Child*, 13: 92–116.

Freud, E.L. (1960) *Letters of Sigmund Freud*. New York: Basic Books.

Freud, S. (1896a) Lettre à Fliess 6.12.1896, in *La Naissance de la Psychanalyse* (trans. A. Berman). Paris: Presses Universitaires de France, 1956, pp. 153–160.

Freud, S. (1896b) Letter 52 from Extracts from the Fliess Papers. *Standard Edition*, 1: 233–239.

Freud, S. (1896c) The aetiology of hysteria. *Standard Edition*, 3: 187–221.

Freud, S. (1897a) Letter 61 from Extracts from the Fliess Papers. *Standard Edition*, 1: 247–248.

Freud, S. (1897b) Letter from Freud to Fliess, October 15, 1897, in Masson, Jeffrey M. (Ed.) *The Complete Letters of Sigmund Freud to Wilhelm Fliess, 1887–1904*. Cambridge, Mass: Harvard Univeristy Press, pp. 270–273.

Freud, S. (1898) Sexuality in the aetiology of the neuroses. *Standard Edition*, 3: 259–287.

Freud, S. (1899) Screen memories. *Standard Edition*, 3: 302–322.

Freud, S. (1900a) The interpretation of dreams. Part I. *Standard Edition*, 4: 1–338.

Freud, S. (1900b) The interpretation of dreams. Part II. *Standard Edition*, 5: 339–625.

Freud, S. (1905) Three essays on the theory of sexuality. *Standard Edition*, 7: 123–245.

Freud, S. (1908) Creative writers and day-dreaming. *Standard Edition*, 9: 141–153.

Freud, S. (1909a) Analysis of a phobia in a five year old boy. *Standard Edition*, 10: 1–149.

Freud, S. (1909b) Notes upon a case of obsessional neurosis. *Standard Edition*, 10: 151–320.

Freud, S. (1910) Leonardo da Vinci and a memory of his childhood. *Standard Edition*, 11: 59–151.

Freud, S. (1911a) Psycho-analytic notes on an autobiographical account of a case of paranoia (dementia paranoides). *Standard Edition*, 12: 9–82.

Freud, S. (1911b) The handling of dream-interpretation in psycho-analysis. *Standard Edition*, 12: 89–96.

Freud, S. (1911c) Formulations on the two principles of mental functioning. *Standard Edition*, 12: 218–226.

Freud, S. (1912a) On the universal tendency to debasement in the sphere of love (Contributions to the Psychology of Love II). *Standard Edition*, 11: 170–190.

Freud, S. (1912b) The dynamics of transference. *Standard Edition*, 12: 99–108.

Freud, S. (1912c) Recommendations to physicians practising psycho-analysis. *Standard Edition*, 12: 111–120.

Freud, S. (1913a) On beginning the treatment (Further Recommendations on the Technique of Psycho-Analysis I). *Standard Edition*, 12: 123–144.

Freud, S. (1913b) Totem and taboo. *Standard Edition*, 13: 1–162.

Freud, S. (1914a) Remembering, repeating and working through (Further Recommendations on the Technique of Psycho-Analysis II). *Standard Edition*, 12: 147–156.

Freud, S. (1914b) On narcissism: an introduction. *Standard Edition*, 14: 73–102.

Freud, S. (1915a) Instincts and their vicissitudes. *Standard Edition*, 14: 111–140.

Freud, S. (1915b) Repression. *Standard Edition*, 14: 141–158.

Freud, S. (1915c) The unconscious. *Standard Edition*, 14: 159–215.

Freud, S. (1915d) Mourning and melancholia. *Standard Edition*, 14: 237–258.

Freud, S. (1915e) A case of paranoia running counter to the psycho-analytic theory of the disease. *Standard Edition*, 14: 262–272.

Freud, S. (1916–17) Introductory lectures on psychoanalysis. *Standard Edition*, 15–16.

Freud, S. (1917) Introductory lectures on psycho-analysis (Part III, General Theory of the Neuroses), Transference Lecture 27. *Standard Edition*, 16: 431–447.

Freud, S. (1918) From the history of an infantile neurosis. *Standard Edition*, 17: 3–123.

Freud, S. (1919a) A child is being beaten: a contribution to the study of the origin of sexual perversions. *Standard Edition*, 17: 177.

Freud, S. (1919b) The 'uncanny'. *Standard Edition*, 17: 218–252.

Freud, S. (1920a) Beyond the pleasure principle. *Standard Edition*, 18: 7–64.

Freud, S. (1920b) The psychogenesis of a case of homosexuality in a woman. *Standard Edition*, 18: 145–172.

Freud, S. (1921) Psychoanalysis and telepathy. *Standard Edition*, 18: 177–194.

Freud, S. (1922a) Dreams and telepathy. *Standard Edition*, 18: 195–200.

Freud, S. (1922b) Two encyclopaedia articles. *Standard Edition*, 18: 235–259.

Freud, S. (1923) The ego and the id. *Standard Edition*, 19: 12–66.

Freud, S. (1924a) The economic problem of masochism. *Standard Edition*, 19: 159–170.

Freud, S. (1924b) The loss of reality in neurosis and psychosis. *Standard Edition*, 19: 171–186.

Freud, S. (1925a) A note upon the 'mystic writing-pad'. *Standard Edition*, 19: 227–232.

Freud, S. (1925b) Negation. *Standard Edition*, 19: 235–239.

Freud, S. (1926a) Inhibitions, symptoms and anxiety. *Standard Edition*, 20: 87–195.

Freud, S. (1926b) The question of lay analysis. *Standard Edition*, 20: 183–250.

Freud, S. (1930) Civilization and its discontents. *Standard Edition*, 21: 57–146.

Freud, S. (1931) Female sexuality. *Standard Edition*, 21: 225–243.

Freud, S. (1937a) Analysis terminable and interminable. *Standard Edition*, 23: 216–253.

Freud, S. (1937b) Constructions in analysis. *Standard Edition*, 23: 257–269.

Freud, S. (1940) An outline of psycho-analysis. *Standard Edition*, 23: 144–207.

Freud, S. (1950) Project for a scientific psychology. *Standard Edition*, 1: 281–391.

García Márquez, G. (1970) *One Hundred Years of Solitude*. London: Picador.

Gell, A. (1992) *The Anthropology of Time: Cultural Constructions of Temporal Maps and Images* Oxford: Berg.

Gesell, A., Ilg, F. L. and Bullis, G. E. (1949) *Vision: Its Development in Infant and Child*. London: Hamish Hamilton.

Gill, M. (1984) Transference: a change in conception or only in emphasis? *Psychoanalytic Inquiry*, 4: 489–523.

Glasser, M. (1979) Some aspects of the role of aggression in the perversions, in Rosen, I. (Ed.) *Sexual Deviation*. Oxford: Oxford University Press, pp. 278–305.

Glover, E. (1924) The significance of the mouth in psycho-analysis. *British Journal of Medical Psychology*, 4: 134.

Gluckman, M. (1972) *The Allocation of Responsibility*. Manchester: Manchester University Press.

Gluckman, M. (1973) *Custom and Conflict in Africa*. Oxford: Alden Press.

Godelier, M. (1958) *Racionalidade e Irracionalidade na Economia*. Rio de Janeiro: Tempo Brasileiro.

Granel, J. (1987) Considerations on the capacity to change, the clash of identifications and having accidents: their interrelations. *International Review of Psycho-Analysis*, 14: 483–490.

Green, A. (1977) Atome de parenté et relations oedipiennes, in Lévi-Strauss, C. (Ed.) *L'Identité*. Paris: Bernard Grasset, pp. 81–98.

Green, A. (1979) L'enfant modèle. *Nouvelle Revue de Psychanalyse*, 19: 27–47.

Green, A. (1983) *Narcissism de Vie: Narcissism de Mort*. Paris: Presses Universitaires de France.

Green, A. (1986a) *On Private Madness*. London: Hogarth Press/Institute of Psychoanalysis.

Green, A. (1986b) Passions and their vicissitudes, in Green, A. (Ed.) *On Private Madness*. London: Hogarth Press/Institute of Psychoanalysis, pp. 214–253.

Green, A. (1991) On thirdness, in Abram, J. (Ed.) *Andre Green at the Squiggle Foundation*. London: Karnac, 2000, pp. 39–68.

Green, A. (1998) *L'Intrapsychique et l'Inter-subjectif en Psychanalyse*. Quebec: Lanctot Editeur.

Green, A. (1999) *The Work of the Negative*. London: Free Association Books.

Green, A. (2000a) *Le Temps Éclaté*. Paris: Les Editions de Minuit.

Green, A. (2000b) The central phobic position: a new formulation of the free association method. *International Journal of Psycho-Analysis*, 81: 429–452.

Green, A. (2000c) What kind of research for psychoanalysis, in Sandler, J. *et al.* (Eds) *Clinical and Observational Psychoanalytic Research: Roots of a Controversy*, Psychoanalytic Monograph 5. London: Karnac, pp. 21–26.

Green, A. (2002a) *Idées Directrices pour une Psychanalyse Contemporaine*. Paris: Presses Universitaires de France.

Green, A (2002b) *Time in Psychoanalysis: Some Contradictory Aspects*. London: Free Association Books.

Green, A. (2004) Thirdness and psychoanalytic concepts. *Psychoanalytic Quarterly*, 73: 99–135.

Green, A. (2007) *Pourquoi les pulsions de destruction ou de mort?* Paris: Éditions du Panama.

Greenacre, P. (1975) On reconstruction. *Journal of the American Psychoanalytical Association*, 23: 693–712.

Greenberg, J. R. and Mitchell, S. A. (1983) *Object Relations in Psychoanalytic Theory*. Cambridge, MA: Harvard University Press.

Grinberg, L. (1962) On a specific aspect of countertransference due to the patient's projective identification. *International Journal of Psycho-Analysis*, 43: 436.

Grunbaum, A. (1985) *Foundations of Psychoanalysis: A Philosophical Critique*. Berkeley: University of California Press.

Guntrip, H. (1968) *Schizoid Phenomena, Object Relations and the Self*. London: Hogarth Press.

References

Habermas, J. (1971) *Logic and Human Interests.* Boston: Beacon Press.

Hallpike, C. (1979) *The Foundation of Primitive Thought.* Oxford: Clarendon Press.

Hamilton, V. (1982) *Narcissus and Oedipus: The Children of Psychoanalysis.* London: Routledge & Kegan Paul.

Hartocollis, P. (1983) *Time and Timelessness: The Varieties of Temporal Experience.* New York: International Universities Press.

Hawking, S. (1988) *A Brief History of Time: From the Big Bang to Black Holes.* London: Bantam Books.

Hayman, A. (1989) What do we mean by phantasy? *International Journal of Psycho-Analysis,* 70: 105–113.

Hayman, A. (1994) Some remarks about the Controversial Discussions. *International Journal of Psycho-Analysis,* 75: 343–358.

Hedeen, P. M. (1983) Gabriel García Marquez's dialectic of solitude. *Southwest Review,* 20: 350–364.

Heimann, P. (1950) On countertransference. *International Journal of Psycho-Analysis,* 31: 81–84.

Hobson, P. (1992) Responses to Professor Daniel Stern's paper 'Phantasy from a Developmental Perspective', unpublished.

Hoffer, W. (1949) Mouth, hand and ego-integration. *Psycho-Analytic Study of the Child,* 3: 49–56.

Hoffer, W. (1950) Developments of the body-ego. *Psycho-Analytic Study of the Child,* 5: 18–24.

Isaacs, S. (1943) The nature and function of phantasy, in Klein, M., Heimann, P., Isaacs, S. and Riviere J. (Eds) *Developments in Psycho-Analysis.* London: Hogarth Press, 1952, pp. 67–121.

Isaacs, S. (1948) The nature and function of phantasy. *International Journal of Psycho-Analysis,* 29: 73–97.

James, W. (1957) *The Principles of Psychology,* New York: Dover Publication.

Jones, E. (1974) *Sigmund Freud: Life and Works,* 3 vols. London: Hogarth Press.

Jelinski, J. B. (1984) Memory and the remembered structure of Cien años de Soledad. *Revista de Estudios Hispanicos,* 18: 323–333.

Joseph, B. (1975) The patient who is difficult to reach, in Spillius, E. (Ed.) *Melanie Klein Today, Volume 2.* London: Routledge/Institute of Psychoanalysis, 1988, pp. 48–60.

Joseph, B. (1985) Transference: the total situation. *International Journal of Psycho-Analysis,* 66: 447–454.

Jozef, B. (1974) *O Espaço Reconquistado.* Petrópolis: Vozes.

Jozef, B. (1996) *Jorge Luís Borges.* Rio de Janeiro: Livraria Francisco Alves.

Kennedy, R. (1998) *The Elusive Human Subject: A Psychoanalytic Theory of Subject Relations.* London: Free Associations.

Kernberg, O. (1975) *Borderline Conditions and Pathological Narcissism*. New York: Jason Aronson.

Kestemberg, J. S. (1966) Rhythm and organization in obsessive-compulsive development. *International Journal of Psycho-Analysis*, 47: 151–159.

Khan, M. M. (1962) Dream psychology and the evolution of the psychoanalytic situation, in Khan, M. M., *The Privacy of the Self*. London: Hogarth Press/Institute of Psychoanalysis, pp. 27–41.

Khan, M. M. (1972) The use and abuse of dream in psychic experience. *International Journal of Psychoanalysis*, 43: 21–31.

King, P. and Steiner, R. (1990) *The Freud–Klein Controversies 1941–1945*. London: Routledge/Institute of Psychoanalysis.

King, P. and Steiner, R. (1996) *Les Controverses Anna Freud Melanie Klein 1941–1945*. Paris: Presses Universitaires de France.

Klein, G. S. (1976) *Psychoanalytic Theory*. New York: International Universities Press.

Klein, M. (1930) The importance of symbol-formation in the development of the ego, in Klein, M. (Ed.) *Love, Guilt and Reparation and Other Works, 1921–1945*. New York: Delta, 1977, pp. 219–232.

Klein, M. (1937) *Love, Guilt and Reparation*, New York: Delta.

Klein, M. (1946) Notes on some schizoid mechanisms, in Klein, M. (Ed). *Envy and Gratitude and Other Works 1946–1963*. New York: Delta, 1977, pp. 1–24.

Klein, M. (1948) On the theory of anxiety and guilt, in Klein, M. (Ed.) *Envy and Gratitude and Other Works 1946–1963*. New York: Delta, 1977, pp. 25–42.

Klein, M. (1952) The origins of the transference. *International Journal of Psycho-Analysis*, 33: 433–438.

Klein, M. (1952a) Some theoretical conclusions regarding the emotional life of the infant, in Klein, M. (Ed.) *Envy and Gratitude and Other Works 1946–1963*. New York: Delta, 1977, pp. 61–93.

Klein, M. (1952b) On observing the behaviour of young infants, in Klein, M. (Ed.) *Envy and Gratitude and Other Works 1946–1963*. New York: Delta, 1977, pp. 94–121.

Klein, M. (1957) Envy and gratitude, in Klein, M. (Ed.) *Envy and Gratitude and Other Works 1946–1963*. New York: Delta, 1977, pp. 176–235.

Kohon, G. (1999a) *No Lost Certainties to be Recovered*. London: Karnac.

Kohon, G. (1999b) Dreams, acting out, and symbolic impoverishment, in Kohon, G. (Ed.) *No Lost Certainties to be Recovered*. London: Karnac Books, pp. 73–86. Also in Perelberg, R.J. (Ed.) (2003) *Dreaming and Thinking*. London, Karnac Books pp. 73–90.

Kohon, G. (2005a) Love in times of madness, in Green, A. and Kohon, G. (Eds) *Love and its Vicissitudes*. London: Routledge, pp. 41–100.

Kohon, G. (2005b) The Oedipus complex, in Budd, S. and Rusbridger, R. (Eds) *Introducing Psychoanalysis: Essential Themes and Topics*. London: Routledge, pp. 66–180.

Kohon, G. (2007) Borderline traces and the question of diagnosis, in Green, A. (Ed.) *Resonance of Suffering Countertransference in Non-neurotic Structures*. London: International Psychoanalytic Association, pp. 203–215.

Korzybski, A. (1941) *Science and Sanity*. New York: Science Press.

Kris, E. (1956) The recovery of childhood memories in psychoanalysis. *Psycho-Analytic Study of the Child*, 11: 54–88.

Kristeva, J. (1995) *New Maladies of the Soul*. New York: Columbia University Press.

Kristeva, J. (1996) *Time and Sense: Proust and the Experience of Literature*. New York: Columbia University Press.

Lacan, J. (1966a) Le séminaire sur 'La Lettre Volée', in Lacan, J. (Ed.) *Écrits*. Paris: Editions du Seuil, pp. 1–61.

Lacan, J. (1966b) *Écrits*. Paris: Editions du Seuil.

Lacan, J. (1977) *Écrits: A Selection* (trans. A. Sheridan). New York: W. W. Norton.

Lacan, J. (1978) *Le Moi dans la Théorie de Freud et dans la Technique de la Psychanalyse: Le Séminaire Livre II*. Paris: Editions du Seuil.

Laplanche, J. (1997) The theory of seduction and the problem of the other. *International Journal of Psycho-Analysis*, 78: 653–666.

Laplanche, J. (1999) *Essays on Otherness*. London: Routledge.

Laplanche, J. and Pontalis, J.-B. (1973) *The Language of Psycho-Analysis* (trans. D. Nicholson-Smith). London: Hogarth.

Laplanche, J. and Pontalis, J.-B. (1985) *Fantasme Originaire, Fantasme des Origins, Origines du Fantasme*. Paris: Hachette.

Laufer, E. (1993) The female Oedipus complex and the relationship to the body, in Birksted-Breen, D. (Ed.) *The Gender Conundrum*. London: Routledge / Institute of Psychoanalysis, pp. 67–81.

Leach, E. R. (1961) Two essays concerning the symbolic representation of time, in Leach, E. R. (Ed.) *Rethinking Anthropology*. London: Athlone Press, pp. 124–136.

Lebovici, S. (1985) *Clinical Studies in Infant Mental Health. The First Year of Life*. New York: Basic Books.

Lebovici, S. and Soulé, M. (1970) *La Connaissance de l'Enfant par la Psychanalyse*. Paris: Presses Universitaires de France.

Leclaire, S. (1975) *On Tue un Enfant*. Paris: Editions du Seuil.

Le Guen, C. (1982) L'Après-coup. *Revue Française de Psychanalyse*, 3: 527–534.

Lepastier, S. (1991) La folie paternelle: un moment dans la constitution du sujet. *Revue Française de Psychanalyse*, 45: 1785–1788.

Lesser, S. O. (1962) *Fiction and The Unconscious*. New York: Vintage Books.

Lévi-Strauss, C. (1947) *The Elementary Structures of Kinship and Marriage.* Boston: Beacon Press.

Lévi-Strauss, C. (1971) *L'Homme Nu.* Paris: Plon.

Lévi-Strauss, C. (1972) *Structural Anthropology 1.* Norwich: Penguin.

Lévi-Strauss, C. (1977) *L'identité.* Paris: Bernard Grasset.

Lewin, B. (1946) Sleep, mouth and the dream screen. *Psychoanalytic Quarterly*, 15: 419–434.

Lewin, B. (1948) Inferences from the dream screen. *International Journal of Psycho-Analysis*, 29: 224–231.

Limentani, A. (1966) A re-evaluation of acting out in relation to working through. *International Journal of Psycho-Analysis*, 47: 274–282.

Loewald, H. (1951) Ego and reality. *International Journal of Psycho-Analysis*, 32: 10–18.

Lorand, S. (1957) Dream interpretation in the Talmud. *International Journal of Psycho-Analysis*, 38: 92–97.

Ludmer, J. (1972) *Cien Años de Soledad: Una Interpretación.* Buenos Aires: Tiempo Contemporáneo.

Malinowski, B. (1922) *Argonauts of the Western Pacific.* Prospect Heights, IL: Waveland Press.

Malinowski, B. (1948) Baloma: the spirits of dead, in Malinowski, B. (Ed.) *Magic, Science and Religion.* London: Faber & West, pp. 149–254.

Mannoni, M. (1968) *Freud: The Theory of the Unconscious.* London: Verso.

Marty, P., De M'uzan, M. and David, C. (1963) *L'Invéstigation Psycho-Somatique.* Paris: Presses Universitaires de France.

Marx, K. (1867) *Capital: A Critique of Political Economy* (trans. B. Fowkes). Harmondsworth: Penguin, 1992.

Masson, J. M. (1985) *The Complete Letters of Sigmund Freud to Wilhelm Fliess (1887–1904)* (trans. J. M. Masson). Cambridge, MA: Belknap Press of Harvard University Press.

Mauss, M. (1938) Une catégorie de l'esprit humain: la notion de personne, celle de 'moi', in Mauss, M. (Ed.) *Sociologie and Anthropologie*, Paris: Presses Universitaires de France, 1973, pp. 333–364.

McDougall, J. (1974) The psychosoma and the psychoanalytic process. *International Review of Psychoanalysis*, 50: 437.

McDougall, J. (1982) Alexithymia: a psychoanalytic viewpoint. *Psychotherapy and Psychosomatics*, 38: 81–90.

McDougall, J. (1986) *Theatres of the Mind.* London: Free Association Books.

McDougall, J. (1989) *Theatres of the Body.* London: Free Association Books.

Middleton, J. (1960) *Lugbara Religion.* London: Oxford University Press.

Miller, L., Rustin, M., Rustin, M., Shuttleworth, J., *et al.* (1989) *Closely Observed Infants.* London: Duckworth.

Mitchell, J. (1982) Introduction, in Mitchell, J. and Rose, J. (Eds) *Feminine Sexuality – Jacques Lacan and the École Freudienne*. London: McMillan Press, p. 1.

Money-Kyrle, R. (1956) Normal counter-transference and some of its deviations. *International Journal of Psycho-Analysis*, 37: 360–366.

Money-Kyrle, R. (1968) Cognitive development. *International Journal of Psycho-Analysis*, 49: 691–698.

Ogden, T. H. (1997) Reverie and interpretation. *Psychoanalytic Quarterly*, 66: 567–595.

Ogden, T. H. (2000) Borges and the art of mourning. *Psychoanalytic Dialogues*, 10: 65–88.

Ogden, T. H. (2004) The analytic third: implications for psychoanalytic theory and technique. *Psychoanalytic Quarterly*, 73: 167–195.

O'Shaughnessy, E. (1992) Enclaves and excursions. *International Journal of Psycho-Analysis*, 73: 603–611.

Parry, J. P. (1982) Sacrificial death and the necrophagous ascetic, in Bloch, M. and Parry, J. (Eds) *Death and the Regeneration of Life*. Cambridge: Cambridge University Press, pp. 74–110.

Parsons, M. (2000) *The Dove that Returns, the Dove that Vanishes: Paradox and Creativity in Psychoanalysis*. London: Routledge, pp. 189–201.

Perelberg, R. J. (1980) *Fronteiras do Silencio: um Estudo de Desvio e Ritualização*. Rio de Janeiro: Achiame.

Perelberg, R. J. (1981) Umbanda and psychoanalysis as different ways of interpreting mental illness. *British Journal of Medical Psychology*, 53: 323–332.

Perelberg, R. J. (1993) 'What can you possibly learn from babies?' on psychoanalytic constructions of primal infants. IPA Congress. Co-Winner of Cesare Sacerdoti Prize, Buenos Aires. *British Psychoanalytical Society Bulletin*, 9(6).

Perelberg, R. J. (1995) A core phantasy in violence. *International Journal of Psycho-Analysis*, 76: 6.

Perelberg, R. J. (1997) Introduction, in Perelberg, R. J. (Ed.) *Psychoanalytic Understanding of Violence and Suicide*. London: Routledge/Institute of Psychoanalysis, p. 1.

Perelberg, R. J. (1998) Introduction, in Raphael-Leff, J. and Perelberg, R. J. (Eds) *Female Experience: Three Generations of Women Psychoanalysts on Work with Women*. London: Routledge, p. 1.

Perelberg, R. J. (1999) The interplay between identifications and identity in the analysis of a violent young man: issues of technique. *International Journal of Psycho-Analysis*, 80: 31.

Perelberg, R. J. (2000) Discussion, in Sandler, J., Sandler, A.-M. and Davies, R. (Eds) *Clinical and Observational Psychoanalytic Research: Roots of a Controversy: Andre Green and Daniel Stern*. London: Karnac, pp. 91–99.

Perelberg, R. J. (2003) Full and empty spaces in the analytic process. *International Journal of Psycho-Analysis*, 84: 579–592.

Perelberg, R. J. (2004) Narcissistic configurations; violence and its absence in treatment. *International Journal of Psycho-Analysis*, 85: 1065–1079.

Perelberg, R. J. (2005) Constructions and de-constructions: a conversation with André Green. Paper presented to the closing plenary to the European Psychoanalytic Federation Conference, Villamoura, Portugal. Unpublished.

Perelberg, R. J. (2006) Controversial Discussions and *après-coup*. *International Journal of Psycho-Analysis*, 87: 1199–1220.

Perelberg, R. J. (Ed.) (2007) *Time and Memory*. London: Karnac.

Perelberg, R. J. and Jozef, B. (2002) Time and memory in Gabriel García Marquez, in Botella, C. (Ed.) *Penser Les Limites*. Paris: Delachaux and Nestlie, pp. 382–390.

Perron, R. (1988) La recherché en psychanalyse et l'Association Psychanalytique Internationale. *Bulletin de la Société Psychanalityque de Paris*, 50: 39–51.

Perron, R. (2001) The unconscious and primal phantasies. *International Journal of Psycho-Analysis*, 82: 583–595.

Pontalis, J.-B. (1974a) Dream as an object. *International Review of Psycho-Analysis*, 1: 125–133.

Pontalis, J.-B (1974b) Bornes ou confins? *Nouvelle Revue de Psychanalyse*, 10: 5–16.

Pontalis, J.-B. (1977) *Entre le Rêve et la Douleur*. Paris: Editions Gallimard.

Pontalis, J.-B. (1979) La chambre des enfants. *Nouvelle Revue de Psychanalyse*, 19: 5–11.

Proust, M. (1913–1927) *À la Recherche du Temps Perdu* (Ed. J.-Y. Tadié), 4 vols. Paris: Pléiade, 1987–1989.

Quinodoz, J.-M. (1999) 'Dreams that turn over a page': integration dreams with paradoxical regressive content. *International Journal of Psycho-Analysis*, 80: 225–238.

Racker, H. (1968) *Transference and Countertransference*. London: Karnac.

Reid, S. (1997) *Developments in Infant Observations*. London: Routledge.

Rey, H. (1994) *Universals of Psychoanalysis in the Treatment of Psychotic and Borderline States*. London: Free Association Books.

Ribas, D. (1999) Communication à l'Occasion du 59 Congrès des Psychanalystes de Langue Française.

Ricoeur, P. (1965) *De l'Intérprétation – Essai sur Freud*. Paris: Editions du Seuil.

Riesenberg-Malcolm, R. (1999) Interpretation: the past in the present, in Riesenberg-Malcolm, R. (Ed.) *On Bearing Unbearable States of Mind*. London: Routledge/Institute of Psychoanalysis, pp. 38–52.

Róheim, G. (1954) *Psychoanalysis and Anthropology*. New York: International University Press.

Rolland, J.-C. (1997) Le rhythm et la raison. *Revue Française de Psychanalyse*, 61: 1589–1651.

Rolland, J.-C. (2005) The metapsychological papers, in Perelberg, R. J. (Ed.) *Freud: A Modern Reader*. London: Wiley, pp. 93–108.

Rose, J. (1997) Distortions of time in the transference: some clinical and theoretical implications. *International Journal of Psycho-Analysis*, 78: 453–468. Also in Perelberg, R. J. (Ed.) (2007) *Time and Memory*. London: Karnac, pp. 23–46.

Rosenberg, B. (1991) Masochisme mortifère et masochisme gardien de la vie. *Monographies de la Revue Française de Psychanalyse*. Paris: Presses Universitaires de France.

Rosenfeld, H. R. (1978) The relationship between psychosomatic symptoms and latent psychotic States. *Bulletin of the British Psychoanalytical Society*, unpublished.

Rosenfeld, H. R. (1987a) Afterthought: changing theories and changing techniques in psychoanalysis, in Rosenfeld, H. R. (Ed.) *Impasse and Interpretation: Therapeutic Factors*. London: Tavistock Publications, pp 267–269.

Rosenfeld, H. R. (1987b) *Impasse and Interpretation: Therapeutic Factors*. London and New York: Routledge.

Roth, P. (2001) Mapping the landscape. *International Journal of Psycho-Analysis*, 82: 533–543.

Sandler, J. (1959) The background of safety, in Sandler, J. (Ed.) *From Safety to Superego*. London: Karnac, 1987, pp. 1–8.

Sandler, J. (1962) Psychology and psychoanalysis, in Sandler, J. (Ed.) *From Safety to Superego*. London: Karnac, 1987, pp. 45–57.

Sandler, J. (1976) Countertransference and role responsiveness. *International Review of Psycho-Analysis*, 3: 43–47.

Sandler, J. (1983) Reflections on some relations between psychoanalytic concepts and psychoanalytic practice. *International Journal of Psycho-Analysis*, 64: 35–45.

Sandler, J. and Dare, C. (1970) The psychoanalytic concept of orality. *Journal of Psychosomatic Research*, 14: 211–222.

Sandler, J. and Nagera, H. (1963) Aspects of the metapsychology of fantasy. *Psychoanalytic Study of the Child*, 18: 159–194.

Sandler, J. and Rosenblatt, B. (1962) The representational world, in Sandler, J. (Ed.) *From Safety to Superego*. London: Karnac, 1987, pp. 58–92.

Sandler, J. and Sandler, A.-M. (1984) The past unconscious, the present unconscious and the interpretation of the transference. *Psychoanalytic Inquiry*, 4: 367–399.

Sandler, J. and Sandler, A.-M. (1992) The past unconscious, the present unconscious and the vicissitudes of guilt. *International Journal of Psycho-Analysis*, 68: 331–341.

Sandler, J. and Sandler, A.-M. (1994a) Phantasy and its transformations: a contemporary Freudian view. *The International Journal of Psycho-Analysis*, 75: 387–394.

Sandler, J. and Sandler, A.-M. (1994b) The past unconscious and the present unconscious: a contribution to a technical frame of reference. *Psychoanalytic Study of the Child*, 49: 278–291.

Sandler, J. and Sandler, A.-M. (1998) *Internal Objects Revisited*. London: Karnac.

Séchaud, E. (1997) L'urgence interpretative. *Revue Française de Psychanalyse*, 41.

Sedlak, V. (1997) The dream space and countertransference. *International Journal of Psycho-Analysis*, 78: 295–305. Also in Perelberg, R. J. (Ed.) (2000) *Dreaming and Thinking*. London: Karnac.

Segal, H. (1980) The function of dreams, in Segal, H. (Ed.) *The Work of Hanna Segal: A Kleinian Approach to Clinical Practice*. London: Jason Aronson, 1981, pp. 89–97.

Segal, H. (1986) *The Work of Hanna Segal*. London: Free Association Books/ Maresfield Library.

Segal, H. (1991) *Dream, Phantasy and Art*. London and New York: Routledge/ Institute of Psychoanalysis.

Segal, H. (1997) The uses and abuses of countertransference, in Steiner, J. (Ed.) *Psychoanalysis, Literature and War – Hanna Segal, Papers 1972–1995*. London: Routledge, pp. 111–119.

Sifneos, P. E. (1977) The phenomenon of 'alexithymia'. *Psychotherapy and Psychosomatics*, 28: 47–57.

Sodré, I. (1997) Insight and après coup. *Revue Française de Psychanalyse*, 61: 1255–1262.

Sodré, I. (2004) Florence and Sigmund's Excellent Adventure, paper presented to the *English Speaking Conference*, unpublished.

Sohn, L. (1985) Narcissistic organization, projective identification, and the formation of the identificate. *International Journal of Psycho-Analysis*, 66: 201–213.

Spence, D. P. (1987) *The Freudian Metaphor: Towards Paradigm Change in Psychoanalysis*. New York: W.W. Norton.

Spillius, E. (1988) *Melanie Klein Today: Volume 2, Mainly Practice*. London: Routledge/Institute of Psychoanalysis.

Spillius, E. (2001) Freud and Klein on the concept of phantasy. *International Journal of Psycho-Analysis*, 82: 361.

Spitz, R. A. (1965) *The First Year of Life*. New York: International University Press.

Steiner, J. (1992) *Psychic Retreats: Pathological Organizations in Psychotic, Neurotic and Borderline Patients*. London: Tavistock & Routledge.

Steiner, J. (2006) Interpretative enactments and the analytic setting. *International Journal of Psycho-Analysis*, 87: 321–324.

Steiner, R. (1992) Some historical and critical notes on the relationship between hermeneutics and psychoanalysis. *British Psychoanalytical Society Bulletin*, 28(10).

Steiner, R. (2003) *Unconscious Phantasy*. London: Karnac.

Stekel, W. (1943) *The Interpretation of Dreams*. New York: Liveright Publishing.

Stern, D. (1985) *The Interpersonal World of the Infant*. New York: Basic Books.

Stern, D. (1995) *The Motherhood Constellation*. New York: Basic Books.

Stern, D. (2000) The relevance of empirical infant research to psychoanalytic theory and practice, in Sandler, J., Sandler, A.-M. and Davies, R. (Eds) *Clinical and Observational Psychoanalytic Research: Roots of a Controversy*, Psychoanalytic Monograph 5. London: Karnac.

Stern, S. (2003) *Time and Process in Ancient Judaism*. Oxford–Portman, Oregon: The Littman Library of Jewish Civilization.

Stewart, H. (1973) The experience of the dream and the transference. *International Journal of Psycho-Analysis*, 54: 359–362.

Strachey, J. (1934) The nature of the therapeutic action of psycho-analysis. *International Journal of Psycho-Analysis*, 15: 127–159.

Thomä, H. and Cheshire, N. (1991) Freud's concept of nachträglichkeit and Strachey's 'deferred action': trauma, constructions and the direction of causality. *International Review of Psychoanalysis*, 3: 401–445.

Tonnesmann, M. (1992) Comments on 'negation'. *British Psychoanalytical Society Bulletin*, 28(2).

Trevarthen, C. (1977) Descriptive analyses of infant communicative behaviour, in Shaffer, H.R. (Ed.) *Studies in Mother–Infant Interaction*: London: Academic Press.

Turner, V. (1972) *Forest of Symbols*. London and Ithaca: Cornell University Press.

Turner, V. (1974) *Dramas, Fields and Metaphors*. London and Ithaca: Cornell University Press.

Vargas Llosa, M. (1971) *García Márquez. Historia de un Deicidio*. Barcelona: Barral Editores.

Viderman, S. (1970) *La Construction de l'Espace Analytique*. Paris: Gallimard.

Wallerstein, R. S. (1988) One psychoanalysis or many? *International Journal Psycho-Analysis*, 69: 5–21.

Whelan, M. (2000) *Mistress of her Own Thought: Ella Freeman Sharpe and the Practice of Psychoanalysis*. London: Rebus Press.

Widlocher, D. (1994) A case is not a fact. *International Journal of Psycho-Analysis*, 75: 233–244.

Widlocher, D. (2002) L'esprit de la recherche en psychanalyse. *Congrès au Palais de l'Uncesco*, Paris, November. Unpublished.

Wilde, O. (1897) *The Ballad of Reading Gaol*. Dover: Thrift, 1992.

Williams, P. (2007) Making time; killing time, in Perelberg, R. J. (Ed.) *Time and Memory*. London: Karnac, pp. 47–63.

Winnicott, C., Shepherd, R. and Davis, M. (1989) *Psychoanalytic Explorations*. London: Karnac.

Winnicott, D. W. (1945) Primitive emotional development. *International Journal of Psycho-Analysis*, 36: 137–143.

Winnicott, D. W. (1949) Hate in the counter-transference. *International Journal of Psycho-Analysis*, 30: 69–74.

Winnicott, D. W. (1956) On transference. *International Journal of Psycho-Analysis*, 37: 386–388.

Winnicott, D. W. (1958) Primary maternal preoccupation, in *Collected Papers: Through Paediatrics to Psychoanalysis*, London: Tavistock Publications, pp. 300–305.

Winnicott, D. W. (1971) Mirror-role of mother and family in child development, in Winnicott, D. W. (Ed.) *Playing and Reality*. Harmondsworth: Penguin, pp. 130–138.

Winnicott, D. W. (1989) The mother–infant experience of mutuality, in Winnicott, C., Shepherd, R. and Davis, M. (Eds) *Psychoanalytic Explorations*. London: Karnac, pp. 251–260.

Wolheim, R. (1984) *The Thread of Life*. Cambridge: Cambridge University Press.

Yorke, C. (1973) Some suggestions for a critique of Kleinian psychology. *Psycho-Analytic Study of the Child*, 26: 129–158.

Index

absence: desire and 20; maternal 1–2, 19, 21, 178–9; mental space and 20–1, 87, 88–95; presence and 1, 10, 18, 72–7, 85; sense of absence in analysis 87, 88–95; *see also* emptiness; loss; separation

accidents: and the avoidance of time 60–2; language of 55–60, 90

aggression, infantile 171, 172, 173–4, 178–9, 180; oral phase and 177–8

agoraphobia 82n7

Althusser, L. 24–5

analytic hystoricization 51

analytic process 53–5, 185–7; communicating the interpretation 133–4; interpretation 20, 71–2, 128, 129, 146–9; psychoanalytic listening 134, 136; transference *see* transference; *see also* projection

analytic site 20, 128; trauma of the analytic situation 132

analytic space 20, 104, 132, 148; Oedipal conflict in 147

Anna Freud Young Adults' Research Group 71

anthropology: Freud's anthropology of time 3, 13–17, 18–19, 25–30, 133–4, 192; research models 189–92; time notions in traditional societies 21–2

après-coup 2n1, 25, 26–30, 62, 106–7, 127–30; clinical examples 125–7,

138–43; the Controversial Discussions and 108–25; descriptive 106, 128, 129; double movement 110–19, 126–7, 130; dynamic 106, 125–7, 129, 149; Freud and 26–32, 107–8; metapsychology and 18, 30–1, 119, 129–30; Oedipus complex and 119–25; reactivation of primal phantasies 18; regression and 110; repression and 179–80; translation 2n1, 30, 107, 108, 112–13; unconscious phantasy and 31–2, 108

atemporality *see* timelessness

attention 16

Aulagnier, P. 104

auto eroticism 18

baby/mother relational development *see* infant/mother relational development

baby observation: at one to two months 165–9; at three to six months 169–71; at eight to ten months 171–7; the clinical and observed infant 176n4, 181–2; psychoanalytic frameworks and 163–4, 183; role of the observer 173

Baby Observation Seminars 164–5, 180, 183

Bachelard, G. 193

Bachofen, J. J. 80

213